BUILDING A PROFESSION

SUNY Series,
The Margins of Literature

Mihai I. Spariosu, Editor

BUILDING A PROFESSION

❀

Autobiographical Perspectives on the History
of Comparative Literature in the United States

Edited by
Lionel Gossman
and
Mihai I. Spariosu

STATE UNIVERSITY OF NEW YORK PRESS

Published by
State University of New York Press, Albany

© 1994 State University of New York

Production by Ruth Fisher
Marketing by Dana E. Yanulavich

For information, address the State University of New York Press,
State University Plaza, Albany, NY 12246

Library of Congress Cataloging-in-Publication Data

Building a profession : autobiographical perspectives on the
  history of comparative literature in the United States / edited
  by Lionel Gossman and Mihai I. Spariosu.
      p.   cm. — (SUNY series, the margins of literature)
    ISBN 0-7914-1799-9. — ISBN 0-7914-1800-6 (pbk.)
      1. Literature, Comparative—Study and teaching—United States.
    2. College teachers—United States—Biography. I. Gossman, Lionel.
    II. Spariosu, Mihai. III. Series.
    PN868.U5B85   1994
    809'.04—dc20   93-3458
                                                          CIP

10 9 8 7 6 5 4 3 2 1

Contents

Foreword   vii

1. *Memories of the Profession*   1
   René Wellek

2. *Comparative Literature at Harvard*   13
   Harry Levin

3. *Experiences and Experiments*   25
   Victor Lange

4. *Versions of a Discipline*   37
   Thomas M. Greene

5. *Am I a Comparatist?*   49
   Thomas G. Rosenmeyer

6. *Reminiscences of an Academic Maverick*   63
   W. Wolfgang Holdheim

7. *How and Why I Became a Comparatist*   75
   Anna Balakian

8. *Comparative Literature, Modern Thought and Literature*   89
   Albert J. Guerard

9. *Comparative Literature, CL, and I*   99
   Thomas R. Hart

10. *Born to Compare*   107
    Lilian Furst

11. On Wanting to Be a Comparatist   125
    Marjorie Perloff

12. Self-Portrait in the Unembellished Mode   141
    Herbert Lindenberger

13. Home Truths and Institutional Falsehoods   159
    Gerald Gillespie

14. Remembering Paul de Man: An Epoch in the History of Comparative Literature   177
    Stanley Corngold

15. Out of a Gothic North   193
    Lionel Gossman

16. Exile, Play, and Intellectual Autobiography   205
    Mihai I. Spariosu

List of Contributors   217

Index   221

Foreword

Three years ago, we learned that René Wellek was in poor health and confined to bed much of the time, but that he continued to work on the last volume of his *History of Criticism*. In the strangely becalmed conditions that seem to have followed decades of theoretical storming, Wellek's steadfast dedication to his monumental project and to his entire conception of the study of literature was impressive. We wondered what might have inspired it, what life experiences, if any, motivate scholars to pursue the disciplines they pursue, what intellectual and ethical passions had moved the older generation of literary scholars in particular. The idea occurred to both of us that it would be instructive to put together some testimonies from notable scholars of Wellek's generation and of the generation he and others like him had trained, and in this way to discover the broader human dimension of their professional careers.

One of us had in mind scholars whose careers have been dedicated to the study of foreign literatures. As he is a comparatist neither by training nor by profession, it did not occur to him to focus on Comparative Literature. The other teaches in a Comparative Literature department and assumed that, as our plan had been inspired by Wellek, we should be thinking primarily of Comparative Literature. It is certainly true that in Comparative Literature— since its beginnings as an academic discipline at the end of the nineteenth century—there is a long tradition of reflection on the objects and methods of the study of literature and on what distinguishes Comparative Literature from the study of the various national literatures or from "World Literature" or "General Literature." Wellek himself has often addressed such questions, most memorably perhaps in his provocative attack on the positivist French tradition of Baldensperger, Van Tieghem, Carré, and Guyard at the Second Congress of the ICLA at Chapel Hill in 1958.

At that meeting Wellek took a resolutely internationalist and cosmopolitan stand, denouncing the traditional conception of Comparative Literature as the "foreign relations" of the national literatures, deploring the deep-seated chauvinism even of its most liberal practitioners, and expressing his own wish that "we could simply speak of the study of Literature or of literary scholarship." It would be preferable, he held, if "there were, as M. Thibaudet proposed,

Professors of Literature just as there are Professors of Philosophy and of History and not Professors of the History of English Philosophy, even though the individual may very well specialize in this or that particular period or country or even in a particular author." Wellek went on to reject the diplomatic compromise by which academic departments of Comparative Literature had undertaken, as the price of admission to departmental status, not to "encroach upon other territories" (namely, the study of the national literatures). "There are no proprietary rights and no recognized 'vested interests' in literary scholarship," Wellek asserted.

> Everybody has the right to study any question even if it is confined to a single work in a single language, and everybody has the right to study even history or philosophy or any other topic. He runs of course the risk of criticism by the specialists, but it is a risk he has to take. We comparatists surely would not want to prevent English professors from studying the French sources of Chaucer or French professors from studying the Spanish sources of Corneille, etc., since we comparatists would not want to be forbidden to publish on topics confined to specific national literatures. . . .The whole conception of fenced off reservations, with signs of "no tresspassing," must be distasteful to a free mind.[1]

Wellek's words made eminent sense to both of us. Even though one of us has spent his career as a teacher of French literature in a Department of Romance Languages, neither of us has felt his scholarly interests must be limited to the particular field he is expected to teach in, be it 17th- and 18th-century French Literature or Modern European Literature. With little discussion or disagreement, therefore, our objective defined itself as a collection of essays, loosely autobiograpical in nature, in which some distinguished senior scholars— not all of them necessarily teaching in a Comparative Literature department, but all sharing Wellek's cosmopolitan and internationalist position—would describe what they think Comparative Literature is, how they came to be associated with it, what the field seemed like to them when they first started out, how it has evolved in the last three or four decades, and finally what they think of it now that they have retired or are well advanced in their careers.

We invited a large number of scholars to contribute. Not all could accept. Many, understandably, were loath to take time out from other projects that meant a great deal to them. To those who accepted, the editors express their gratitude. Indeed, we were moved by their generosity to lay ourselves on the line along with them, and our own statements will be found at the end of the volume. Obviously, it is our hope that readers too will be thankful for these testimonial documents from a generation that contributed greatly to the present prosperity and popularity of Comparative Literature in the university. All of them shed light on the history of the field in this country, on the changing character of the American university in the last sixty or seventy years, and more broadly still on the vast social and cultural transformation undergone by the United States since World War II; but in addition, many will be enjoyed as lively, witty narratives of human experience and ingenuity, each of them carrying the imprint of its author's personality. We wish therefore to emphasize that we conceived the volume as a collection of personal testimonies contributing to the history of scholars and scholarship, rather than to the theory of literary study.

Because of their personal character, the essays will largely present themselves and do not need an extensive introduction. One may, however, briefly point out several general features that they have in common. Most of the essays illustrate a close intertwining of lived experience, theoretical reflection, and institutional and communal concerns. Several of the contributors have been German or East European nationals seeking refuge from Nazi persecution or from World War II and its devastating consequences, with all the emotional and intellectual turmoil that such exile entailed. Others were sons and daughters of immigrants and had a first-hand experience of exile and uprootedness in their homes. There are also those who made the reverse trip to Europe with a victorious American army either during or shortly after the war. It is therefore fair to say that an experience of uprootedness and exile occasioned by war lies at the basis of the very being of many of the contributors. They were "born to compare," as Lilian Furst suggests, and some of them had no other choice. They came or returned to America and founded or refounded a discipline to match their cosmopolitan, international experiences, their familiarity with boundary crossings, and at the same time their desire for a new kind of community, arising out of the experience of uprootedness and estrangement itself. Comparative Literature became for them the place where colleagues of diverse backgrounds and interests were united by deep-seated opposition to the "fenced off reservations" with their "no trespassing" signs, from which many of them had had to endure so much suffering, and by the conviction that greater understanding and—dare one say it?—a higher degree of humanity would be the prize for venturing into a world where frontiers were crossed rather than respected.

Their experience illustrates the ambiguous nature of any foundational act. On the one hand, as young men and women these scholars experienced America anew, as a land of unlimited possibilities and with an exhilarating sense of freedom, allowing for the creation of a novel self and novel institutions. On the other hand, they experienced the deep-rooted, often unconscious fear of constant change and ceaseless upset that inevitably accompanies exile, and that fear was eventually mediated in personal and institutional terms as a need for continuity, for upholding a humanistic tradition that had nourished them and their predecessors. In this sense, the most prominent of them were in their own modest way like the Byzantine scholars who after the fall of Constantinople took refuge upon the shores of Italy and were instrumental in bringing about the cultural Renaissance.

From this perspective, one can also understand the ambiguous feelings most of these scholars share in regard to theory, understood as will to order, on the one hand, and as ceaseless reflexivity, questioning, and self-questioning, on the other. In his 1958 ICLA address, for example, Wellek employed theory in order to challenge the traditional, positivist conception of Comparative Literature and the dominance of national language and literature departments. It is clear, then, that from early on Comparative Literature in the United States went hand in hand with theory, even though several accounts in this volume and elsewhere consider the association of the two a later development dating only from the end of the sixties and the importation of French structuralism and post-structuralism. In fact, ironically, it was to no small extent the avant-garde action of Wellek and his students that prepared the terrain for the later massive infiltration of postwar French and German theory into Comparative Literature. To some extent, therefore, the original theorizers became victims of their own success.

Several contributors express disappointment and occasionally even bitterness over the ideological divisions that have lately plagued the field without pausing, perhaps, to consider that spirited controversy has been a built-in component of Comparative Literature virtually from the outset and that the very nature of theory is agonistic, since it is closely related to questioning and debate about the nature and boundaries of literature and literary study. Other contributors display the same wise tolerance toward the most recent theoretical "excesses" that some of their open-minded teachers had displayed toward their own when they first started out; they view these excesses simply as part of the continuing challenge of any vigorous field of intellectual inquiry.

Having said this, however, we also ought to point out that the older generation of theorists by and large preserved intact their ties to the literary work and its historical contexts and, therefore, kept in check theory's *esprit de système* or will to order, which is not only potentially tyrannical and oppressive, but also ultimately the mirror of the will to disorder or chaos. From Wellek's delightful reminiscences, in this volume, of Princeton in the late 1920s, it seems that the only professor at Princeton at that time who had a theoretical interest—Morris Croll—was also the most intolerant of strong positions other than his own. When theory is not mediated by literary history and literary texts, it can easily turn into a pure power mechanism—a disturbing development that Stanley Corngold, among others, addresses eloquently in the present collection.

Another feature of the old comparatist school that appears to have lost ground among their successors is its free-spirited cosmopolitanism. The danger of turning Comparative Literature into a pure political agenda for special interest groups may be overdramatized in some of the essays, but is nevertheless real. Comparative Literature, as a number of the essayists point out, is naturally sympathetic to cultural and ethnic diversity and pluralism. Comparatists should not lose sight, however, either of their own scholarly and human limits (*ars longa, vita brevis*), or of the conflictive and exclusive nature of difference, including difference of the ethnic, cultural, and sexual kind, when it is no longer contained by a larger transcendent category, such as reason, humanity, or literature. What is needed, several contributors suggest, is greater generosity, openness, and tolerance all around. That, in the end, had been the objective of the founders, even at their most combative and provocative.

NOTES

1. René Wellek, "The Crisis of Comparative Literature," *Proceedings of the Second Congress of the International Comparative Literature Association* (Chapel Hill: University of North Carolina Press, 1959), 155–56.

1

Memories of the Profession

René Wellek

I am eighty-eight years old, retired since 1972, and thus can hardly advise on how to "build a profession." But I can supply, I hope, reflections and reminiscences about the profession which I have experienced in three different countries, in several subjects and several institutions. I should explain my background. I studied at the Czech University of Prague what was called Germanic Philology, that is, German and English literature and language, and received a D. Phil. in 1926. I had been to England several times but never received any formal instruction there in the history of English literature, which was my main passion. I thus was delighted that in 1927 I received a Procter Fellowship to the graduate school of Princeton University with a stipend of fifteen hundred dollars. My father lent me the money for the trip and I took the Dutch ship *The New Amsterdam* in September 1927 to New York.

I was late for the opening of the fall term at Princeton, partly because of bad weather on the ocean. After landing at Hoboken I immediately took a train to Princeton where I was assigned a very nice suite in the newly opened expansion of the graduate college. I was too tired to see anybody until the next morning, when I called on Professor Robert Kilburn Root, the head of the English Department. He welcomed me and asked me what my interests were, and I said that I wanted to study the English Romantic movement, Wordsworth and Coleridge in particular. He said, "Pick out the courses which you may like," and showed me a table of the courses. I did not know a single person except for George MacLean Harper, into whose two-volume biography of Wordsworth I had dipped. Mr. Root, when I mentioned Harper, waved him aside and said: "You will take a course with me on Pope, one with Mr. Thomas Marc Parrot on Shakespeare, and a seminar on Edmund Spenser with Charles Grosvenor Osgood." As I knew nothing about any of the people listed, I meekly accepted my schedule and started that very afternoon with Mr. Osgood's course on Spenser, which met in his house on Stockton Street.

1

Mr. Osgood, a man in his fifties, sat in a rocking chair in his book-lined study and listened to reports silently. When he did not like something he suddenly would start to say "Tut, tut," but never said a comprehensible word. I received for a report the topic "Spenser's Irish Rivers." I went to the library and pored over maps and dictionaries and composed what I thought was a decent account of the different rivers mentioned in *The Faerie Queene* and *The Shepheardes Calendar.* Colleagues commented that Mr. Osgood had maliciously given me a topic as far removed from my own interests as possible. Ireland had little to do with Bohemia, and Irish rivers with anything important in English literature. I, however, soon came to the conclusion that Mr. Osgood simply had a list of topics and assigned the Irish rivers to me as the next item and was hardly aware whether I came from Bohemia or the moon.

Mr. Parrot's course on Shakespeare amounted to a word-by-word comparison between the quarto and the folio of *Hamlet.* No attempt was made to discuss anything about what happened in *Hamlet,* but merely the verbal differences between the two versions were noticed and recorded. I frankly thought the course a bore. But luckily I met Mr. Parrot later and discovered that he was a widely educated and traveled gentleman who liked to go to Europe and knew a great deal about conditions in Germany, France, and England. I struck up lively conversations with him, and in 1935, on a trip to Europe, he made a special point of seeing me in Prague. I invited him and his son to our house for dinner and he was delighted to meet natives who were interested in the political situation which at that time had changed completely with the victory of the Nazis. He had been in Germany that summer and detested the Nazis and the whole German atmosphere. Mr. Parrot turned out to be very important in my later life when he made my move to the United States possible.

To come back now to 1927 and the situation at Princeton, I was frankly disappointed because at Prague we had lively debates and quarrels about literary history. Coming to Princeton was like being sent back to the later nineteenth century. Mr. Root was a very learned student of Alexander Pope who had a very (to me completely) new philosophy or rather outlook behind him. He called himself a "new humanist," which he combined with a fervent adherence to Anglo-Catholicism. I had never before met anybody who combined a Neo-classicism in literature with an orthodoxy in which King Charles I appeared as a martyr unjustly condemned by the Puritans.

Soon after I came to Princeton I was warned not to praise President Wilson. They rightly assumed that I, as a Czech, would praise the Fourteen Points, which were legal background for the establishment of the Czechoslovak Republic. At Princeton there were two factions: one which admired Wilson, who as president of the university had introduced the tutorial system, and to which Root, Osgood, and Parrot belonged, and another faction which was deeply rooted in the South and its ideology and condemned Wilson as a traitor. In this first year at Princeton I kept very quiet about politics and avoided conversations on the subject, pleading absorption in my courses.

I must not forget that at the recommendation of my fellow students I took a fourth seminar with Professor Morris Croll ostensibly devoted to the lyric. Mr. Croll assigned immediately the whole first part of Croce's *Aesthetics* for intensive study and discussion. I am afraid I shocked him, as I was the only student who had many reservations and arguments against some of Croce's main tenets. Mr. Croll thought of Croce's aesthetics as something like the Holy Bible. He found it extremely offensive that I had my doubts and he rather bruskly interrupted me and tried to silence me. I did not want to offend him and pretended to swallow Croce almost whole, also because I wanted to hear Mr. Croll on metrics, for he was one of the first professors who adopted Thompson's metrical annotation, which still has adherents even today. The Yale professor John C. Pope published a book, *The Rhythm of Beowulf* (1942), which works with this metrical theory, apparently very successfully.

On the whole, I had a very good year as a graduate student, partly because I wanted to learn to write in English and to grasp something of the methods and interests of the Princeton professors, which were by no means confined only to Princeton. Yale had many related students combining also literary classicism with fervent Anglicanism.

I wanted to stay on in the United States, as the rules of the University of Prague, which were then the same as at German universities, required the student to wait three years after the D. Phil. before he could present himself for a new examination, which required an oral lecture and a published book, in order to become Docent of English or German literary history. I thus asked my Princeton friends to find me a job, but there was nothing in Princeton for which I could be qualified—in practice, German language—but by looking through the professional journals I learned that Smith College in Northampton, Massachusetts, was looking for a teacher of German. I wrote a letter to the chairman of the German Department at Smith, Mr. Heinrich Mensel, and was invited to present myself for an interview. I took the train to Northampton, which was then still a station stop. When I left the train Mr. Mensel saw me getting out and walked up to me with his hands stretched out and said (I swear that these were his first words): "I see you are not a Jew." He then took me on a short tour of the college and finally to the office of the president of the college, Mr. William Allan Neilson. There a contract was laid out for me to sign, which I did, of course, happy to have a job for the following year. If I had been a Jew, Mr. Mensel would have taken me on a tour of the campus but sent me back to New York or wherever without calling on President Neilson.

I was of course confronted with the problem of registering at a university in order to protect myself against the immigration authorities, who could have expelled me. At the next opportunity I went up to Harvard and registered for a graduate course with John Livingston Lowes on Coleridge which met at a time when I could, with an effort, commute from Smith College. At Smith I taught two courses of German reading which amounted to translating and commenting on two harmless stories, Theodor Storm's "Immensee" and Eichendorff's "Aus dem Leben eines Taugenichts." Besides, I had a seminar on modern German poetry attended by one student, a German woman who liked George and Rilke.

On the whole, the year at Smith was a leisurely time. I remember best an excursion to Toronto where the Modern Language Association met as usual after Christmas. I took a train with other teachers from Smith to Toronto and was somewhat apprehensive that the American border guard would object to my passport which contained a visa explicitly valid only for the United States. But nothing happened. I got through to Toronto without any trouble and could not but be amazed at how the trainload of teachers from New York and other places on the way threw themselves at the banks which were about to close in order to get coupons that allowed them to buy liquor. This was the Canadian version of Prohibition, much softer than the American which was then still in force. All the American teachers got hold of coupons and bought any amout of whiskey and gin. We were then taken to the campus of the University of Toronto and put in a dormitory where there were big signs, "Drinking strictly prohibited"—but the company I was with immediately set about opening their bottles. They had no corkscrews or bottle openers, but they solved this problem by putting the bottles into the hinges of the doors and breaking the necks. Quantities of liquor poured out all over the floor, smelling up the place for the night. Otherwise, I do not remember the meeting.

In the summer of 1929 Professor G. M. Priest, the head of the German Department at Princeton, took a sabbatical and suggested that I be asked to fill his place for the year, expressly saying that the appointment would be for that year alone. I accepted, as I planned to return to Prague anyhow in 1930. I had again to devise a scheme that would allow me to register as a graduate student at some university while teaching as an assistant professor at Princeton. I got in touch with Mr. John Herman Randall, who was then an assistant professor of philosophy at Columbia. He had written a very successful book, *The Making of the Modern Mind* (1926), a skillfully organized and clear history of ideas mainly in the sixteenth and seventeenth centuries leading up to Romanticism. I visited him at Columbia and agreed to submit an elaborate paper on the Platonic, or rather Neoplatonic, tradition in English literature. I had to study Shaftesbury and the Cambridge Platonists and submitted finally a paper which met with his strong approval. At Princeton I taught elementary German grammar and syntax from current textbooks, a routine job which allowed me to cultivate the company of the younger faculty members. I met there people with whom I struck up an intimate friendship, such as John Ellis Baker, who wrote a thesis on the Oxford Movement and who later was the only person I knew in Iowa City, where he had found a job in English.

In the summer of 1930 I returned to Prague, as my father had warned me that a rival could have occupied the slot for a Docent in English literature if I did not return. Professor Mathesius, who was professor of English at the Czech University, obviously preferred me to the competitor and appointed me assistant professor to take over his courses, as he had to take a leave of absence because of a serious affliction of sudden blindness. I heard that he called on an ophthalmologist who shook his head when he saw that there was a tumor on the back of his spine and sent him to a specialist in tuberculosis. Mathesius had to quit teaching for years but did not resign his professorship for reasons which were purely financial. He could not have lived on his pension, as he had to support a family and pay the extra expenses at the gratis government hospital. I saw him there, lying under a big beam to which his arms were tied. I taught four years as a substitute for Mr. Mathesius, following his plan of lecturing on English literature from the middle of the eighteenth century to the end of the nineteenth. These four years taught me much literary history and forced me to formulate my knowledge in Czech.

Mathesius realized that I was poorly paid in a low position, and he managed to persuade the Ministry of Education to appoint me lecturer in Czech at the School of Slavonic Studies at the University of London. The director of the School, Sir Bernard Pares, received me cordially, but stuck to the reservation that the School could dismiss the lecturer with only a year's notice. It meant for me that every year there were certain doubts about my staying on. But Sir Bernard was apparently satisfied with me and I stayed there until the invasion of Prague by Hitler on 15 March 1939. The Germans immediately stopped my pay. My wife Olga and I had somewhat foreseen this catastrophe and managed to save enough money to pay for passage to New York. We did not even think of returning to Prague. Even before the invasion I had written to my former teachers at Princeton asking for some help in acquiring a non-quota visa, which required that I have the definite promise of a position in the United States with exactly the same rank and salary as I had in London. Mr. Root wrote me bluntly: "Go back to Prague. There will be no war. There's no reason to emigrate." But Mr. Parrot, who understood the situation better, wrote a letter to Professor Norman Foerster, who was the head of the School of Letters at the University of Iowa, not only recommending me but sending a copy of my first published book, *Immanuel Kant in England*, which had come out in 1931. Mr. Foerster was impressed by my book and by Mr. Parrot's praise, and I received an offer of a position at Iowa in the spring of 1939.

We went first to New Haven, as the nearest city to New York with the reputation of a great library. I used that summer to finish the manuscript of a book I had prepared in London, which was published in 1941 as *The Rise of English Literary History*. That summer at Yale I made the acquaintance of James Marshall Osborn, a private scholar who worked on the history of English studies and thus shared many of my interests. His good words must have played a role in the offer from Yale in 1945.

We arrived in Iowa City on 1 September 1939, when boys with extra editions of an afternoon paper told of the outbreak of European war. We settled in a modest house and the next day I called on Mr. Foerster, who welcomed me cordially and then introduced me to his new professor of English, Austin Warren, who had come from Boston University. Iowa City was a very small town, ten thousand people at that time. We communicated largely by word of mouth or by telephone. Mr. Foerster called together Mr. Warren; me; a linguist, John C. McGalliard; and a professor of English who taught what was called creative writing, Wilbur Schramm. We met in Mr. Foerster's rather stately house regularly and composed fairly quickly a book which came out in 1941 as *Literary Scholarship*, published by the University of North Carolina Press, with which Mr. Foerster had old contacts. I also sent my manuscript to North Carolina, where *The Rise of English Literary History* came out also in 1941.

All this may sound idyllic, but actually Iowa City was divided into at least two factions: those who supported Mr. Foerster's humanism or neohumanism, mainly in the wake of Irving Babbitt, and those who rejected all these newfangled trends in scholarship and insisted on a knowledge of facts, sources, titles, and sometimes biographies. Mr. Baldwin Maxwell, the head of the English Department, had written very specialized articles on details of the history of the English drama; the title of one piece, "The Date of 'Wily-Beguiled,' " lent itself to satirical comments. The other faction was extremely and even malevolently hostile. The tone of department meetings can be illustrated by quoting Professor Pfuhl, who told us that we were "despised" all over the country and that we did not belong to a university at all. To understand this, one has to realize that Mr. Foerster had been brought in as director of the School of Letters with the (at that time) fabulous salary of thirteen thousand dollars, while the next professor, Mr. Maxwell, got only five thousand. I remember an occasion when the dean of the graduate school told an assembly of the members that he could fire us all and rehire us for half-pay. But nothing ever happened.

The whole atmosphere was poisoned also by the sharp division between isolationists and supporters of the Allies. The table conversations often became acrimonious. Students carried placards with the inscription "The Yanks are not coming." Things changed of course with Pearl Harbor on 7 December 1941. When I suggested at the luncheon table that the speech announced by Hitler would contain a declaration of war against the United States, I was laughed at. Still, I won a very moderate bet the day Hitler delivered his anti-American harangue.

I was assigned a graduate course on the German influence in English literature. I had a small group of students and was surprised by the eagerness with which one of them, a Quaker from Pella, Iowa, Arthur Wormhoudt, took up the question of Jakob Böhme's influence in England in the seventeenth and eighteenth centuries and submitted a solid, well-argued, convincing paper which later led to his receiving a Ph.D. under my direction.

Teaching at Iowa was interrupted by the establishment of language and area courses by the Army in order to train interpreters. I was assigned a section in Czech which required my complete attention from September 1942. The Army had assigned thirty-five young sergeants and corporals to learn spoken Czech in case the Army reached Czechoslovakia. As there was no textbook, I had to compose a textbook of my own. I taught seventeen hours of Czech each week and had to find additional teachers to support me. I got a young man, Milič Kybal, from Whittier College in Los Angeles and another, Milič Čapek, who was stranded in a physics lab at the University of Pennsylvania. We three worked very hard for seven months, but when we were about ready to have the students graduate with a fair knowledge of Czech, Mr. Henry Stimson, the Secretary of War, suddenly abolished all these programs and sent the young men back to the ranks. The result was that when General Patton's army reached Czechoslovakia in the spring of 1945 they had no interpreters and had to hire local Germans with some knowledge of Czech. Some years later when I was at Yale a young man from Bridgeport named Dybicz, who had been in my course at Iowa City, appeared at my office and told me that he spent the war as an MP in Marseilles—not a good place to exercise his Czech.

The two books I published in 1941—my contribution to the symposium *Literary Scholarship* and my monograph on *The Rise of English Literary History*—were received with great interest at the Huntington Library in San Marino, California. The director, Louis B. Wright, appointed me to a fellowship for the summer of 1942. My wife and I went out and were given an apartment in the Atheneum of the California Institute of Technology, which was in walking distance of the library. We could not stand it there, as the Atheneum was filled with Navy officers who were ready for shipment on battleships and cruisers; they were assembling for what turned out to be the Battle of Midway which changed the course of the Pacific war. The secretary at the Huntington Library gave us the address of a lady on Rosalind Road who rented a porter's lodge for the summer. My wife went out and was met by the owner, Mrs. Donleavy, whose husband, we found out later, was the owner of the *Saturday Evening Post* and several other periodicals. The lodge was a newly equipped little house of great charm with access to the large garden inhabited by flocks of quail. My wife asked Mrs. Donleavy how much she was asking for this porter's lodge and she replied that her agent had said five hundred dollars a month. As our fellowship to the Huntington Library amounted to only nine hundred dollars for two months, paying this sum was out of the question. But Mrs. Donleavy talked to my wife and found out that we were recent refugees from Czechoslovakia. She apparently took to her and said, "I don't care for money. Would you like to have it for fifty dollars?" So we did.

The summer at the Huntington Library was very profitable. I read books I had never seen before and met people in the profession, such as Merrit Y. Hughes, the famous Milton scholar, and Ruth Wallerstein, who had written on seventeenth-century poetics. At the end of the summer of 1942 we returned by train to Iowa City, not stopping anywhere on the way, as my wife expected a child. My son Alexander was born on 5 March 1943 in Iowa City.

The good impression of my work must have stimulated Dean William C. DeVane of Yale University. At the meeting of the Modern Language Association in Chicago at Christmas 1944 Mr. DeVane asked me to call on him and he offered me a professorship of Slavic and Comparative Literature at Yale with the reservation that I would first give an acceptable lecture. I remember that I hesistated to consider the offer, as definite as it sounded. There was the question of selling the house in Iowa City and buying a property in New Haven. For me this offer was decisive. I had friends in New York who had very good information about conditions in Czechoslovakia just after the war, and they confirmed me in the view that I should reject any offer from Prague. I decided to become an American citizen, and went to the Iowa City courthouse where I was askcd whether I could read and write! I got naturalized, though my wife did not, but stayed a Czechoslovak citizen until 1948 when the Communists took power. She then ran down to the courthouse in New Haven to get naturalized, in great haste.

In February 1945 I made a trip to New Haven and gave a lecture on "The Revolt against Positivism in Recent European Literary Scholarship." It was apparently well received by the rather small audience that listened to it. This audience included John C. Pope, Mr. Pottle, Mr. Menner, Henri Peyre, and other prominent humanists. Dean DeVane assured me that my appointment was definite. We sold our house in Iowa City and I rented a house for the summer in Woodbridge, commuting by bus to town to work in the library. After a long search I discovered a shingled house on Ridgewood Avenue in Hamden which I could afford. The owner, Mr. Menzies, wanted an agreement within two hours. My wife and little son were still in Iowa City and I had to phone there to get her consent. We moved into the Hamden house in September 1945, and I started teaching at Yale, announcing a course on Russian literature and a seminar on the history of criticism. The course on the Russian novel became a grcat success. It attracted some one hundred twenty-five students and caused some trouble because I had to have two assistants to grade the papers. These assistants were sophisticated graduate students—one of them an Englishman, Tony Thorbly, and Thomas R. Hart from the University of Oregon. They often wrote sarcastic comments on the examination papers which in turn elicited loud protests and long arguments with the reader and finally with me, who had to be the arbiter.

I taught this course on the Russian novel till 1962, when I used the occasion of a leave of absence to give the course to a newly appointed assistant professor of Russian, Robert L. Jackson, while I more and more concentrated on graduate seminars in the history of criticism or on some problem of comparative literature. In 1952 President Whitney Griswold had given me the title of Sterling Professor of Comparative Literature, and I could then shed the original emphasis on Slavic literature. I continued in this way until my retirement in 1972. I can say that the Yale administration has always treated me well and fulfilled my wishes, particularly when I accepted an offer to move the whole department into the seventh and eighth floors of Bingham Hall, where the department took over a large German library collected by a Professor Schreiber. We were not allowed to destroy or remove any of the books he had collected, but I managed to put old textbooks of German into boxes and to move into the front complete editions of the classics. When Adam Milman Parry and his wife, both professors in the Classics Department, died in a motorcycle accident they left their books to the Comparative Literature library. We had now a solid collection of the main Greek and Latin classics, and I managed to persuade the administration to give us a small sum of five or six thousand dollars a year to buy books which would supplement the German library with relevant books on comparative literature or on issues in criticism. The students can have free access there to the writings of such great scholars as Auerbach, Curtius, and Spitzer. I had learned in Prague that even a small freely accessible seminar library is worth more than the treasures of Beinecke or Sterling Library if we judge it from the point of view of a diligent graduate student.

The library was soon used also as a place for discussions and lectures. We brought in even very prominent scholars. I feel that we have there an excellent basis for teaching on a high level within a tradition of scholarship which still pays attention to the demands and wishes of the students. Discussions swirled around the lecturers, and soon many students from other departments came to listen and to take part in the discussions. The students of comparative literature had begun to form quite a community of their own and were able to look back to a group of eminent members of the first several years of the Comparative Literature program. I do not want to be invidious about this new, more numerous group, but rather to comment on the very first students of the program. Oddly enough, an Italian, Pier Pasinetti, was the first Ph.D., who wrote a sensitive thesis on the image of the poet in modern literature which won the Porter Prize. Pasinetti later became a very well known Italian novelist who taught Italian literature at UCLA for many years.

Lowry Nelson, Jr., wrote a Ph.D. thesis on Baroque poetry, with an emphasis on Spanish Baroque and particularly on Gongora. He left us for the Harvard Society of Fellows, from where after several years he went out to UCLA as a younger colleague of Pasinetti, teaching Spanish. When I left for my sabbatical in 1962 I offered him a visiting professorship in our Comparative Literature department, and he was so well liked and admired that we were able to keep him. He is even now with us.

The third Ph.D. was an Englishman, Anthony Thorbly, who returned to England, served in the army, and founded a Comparative Literature department at the University of Sussex at Brighton, the only department in England that called itself "comparative." As other British universities followed, Thorbly can be called the founder of Comparative Literature studies in Great Britain, at least in an official sense.

Another early student was a young woman, Dorrit Hale, a refugee from Vienna who passed her orals with distinction, but left us then to marry Robert Cohn, who later became well known for his writings on Mallarmé. She had children with him, but after several years took a Ph.D. with Edgar Lohner, the translator into German of my *Theory of Literature*. Surprisingly, after a short stay at Bloomington, Mrs. Cohn was called to Harvard with a book, *Transparent Minds* (1978).

Thomas R. Hart wrote a thesis on the early histories of Spanish literature, which were all by non-Spaniards: Bouterwek, Sismondi, Ticknor. Mr. Hart went out to his alma mater, the University of Oregon, and became there professor of Comparative Literature. He not only taught but also edited the periodical *Comparative Literature*, founded by the Modern Language Association, for over forty years, and wrote very important monographs on Giles Vincente.

The students at the university can be proud of the scholars who taught them and upheld an ideal of the union of teaching and scholarship. Only recently, new dark clouds appear on the horizon, not only of Yale but of most American universities. Part of the troubles are political and have been described in several books, such as *Illiberal Education* (1991) by Dinesh D'Souza, a young Indian who edited the *Dartmouth Review* for a time and is now with the American Enterprise Institute in Washington. There, on page 177, Mr. D'Souze says that my and Austin Warren's "influential book *A* [?] Theory of Literature (1949) . . . maintained that the definition of literature was problematic and posited circumstances under which Shakespeare might be displaced by the Manhattan phone book or by graffiti." The notes contain no page reference, but could not have such a reference, as I never believed in anything so foolish as that Shakespeare could be displaced by the Manhattan phone book. I have always taught and written with a completely opposite point of view, always defended the need of judgement in literary criticism and analyzed and appreciated the great writers of the past. I do not want to be called "one of the cofounders of the *au courant* scholarship" (p. 39).

But I do not at this point want to enter into the thicket of these controversies. Rather, I want to express my fear about the rumors of an assault on the union of scholarship and teaching which I hope we have established at Yale. I hear of proposals to make Yale a first-class undergraduate college, returning it to the status of the nineteenth century, downplaying the achievements of historical and literary scholarship. This seems to me a horrible mistake, an assault on what is the best in a place like Yale, which must be considered somewhat apart from others. We have at Yale first-class libraries of irreplaceable manuscripts and first editions. Yale is the right place to bring scholarship together with teaching in the conviction that no teaching is of much value which is not based on first-hand scholarship, at least of the teachers. They should uphold, in practice and by their own example, the concept of historical and literary scholarship which has grown over the centuries and has created great works and deep insights into the past and even the present of humanity. To abandon this ideal seems to me a real crime against Yale University, the American university tradition, and even the reputation of America abroad.

I hope these fears are exaggerated. Scientists will always want to have their labs and computers and will defend the ideal of an exact empirical knowledge. History and literature have in their eyes the disadvantage of inexactness or arbitrary individualism. But history and literature have their own ideal of exact knowledge, which cannot be simply dismissed as caprice but is a concept of knowledge that is in some way wider than that of the sciences, as it embraces the whole man, his feelings and even prejudices included. Both history and literature uphold the ideal of a total man and should be defended as the basis of a rounded education. Scholarship cannot be divorced from teaching. The real scholars are the best teachers, if only as models. One could reject this view and argue that many members of the Yale Corporation were only undergraduates at Yale, but they were taught precisely by scholars and must have recognized this ideal of the union of scholarship and teaching, as otherwise Yale would have declined into an undergraduate college of the sort prevalent in the nineteenth century, where scholars were only occasional lucky exceptions. I greatly hope that this attack on the ideal of the humanities as the union of scholarship and teaching will fail.

2

Comparative Literature at Harvard

Harry Levin

The systematic recognition and study of literature as such came gradually to the universities. It is true that their traditional curriculum was principally based upon great books in ancient languages: Greek and Latin, plus—in the Puritan canon—biblical Hebrew. But, under a program dedicated originally to the training of future ministers, lawyers, and teachers, the pedagogical emphasis fell upon the practice of rhetoric. It was not until 1876, two hundred and forty years after the founding of America's oldest college, that Francis James Child relinquished its Boylston Professorship of Rhetoric and Oratory in order to become Harvard's first Professor of English. Living foreign languages had been introduced early in the nineteenth century, largely through the efforts of George Ticknor, the Dartmouth graduate who returned from postgraduate studies in Europe to become Harvard's first Smith Professor of the French and Spanish Languages. Some degree of comparison, some approach to the more synoptical purview of Romanistics, seems to have been implicit in the terms of that appointment. Ticknor was succeeded by Henry Wadsworth Longfellow and in turn by James Russell Lowell, both of them cosmopolitan men of letters—as had been their predecessor, the pioneering historian of Spanish literature. Longfellow branched out into Italian, moving toward his translation of Dante's *Commedia*; Lowell, under the heading of "Belles Lettres," contributed an extracurricular sequence of lectures which pointed toward his published essays on European writers.

As the respective departments were developed (English, Romance, Germanic, later Celtic and Slavic), they would be subsumed within a Division of Modern Languages, an examining and degree-recommending body which paralleled and complemented the Division of Ancient Languages (comprising the Greco-Roman Classics and Indic Philology). It was among the modern language offerings in the catalogue of 1892–93, closely bound together by a common background in philology and consequently by a temporal focus upon the Middle Ages, that the new rubric made its first appearance. Arthur Richmond Marsh, a Harvard graduate of 1883 who had studied abroad and taught at the University of Kansas, had just been designated Assistant Professor of Comparative Literature and was now offering two courses: "Latin Literature in the Middle Ages with especial reference to France and Provence" and "Mediaeval Literature in the Vulgar Tongues." He would justify the curricular innovation with an article in PMLA (1896), "The Comparative Study of Literature." Defining this as a method rather than a subject, as a somewhat more scientific alternative to the naive estheticism of existing critical approaches, he broadly sketched a line of historical precedents that centered on the rhetorical conception of *eloquentia*. More prophetically, he exemplified by referring to the Homeric Question, which involved its exponents in the conditions of authorship, the nature of genres, the generation of myths, and cross-reference to analogous compositions from different cultures.

But it was not Marsh's destiny to fulfil the prospects that he had outlined. Though he was elected a corresponding member of the Spanish Academy, and was promoted to a full professorship in 1898, he unexpectedly resigned from Harvard in the following year. That academic anticlimax led to a mercantile climax, when his subsequent career in business culminated with the presidency of the New York Cotton Exchange. Some of his teaching was taken over by colleagues from Romance Languages, notably E. S. Sheldon and M. A. Potter; the latter directed graduate studies and established two essay prizes. The program's chronological scope was extended from the Middle Ages to the Renaissance by J. B. Fletcher, who was soon called to Columbia University. Members of the English Department were increasingly active: Barrett Wendell with an introductory survey of European literature, Bliss Perry and George Pierce Baker with generic courses in fiction and drama, and William Allan Neilson on allegory. Already in 1891 George Edward Woodberry, a poet-critic who had graduated from Harvard (where he is commemorated by a Poetry Room in the Lamont Library), had begun to teach his version of Comparative Literature at Columbia. He would be named professor of a new department in 1900, start a *Journal of Comparative Literature* that appeared for four issues in 1903, and then resign to pursue his own writing in 1904.

He was succeeded by his former pupil, Joel Elias Spingarn, who had made an outstanding scholarly contribution with his *Literary Criticism in the Renaissance*. Spingarn would leave academic life quite suddenly in 1911, after a disagreement on administrative policies that would end with the annexation of Columbia's Department of Comparative Literature to its Department of English. Meanwhile Harvard had conferred its initial doctorate in Comparative Literature (1904), and in 1906—by a vote of the faculty on a motion from F. N. Robinson, the Chaucerian scholar and Celticist—set up a separate department under the Division of Modern Languages. Its chairman, appointed at the same time to the vacant chair in Comparative Literature, was W. H. Schofield, who had graduated from the University of Toronto and taken a Harvard Ph.D. in English philology. A Canadian with a great many European connections, a well-rounded medievalist primarily concerned with the history of Middle English literature, Schofield had additional interests in Scandinavian culture from the Icelandic Eddas to Dano-Norwegian drama. Though his own career would be cut short by illness in 1920, it was he who founded and helped to subsidize the *Harvard Studies in Comparative Literature*. This series, a continuing publication of the Harvard University Press, has brought out forty-one titles to date, which denote both particular researches within the Department and programmatic tendencies in the field at large.

These *Studies* began, upon the unique intellectual plane of George Santayana, with his *Three Philosophical Poets: Lucretius, Dante, Goethe* (1910). Continuation included two volumes by Schofield himself, along with others reflecting a departmental concern with the Nordic sphere: *The Comedies of Holberg* by O. J. Campbell, *Angevin Britain and Scandinavia* by Henry Goddard Leach. Two more volumes by B. J. Whiting, dealing with proverbs in their literary contexts, linked folklore with Comparative Literature—as, in another vein, did *Virgil the Necromancer* by J. W. Spargo. Still another vantage-point, with a broadening outlook on intercultural relations, would be represented by E. J. Simmons's *English Literature and Culture in Russia (1553–1840)*, as well as by the volumes that came out in French during the general editorship of Fernand Baldensperger. A later phase was heralded by the collective volume, *Perspectives of Criticism*, which I undertook to gather mainly from the new members of a reestablished department, and would attempt to supplement with two volumes of my own essays, particularly devoted to critical method and the definition of terms. Albert Lord's elucidation of his extensive fieldwork, *The Singer of Tales*, tracing the Greek epos to its bardic origins, has had a substantial impact. So has the symposium *On Translation*, edited by Reuben Brower with contributions from Dudley Fitts, John Hollander, Rolfe Humphries, Roman Jakobson, Willa and Edwin Muir, Vladimir Nabokov, Justin O'Brien, and Willard V. Quine.

Often a doctoral thesis, emerging as a printed monograph, has marked the emergence of its author as a scholar or critic of some authority: *The Testament of Werther in Poetry* and *Drama* by Stuart Atkins, *Vissarion Belinski, 1841–1848* by Herbert Bowman, *Praisers of Folly: Erasmus, Rabelais, Shakespeare* by Walter Kaiser, *Rogue's Progress: Studies in the Picaresque Novel* by Robert Alter, *Dostoevsky and Romantic Realism: A Study of Dostoevsky in Relation to Balzac, Dickens, and Gogol* by Donald Fanger, *The Icelandic Family Saga: An Analytic Reading* by Theodore Andersson, *Roman Laughter: The Comedy of Plautus* by Erich Segal, *Pan the Goat-God: His Myth in Modern Times* by Patricia Merivale, *The Renaissance Discovery of Time* by Ricardo Quinones, *Comparative Studies in Greek and Indic Meter* by Gregory Nagy.

Contributors from other institutions have added their distinction to Harvard's list: Lilian Furst, *Fictions of Romantic Irony: Jane Austen, Flaubert, Byron, Jean Paul, Diderot, Sterne;* Virgil Nemoianu, *The Taming of Romanticism: European Literature and the Age of Biedermeier*; Jean Starobinski, *The Living Eye* (translated from the original French). Among the latest volumes are numbered Stephen Owen's study in modern Chinese poetry (*Milou: Poets and the Labyrinth of Desire*), Jurij Striedter's correlative interpretation of Russian Formalism and Czech Structuralism (*Literary Structure, Evolution, and Value*), and Svetlana Boym's explorations of poetic subjectivity in French and Russian (*Death in Quotation Marks: Cultural Myths of the Modern Poet*).

But to glance across that whole shelf is to overleap matters of personnel, to which we must return. During a long generation, from the late eighteen-nineties through the early nineteen-thirties, the most influential teacher and predominant personality—Harvard's Dr. Johnson—was Irving Babbitt. Nominally a professor of French, he took over two courses that had briefly been inaugurated by Lewis E. Gates: one on the Romantic Movement, the other on the history of literary criticism. He originated another, on Rousseau and his influence, which became his most characteristic forum and would inspire his central book. (His other books dealt with French critics, aesthetic theory, higher education in America, and the social problems of democracy; and there were also two collections of sharply pointed essays.) Babbitt's own influence, especially upon undergraduates, has been well attested by such former pupils as T. S. Eliot and Van Wyck Brooks. For a while it almost became a movement in itself, promulgated by his more academic disciples—Paul Elmer More, Norman Foerster, Stuart P. Sherman—and rallying to the watchword of "New Humanism." Generally speaking, this was nothing less than a critique of unbridled modernism from the standpoint of ethical tradition or political neo-conservatism. From an educational perspective, it could best be understood as a rear-guard action on behalf of the endangered humanities. It was encyclopedic in its viewpoint, drawing upon Babbitt's personal knowledge of Sanskrit and looking forward to a wider acquaintance with Asiatic thought.

Recognizing the gap left by Babbitt's death, the University made a distinguished outside appointment. It could not have chosen a more official *comparatiste* than Fernand Baldensperger, who had just retired from his Institut de Littérature Comparée at the Sorbonne. But the ensuing years (1935–40) would not be very propitious for international relations of any kind. Baldensperger proved an urbane and friendly senior colleague, offered comprehensive but sparsely attended courses in world literature, and then moved on to a second American quinquennium at the University of California, Los Angeles. The interval of the Second World War was a limbo for Comparative Literature at Harvard. Courses were suspended or relocated; two or three graduate students straggled toward the doctoral degree; several of us formed a sort of temporary holding company by lunching together weekly at the Faculty Club. Shortly after the war an unsympathetic chairman of the Division recommended that the Department be formally abolished. His foremost predecessor, George Lyman Kittredge, had once declared it his pontifical duty to dissuade any aspirants for its degrees. Such suspicious attitudes have been quite familiar to those who laid the groundwork for our specialty. Departmental rivalries opposed it; professorial elders viewed its programs as overextended or superficial—which, alas, they could sometimes be. But it was ironic to face opposition from what Babbitt had termed "the philological syndicate"; for Harvard's medievalists and folklorists had, within their self-limited domain, taken the earliest steps toward this cross-cultural interchange.

Yet Comparative Literature must, by definition, be a collaborative endeavor; most of its departments could just as well be regarded as interdepartmental committees; and most of our divisional colleagues wanted to see Harvard's department revived, reorganized, and brought up to date. In 1946 a subcommittee consisting of André Morize (French), Karl Viëtor (German), and myself (English) drew up some tentative plans. Our report was unanimously adopted, and the recently tenured junior member—despite, or perhaps because of, his administrative inexperience—was relegated to the chairmanship. On all sides the time was ripe for an enlarged commitment to the evolving discipline; postwar fellowships were sending Americans abroad and welcoming foreign visitors to our campuses; curricular revision was creating a need for younger teachers who could lead discussion on Great Books from various countries. The National Defense Education Act would provide eventual reinforcement for the study of languages. The European-American diaspora, which had brought Morize and Viëtor to Harvard, would bring Werner Jaeger from Germany, Roman Jakobson from Russia, Paul Bénichou from France, and Amado Alonso from Spain. The profession itself was spreading so widely that, by 1949, the University of Oregon could launch the journal *Comparative Literature*. In 1952–53, while lecturer on exchange at the Sorbonne (where Schofield had been my predecessor some forty years before), I was invited by Jean-Marie Carré to express a *"point de vue d'outre-Atlantique"* for a symposium sponsored by the *Revue de littérature comparée*.

Nineteen sixty saw the founding of the American Comparative Literature Association. Its first president was W. P. Friederich, a native of Switzerland who had taken a Harvard Ph.D. with a thesis on *Die Diesseits-Jenseits Problem in der Englischen Barocklyrik*, and had occupied his veteran post in the established department at the University of North Carolina since 1936. The second president was René Wellek, the third myself; the second triennial meeting took place at Cambridge in 1965. By 1964 our unifying phrase had been invoked to cover such numerous and diverse activities that the Association asked some of us to report on professional standards. The year of Harvard's reorganization, 1946, had also witnessed the beginning of Yale's conspicuous role, when Wellek became its professor of Slavic and Comparative Literature, leaving his professorship of English at the University of Iowa. Such a joint appointment, almost simultaneously, had been accepted at Harvard by Renato Poggioli. Professors operating in Comparative Literature have likewise tended to be part-time specialists in one basic area; and it is significant that, in both of those instances, that base had shifted to the Slavic languages. Harvard was then reorganizing its Department of Slavic, and Poggioli's call was equally due to his competence in Russian literature. He had been trained in Italy as a Slavicist, gone on to teach Romance Languages in Poland and Czechoslovakia, coedited the quarterly *Inventario*, and translated poetry into Italian from a dozen other languages—an auspicious preparation for a comparatist.

My own apprenticeship, on the other hand, had never been entirely disengaged from my local alma mater, although a year on one of its travelling fellowships and five years in its incipient Society of Fellows had encouraged me to stray beyond the collegiate borders of Classical and Anglo-American literature. Baldensperger had benignly allowed me to work up an experimental course on Marcel Proust, James Joyce, and Thomas Mann (which would be recollected by Norman Mailer in his first novel, and audited by Jacques Derrida as an exchange fellow from the Ecole Normale Supérieure). Poggioli, along with his alternating courses in the Romanticists and the Symbolists, regularly gave a proseminar in Theory of Literature, which became our propaedeutic requirement for first-year graduate students (utilizing the recent handbook of the same title, by Wellek and Austin Warren, as a well-timed syllabus). He became chairman in 1952, and served for a decade; I was meanwhile chairing the Division, but reverted to the Department's chairmanship—after his tragic death by motor accident—in 1963, and would serve in that capacity off and on for a total of seventeen and one-half years. Part of our great loss lay in Poggioli's teeming file of uncompleted projects; but he had left a rich legacy of usable ideas through the English translation of his *Teoria dell' avanguardia* and the posthumous publication of his versions of pastoral, *The Oaten Flute*. His *Poets of Russia: 1890–1930* had won the Faculty Prize of the Harvard University Press in 1960.

The Harvard administration of President James B. Conant and Provost Paul H. Buck, committed as it was to General Education, to interdisciplinary cooperation, and to broadening the preliminary courses in the Humanities, likewise lent its institutional support to Comparative Literature. Conant's successor, President Nathan M. Pusey, who had studied with Irving Babbitt as an undergraduate, created a professorship in his memory, which was entrusted to me as another former pupil (while Poggioli became the Curt Hugo Reisinger Professor of Slavic and Comparative Literature). Francis P. Magoun, the medieval philologist who inherited Schofield's title as well as his courses, had clarified a changing situation by gracefully stepping back into the English Department. (There would be a further clarification when another department, Comparative Philology, updated and retitled itself as Linguistics.) Albert Lord had taken his doctorate in 1949, carrying on toward completion and formulation the interrupted researches of his classical mentor, Milman Parry. Lord's final examination was truly a *soutenance de thèse*, since oral composition was its thesis in the most controversial sense of the word, and had then to be defended against received Homeric opinion. That event was conducted before a large and notable committee of examiners, including C. M. Bowra and Roman Jakobson. Magoun, who had started out as the sharpest challenger, ended by being converted to the advancing position, and went on to adopt it in his own later work on the *Beowulf* and other Germanic lore.

J. C. LaDrière, an early Ph.D. in Comparative Literature from the University of Michigan, had been a Junior Fellow at Harvard, and had been training comparatists at the Catholic University of America (Washington) before returning to Cambridge in his later years (1965-78). Unfortunately these turned out to be years of declining health, which kept him from book-length consolidation of those penetrating ideas which he had put forth in well-informed articles on comparative metrics and critical theory. In the latter subject, through the proseminar, he made some devoted disciples; and it was at that time—in response to suggestions from students—that we added a complementary proseminar on critical methods, which I would teach in its opening rounds. This was very capably continued by Harold C. Martin, our recent alumnus who had charge of the freshman writing program (1955-65), whence the practical gifts he had manifested took him off to administrative responsibilities in other spheres (as president, in succession, of Union College and of the American Academy at Rome). At the level of part-time lecturer, we were briefly joined by Paul de Man (1957-60), who taught small groups effectively, and whose dissertation on Yeats and Mallarmé would be expanded into a subsequent book. Nothing that he ever did or said, as a graduate student or junior colleague, hinted at the disconcerting revelation about his youthful Belgian writings— though one might retrospectively interpret his post-structural metaphysics as a defensive argument that writers do not actually mean what they say.

From 1970 to 1980 the Department benefited from the presence of Jean Bruneau, who served as chairman for four of those years. Half of his teaching was in French literature, and his principal publication would be the definitive Pléiade edition of Flaubert's *Correspondance*. He was thoroughly at home in the United States, where his wife had studied at Radcliffe College; but he had been Carré's *assistant* in Comparative Literature at the University of Paris, and would go back to reassume the oldest French chair in the field (established in 1897)—occupied earlier by his grandfather, Edmond Estève, at the University of Lyons. Bruneau's chairmanship with us was preceded and followed by that of our alumnus, Walter Kaiser, who has latterly moved on to the directorship of the Villa I Tatti at Florence, formerly the estate of Bernard Berenson, now the Harvard University Center for Italian Renaissance Studies. Another of our alumni, Claudio Guillén, who had been teaching previously at Cologne,

Princeton, and San Diego, and had lectured and published widely on problems of methodology, spent a few years as chairman at Harvard before retiring early to his ancestral Spain. His successor in the chairmanship, Joaquim-Francisco Coelho, a native Brazilian who took his doctorate in Comparative Literature at the University of Wisconsin, is Harvard's Nancy Clark Smith Professor of the Portuguese Language and Literature. The present chairman, Judith Ryan, a native Australian with a doctorate from the University of Münster, is Robert K. and Dale J. Weary Professor of German and Comparative Literature, specializing in modern European fiction and poetry.

In an opportune year for reorganization, 1984, following some retirements, departmental standing and titles were extended to a number of cooperating professors from other departments. Tenured posts have also been accorded to Barbara Johnson, who has cultivated a timely range of theoretical interests, and to Jan Ziolkowski, who ably carries on the traditions of E. K. Rand and Herbert Bloch in medieval Latin scholarship. At the moment there are other openings to be filled. The pursuit of folklore, which began with Child's ballad-collecting, which was augmented by such Harvard-trained scholars as Stith Thompson, and reached so high a point in the Parry-Lord studies of oral composition, has now propagated a major of its own, with the establishment of a Faculty Committee on Undergraduate Degrees in Folklore and Mythology. (Lord himself, who died in the past year, played a leading part as Arthur Kingsley Porter Professor of Slavic and Comparative Literature.) Having enjoyed a friendly relationship with Harvard's authoritative Department of East Asian Languages and Civilizations, we have conjointly turned out a succession of Ph.D.s in East-West literary relations. Latin-American studies have, obviously, become more and more important. History of ideas, which Babbitt had practised in his own way, was given further impetus when Arthur Lovejoy delivered the first series of William James Lectures (on *The Great Chain of Being* in 1933). Our seminar in thematics was set up with the cordial and stimulating collaboration of Henry A. Murray, the professor of clinical psychology who had devised its Thematic Apperception Tests.

At Harvard there has never been an undergraduate major—or field of concentration, as we call it—in Comparative Literature, denominated as such. But this does not mean that it could not have been pursued, as a focal subject, by interested undergraduates. It has been possible for honors students to major in History and Literature, long under the tutorial leadership of F. O. Matthiessen, by combining two or three related cultures within a given period. Another possibility, initiated by Babbitt, was Literature, a variation on Classics, which normally comprised both Greek and Latin, but under this dispensation could be either the one or the other, together with a modern language-and-literature as its interrelated complement. That program has been broadened, so that its concentrators may now put together combinations of virtually any two modern literatures, interconnected and structured through the perspectives of criticism.

Needless to say, these options have had to be taught, examined upon, and administered by the same faculty members that handled the candidates for the higher degrees in Comparative Literature. It was our feeling, however, that very few undergraduates would be linguistically qualified to cover more than two literatures at first hand (and our doctorate requires three at least). We were not anxious to foster the sort of college major that has all too often depended upon cursory name-dropping and insecure translation. Better to be at home in a single literature as a whole, before proceeding to explore its counterparts in other literatures.

On the other hand, the Department has fostered individual lecture courses that have attracted a wide attendance by undergraduates, such as those of Babbitt—or again, for some years the most popular course in the college, instruction in the English Bible by its eloquent British interpreter, Kirsopp Lake. Visiting scholars have been frequently welcomed for occasional lectures, and a regular lecture on European Literature has been annually scheduled in memory of Renato Poggioli. Among the many guest professors, sometimes invited by the Department itself, sometimes present on a neighboring appointment (such as the Charles Eliot Norton Professorship of Poetry) but generously willing to teach with us as well, there have been warmly remembered visits from Maurice Bowra, Patrick Brady, Douwe Fokkema, Joseph Frank, Northrop Frye, Lilian Furst, Wlad Godzich, Frederic Jameson, Jean-Jacques Mayoux, Czeslaw Milosz, John Frederick Nims, Thomas G. Pavel, Edward Said, George Steiner, Edward Wasiolek, René Wellek, and Edmund Wilson. For several years we too, in conjunction with the Hispanic programs that brought them to Harvard, could take advantage of successive courses from Octavio Paz and Carlos Fuentes. During the transitional period when the Department was being reestablished, from month to month it held a lively colloquium, a less formal exchange between students and faculty than in the classroom. Such discussions have since been multiplied, and have now been institutionalized at Harvard's Center for Literary and Cultural Studies, which promotes a wide variety of extracurricular seminars.

Wherever it might be practical, perhaps through the Fulbright exchanges or similar opportunities, we would encourage American students to include some overseas experience in their preparation. Our Graduate School of Arts and Sciences has been helpful in awarding scholarships where they are needed, and two of these—the Sears and the I. H. Levin Fellowships—have specifically been earmarked for this department. Since we have never had an undergraduate field of concentration, we have not controlled the assignment of very many teaching assistantships. Yet since we consider the doctoral candidacy to be a pedagogical, as well as a scholarly, apprenticeship, we could fortunately depend upon sister departments to employ our candidates part-time as readers, tutors, or section-instructors. Records show that, from the outset through the commencement of 1991, Harvard has altogether conferred 210 doctorates in Comparative Literature. The fact that 191 of these have been obtained since

1949—during the second half of the period under review—bears witness to the development of the subject and documents the expansion of the field. A closer look would show increases in the number of foreign students working for Harvard's advanced degrees. It could also indicate the extent to which some of our Ph.D.'s have been pursuing their mature careers in other countries: within this hemisphere (Canada, Latin America), in Europe (France, Belgium, Italy, Spain, Austria, Greece), and farther eastward (Turkey, India, China). This lends some warrant to the hopes we hold for comparatists as potential fellow citizens in an international Republic of Letters.

I cannot list the whole roster, though I have come to look upon much of it with a vicarious pride. But I should like to mention a handful of names, leaving out those mentioned here already in some other connection, and trusting in the knowledgeable reader to recognize some of the positions held or contributions published by those named. A chronological listing too, since by now it spans nearly a century, may signalize new trends and changing directions. Among the Harvard Ph.D.'s in Comparative Literature, then, let me—arbitrarily and apologetically—cite the following fifty: Henry Wadsworth Longfellow Dana, Samuel Hazzard Cross, James B. Munn, Bernardo Gicovate, Irving Massey, Ralph Matlaw, Alain Renoir, Leo Bersani, Robert M. Durling, Achilles Fang, Burton Pike, Arnold Band, John Simon, Howard Clarke, Robert Tracy, Charles Witke, Barry Jacobs, Peter Brooks, Nancy Dersofi, Lily Chou, Margery Sabin, George Szanto, Maire Jaanus, Arnold Weinstein, Roberta Frank, Clayton Koelb, Deborah Heller, Robert Torrance, D. K. Banerjee, Daniel Javitch, Susan Kirkpatrick, Laurence Senelick, George Slusser, Charles Bernheimer, Steven and Janet Walker, George Grabowicz, Arthur Holmberg, Raymond Fleming, Michael Palencia-Roth, Richard Sieburth, Katherine Harrington, John Leyerle, Kristiaan Versluys, Christopher Benfey, Siegfried de Rachewiltz, Sandra Naddaff, Liliane Weisberg, Ana Fernandez Sein. Some, like Haskell Block or Nabaneeta Sen, spent a year or two with us and took a doctorate elsewhere. Others, like Renata Adler, Maxine Kumin, John Train, David Kuhn (writing under the pseudonym of David Mus), and Dana Gioia, went on from our master's degree to careers as professional writers.

It has now been exactly one hundred years since the term "Comparative Literature" first appeared in Harvard's catalogues, and that span has roughly coincided with the distinctive existence of the field itself. Looking back across the shifting paradigms and the reshuffled canons, we may note how it has been making its way from a marginal to a central place in literary studies. Insofar as these have been traditionally framed and subdivided by historic and linguistic circumstances, it has been their habit to dwell upon the uniqueness of their objects at the expense of the underlying principles. To broaden and to vary their frame of reference is to proceed toward a philosophical overview, from which we can more expressly discern the processes at work and formulate the critical theories. English literature is incomparably rich in masterpieces, but

French literature may have somewhat more to tell us about the dynamics of artistic movements, and we may learn somewhat more about the articulation of genres by studying the Classics. All of those cultures are closely interrelated, to be sure; and, in an era of multicultural awareness, we should also be interested in literatures that derive from independent roots. Comparisons can be all the more revealing when there are no ethnic continuities: e.g., the Anglo-Italian Punch and the Turkish Karaghiosis. Moreover, it is to Comparative Literature that we must turn when we are called upon to consider—as we are so often today—the interdisciplinary linkages between the various arts or the esthetic status of such up-to-date arts as the cinema.

The starting point of the ACLA Report on Professional Standards (1964), responding to the sudden proliferation of new departments, was a heart-searching caveat: that no institution should be taking such a step unless it could already count upon a strong library, an influx of well-qualified students, and a group of committed and competent professors in literature and languages. Harvard had been lucky enough to meet those three conditions, which enabled it to take some of the initiatives in the American growth of our subject. Nonetheless, we have always considered this to be not only an international and inter-departmental, but also an inter-university undertaking; therefore we have highly valued, and done our best to instigate and sustain, contacts with colleagues far and near. We have never believed, as some of them have, in embracing or imposing a set of doctrines; indeed we strive toward a critical pluralism, wherein the whole spectrum of relevant views can be fairly presented. We do feel that, with the acceptance and advance of Comparative Literature, its proponents no longer need to engage in what I once ventured to characterize as "paracom-paratism." It was doubtless useful, while the way was still being prepared, to have so many prospectuses and prolegomena, so much methodological shop-talk (attempts to distinguish French and American schools, for instance). But those battles have been won, and we should make better use of the larger opportunities that they have gained for us by moving on from the peripheries to the substantive core of our subject-matter.

3

Experiences and Experiments

Victor Lange

No aspect in the work of a modern teacher of literature and that of his students has been so surprising—and galvanizing—as the eruptive shifts during the past century in the perspective of long established forms and purposes of literary criticism. Nearly every assumption, every definition, every notion of the premises and objectives of literary pedagogy, above all of the modes of impact of literature upon the reader, individually and collectively, has changed from the certainties of a long prevailing critical canon to a barely surveyable variety of assessment of the objects as well as the subjects of literature.

While this issue has been familiar, welcomed either as an extension of the tradition, or condemned as an historical whim, it has seldom been described as a process of cause and effect in the attitudes of teachers and students. During periods of exceptional unrest they were challenged by extraordinary shifts in the circumstances of their private or, even more disturbing, their political lives.

To gauge the scope and the underlying motives of these changes, it may be useful to consider the academic background, and the phases in my own intellectual development: a young German who was, after his apprenticeship in Leipzig and Munich as a student of English, invited in 1931 to join the German faculty of the University of Toronto. Until my retirement in 1977 I was a professor of German literature, an "honorary" professor at the Free University of Berlin, and a frequent visiting professor in this country and abroad, an active observer and participant in the curious if remarkable evolution of contemporary literary critism.

During my student years the views I held of the categories of literary judgment were determined by the deeply ingrained convictions of my European education, by its historical axioms and its cumulative, inductive method. What in the early nineteen-twenties I had learned at the venerable Thomasschule in Leipzig was based on a firm belief in the philological discipline. Within that

25

severely defined "classical" curriculum and pedagogical design the inestimable revolution that had during the previous decades taken place in nearly all humanistic and scientific fields was not seriously brought to bear upon the materials and approaches of our superbly trained and dedicated teachers. Neither scientific nor mathematical studies were at the core of my education at the Gymnasium, but chiefly literary interests, firmly founded on the great Greek and Latin writers and the conspicuous documents of the European tradition, defined essentially within a framework of historical information, and sustained at a school where Bach had been cantor by the practice and theory of music.

Not until I entered the university did it become evident that the monolithic classical assumptions had for some time, conspicuously in Germany, been challenged by divergent theories in the sciences, in psychological and sociological studies, in philosophy and historiography. The enormous political and intellectual revolution before and after the First World War, set decisively in motion by the provocations of Nietzsche, now provided the climate of my encounter with the academic life of the late twenties and early thirties. Historians such as Brandenburg, Walter Goetz, or Joachimsen still seemed to insist on the lucid creed of the truth in facts; but to attend the Hegel-seminar of Joachim Wach provided the first historically coherent material of what was soon to become the theory of that hermeneutical "understanding" of intellectual and aesthetic issues which was to culminate thirty years later in Hans-Georg Gadamer's *Wahrheit und Methode* (1960).

A Kant-Vorlesung by the biologist Hans Driesch, a stirring series of reflections on medieval German art by Wilhelm Pinder or an introduction to modern sociology by Hans Freyer suggested the growing interdependence of academic disciplines. The Leipzig Germanist August Hermann Korff and Fritz Strich in Munich had fascinated me by the elegance and scope of their interpretation of the "Goethe-period."

In the end I chose philosophy and history as my minor fields, English— only cursorily taught at school—as my major. In Levin Schücking, the editor of Beowulf and of Shakespeare, I found a severe master of the philological craft. A cultivated Westfalian with a deep and active sense of political and social responsibility he was committed to the conviction that the spirit is not a free-floating element or a subjective construct, but a substance made tangible in the living institutions of a given time. With his contributions to the history of literary "taste," Schücking was one of the first to insist on the sociological premises of the aesthetic judgment. Despite his intense interest in modern English life, he held to the traditional belief that contemporary letters neither should nor could be the object of critical research: when I began my academic life, first as an exchange student, later as a member of the faculty of the University of Toronto, my scholarly familiarity with English literature ended, on the basis of Schücking's lectures and seminars, with Oscar Wilde and Shaw. My spoken English was limited, I knew my Shakespeare but was woefully ignorant of *Alice in Wonderland* or the familiar quotations, or the information in such incomparable treasure-chests as Brewer's "Dictionary of Phrase and Fable."

It was assumed that, as a native speaker, I was competent to teach the German language. However, my knowledge of German grammatical theory was slight, and with my slim grasp of English, nearly impossible to convey. In those early years, the rich echoes of my German education still alive, my teaching of literature was either cautiously descriptive or consisted, with a few well-prepared students, of a discursive reading of selections of older or more contemporary German texts, set in the matrix of biographical and historical information. As in English or German universities, the acquisition of an oral fluency was nearly irrelevant: what mattered was, by becoming acquainted with the foreign document, generally to stimulate literary sensibility, to "translate" the German text into something approaching the admired style of Stevenson or Hardy, in short, to turn the German text into an English one. On the basis of long established "set" passages, the annual exams tested this skill as well as the command of the staples of literary history.

I was by choice or instinct not a "linguist" but more inclined toward literary criticism and its relationship to philosophy and history. It was much later that I thought it defensible to separate in the curriculum the linguist's newly developed techniques of teaching the modern languages from those dealing with literature in critical terms. I have since become doubtful of the wisdom of such a practice, which was later institutionalized at Cornell by creating the "Divisions" of language and of literature, independent of one another in staff, purpose, and method.

The acquisition of a new language and an intensified interest in its theoretical scaffolding was one of the reasons for an increasing awareness of the centrality of language as the decisive philosophical vehicle of articulation and definition. But while this insight moved my speculative interests toward more pragmatic ways of approaching the literary object, it was far from producing a coherent sense of method.

One impressive type of "method" I had not encountered before, was that practiced by the most memorable of Canadian teachers of German literature, my chairman and friend, Barker Fairley. Fairley was a reader and interpreter of quite uncommon literary perception, concerned with literature not primarily as a field of academic enquiry but as a life-enlarging universal phenomenon. He surprised me when he confessed that he had little sympathy with the Germans among whom he had lived as a Lector at Jena, but that he was prepared to speak of the stirring examples of their literature with critical enthusiasm and in terms that disavowed all national rhetoric. He had published a superbly sensitive study of Goethe—personal, free of pedantry, and totally indifferent to the vast and ponderous canon of German Goethe-criticism. He implicitly endorsed the work of Professor E. M. Butler at Cambridge, who had, in her skeptical study *The Tyranny of Greece over Germany (1935)*, challenged the hagiographical German view of its classical antecedents.

Fairley's roots were profoundly English: he had written the first critical assessment of the great traveller in Arabia, Charles Doughty, whose force and delicacy of poetic speech he defended with passionate conviction. He seemed to disregard the relevance of cultural differences as an essential prerequisite of literary criticism. His curiosity was directed at two facets of "reading": one, the manner in which a work was "made," and the other, whether that process of making had produced an aesthetic object that could be measured and weighed by the presence and wealth of its resonant relationships and the resulting widening of the reader's perception. Neither mystical radiance nor vaporous enthusiasm were for Fairley legitimate conditions or objectives of the aesthetic process.

Although he wrote a study of the German novelist Raabe, who seemed to him to have technical and aesthetic characteristics comparable to those of Chekov, he was not interested in the emerging claims of "Comparative Litera-ture," a pompous administrative category, he felt, without an unambiguous theory, that had in any case for long been resonant in the inclusive and rich term "literature." His gauge for the best in the world of letters was the strength of "poetic" energy, the craft of turning experienced life into a stirring verbal concentrate of perception.

For long a dedicated admirer of the Canadian "Group of Seven," painters affirming a strong feeling for native qualities, he later developed his own personal style of painting, defying prevailing European conventions, angular and intent on shaping the interplay of line and color. He was, when he died in 1986 at the age of ninety-nine, a distinguished scholar of German literature as well as one of the admired Canadian artists.

The early years of my teaching strengthened the conviction that my task was not merely to communicate the text-book topography of a long-established view of German literature, but to convey the fundamental need—and valid and useful categories—of attempting to articulate and interpret alternative ways of looking at a text or a work of art. It was this gradually emerging understanding of unexpected modes of approach that represented the first of those fresh convictions which I sought to make effective in myself and in the critical operations of my students. I wanted new manners of approach and insight to modify the often elusive disparities between national dispositions. In such presumed differences, students seemed primarily interested, and traditional teachers considered these, even in the technical pursuit of language learning, the most engaging and rewarding part of their work.

In the University of Toronto faculty at large, I could not have been in more impressive or dedicated company. All departments imparted the body of their information within an unquestioned Arnoldian faith in the absolute value of great literature as a guiding focus within the life of a society. The prescription of "set books" defined and confined the curriculum and, to some extent, produced a sameness of point of view and examination questions which were given at the end of the year to hundreds of students. The tenor of the Toronto faculty was Anglo-Saxon, pragmatic in its teaching and never strained by fashionable idiomatic speculations. Disputes on varieties of critical approaches were rare; Saintsbury's canonical *History of Criticism and Literary Taste* offered little methodological direction. I. A. Richard's anti-impressionistic *Principles of Literary Criticism* had appeared in 1929: its novelty was only slowly recognized.

A number of distinguished scholars (not only in the natural sciences, where Banting and Best, the discoverers of Insulin, had been awarded a Nobel Prize), offered the kind of pragmatic learning which seemed to ignore the intellectual commotion across the Atlantic. Still, there were several critical colleagues: F. C. Green was a superb narrative historian of French literature, A. B. Woodhouse a magnificent Milton scholar; there were able historians and political and economic scientists. The discriminating collector of English literature ancient and modern, was Herbert Davis, the editor of the works of Swift. It was from him that I learned the meticulous and exhilarating craft of textual criticism, a discipline of which at the end of his life, Davis became a Reader at Oxford.

In Davis's circle of students and friends, such as Northrop Frye, later a distinguished Blake scholar and (in 1957) the author of the *Anatomy of Criticism*, I began to feel the creative impact of a humane and firmly oriented teacher upon his students. It was Herbert Davis who persuaded me to follow him to Cornell, where he was to be chairman of the English department and I a member of the Department of German Studies.

The change turned out to be significant beyond all expectations: Toronto had represented a carefully structured British pedagogical ethos and practice; Cornell was an academic community of quite different, fluid, experimental, and aggressively "American" aims. It was a moment at which in all the sciences German and Austrian refugees of distinction introduced "European" scholarly convictions and techniques; they brought to the humanities a strong emphasis upon historical and hermeneutical approaches. There prevailed a stubborn current of opposition to European modes of thought and a militant emphasis upon the "native" American heritage which the books of Van Wyck Brooks and others had summarized.

In 1949 the Goethe-Bicentennial celebrations at Aspen represented the most memorable encounter, the first after World War II, of several groups of European and American scholars in many fields of the humanities and the social sciences. It enabled them to resume the discourse that had for so long been interrupted. Theologians and historians, literary critics and artists, spoke before large audiences and in the spirit of Goethe gave testimony to the current state of learning. The most admired critic apart from spectacular figures such as Albert Schweitzer—was Ernst Robert Curtius, the German scholar of Romance Languages, who had just published his monumental *European Literature and the Middle Ages*. His influence as a historian of the overriding intellectual relationships and attitudes reflected in medieval literature has continued in part through the work of his students and disciples at Johns Hopkins University. At the same time one of the most impressive German refugee scholars, Leo Spitzer, reasserted a modern theory of stylistics through his collection of essays (1948) on *Linguistics and Literary History*—with an emphasis on "interpretation," close to the details of the text, and resolutely opposed to the descriptive assumptions of contemporary linguistics.

What had, at times with a pointed animosity to historical forms of reading a text, made the specificity of literary criticism a challenge of sudden urgency, were the fascinating tenets of the "New Criticism." In 1938 Cleanth Brooks and Robert Penn Warren had in their anthology *Understanding Poetry* urged students to approach the poem with a sharper eye upon the functioning of detail and poetic strategy, on the poem itself, instead of its historical context. As an attack upon unexamined convention the "New Criticism" had its notable effect, however limited it proved to be in that explosive complexity which became the substance and impulse of all future literary theory.

To define the character of a literary text not primarily as a vehicle of information or of inspired "confession" but as a document of a particular linguistic or rhetorical character and tradition was in broader perspective the aim of Wellek and Warren's *Theory of Literature* (1949). The influence of this incisive work upon teachers and students alike (a rich collection of essays, *Concepts of Criticism* followed in 1967), was of inestimable consequence: by recalling the European romantic resolution to test the inherited forms and purposes of literature, Wellek demonstrated the historical continuity and legitimacy of a distinct discipline of literary criticism.

The debate on the definition and delineation of the nature of the literary work was at Cornell and elsewhere one of the chief preoccupations of English (and Modern Language) studies. The other, more radical and far-reaching, was the emerging emphasis upon questions concerning the very character of language itself. The fresh reading of Ferdinand de Saussure's *Course in General Linguistics* (1916) opened a broad and influential field of linguistic questions and introduced by implication the enormously wideranging topoi of verbal and textual "intentionality."

In the discussion of these issues, faculty and students at Cornell became equally involved. In the forties the humanistic part of that sprawling institution (with nearly equal interests in agriculture, history, and letters) had a varied and lively faculty: it included conservative as well as innovative scholars such as Lane Cooper and F. Solmsen, the musicologist and Librarian O. Kinkeldey, M. Abrams, David Daiches, Robert Adams, R. C. Bald, and Morris Bishop, as well as, in an ill-defined but stimulating role, the writer Vladimir Nabokov.

What became a vaguely structured but altogether effective pedagogical device was the practice, urged by the resolute dean of Arts and Sciences, C. W. de Kiewiet, to draw senior members of all humanistic departments into the teaching of an introductory course in English of select European literary masterpieces. It was not the kind or scope of the offered texts—since then widely adopted in many colleges—as the fact that all participating instructors taught all prescribed texts, not only those of their scholarly specialty. Knight Biggerstaff, the professor of Chinese Literature, dealt with the *Divine Comedy*; the Professor of Classics shared in the discussion of Ibsen's plays. Weekly meetings of this—sometimes uneasy—"team" developed and exchanged differences of taste, judgment, and methodological assumptions—a perceptible cause for an interest among students in an evolving variety of theoretical reflections. The text remained the central object of critical concern: "theory" had not yet emancipated itself from the presumably compelling totality of the work itself.

The Cornell students were at that time remarkably alert, inquisitive and restless—quite different from the more homogeneous and conventional students at Toronto. Many of them came from the superior New York schools, such as Erasmus High or the High School of Science and Arts, both with strong interests in arts and letters. It has seemed to me indicative of the challenging nature of the Cornell program that several of our students—Harold Bloom or E. D. Hirsch—became themselves effective teachers and influential contributors to the articulation of new theories of literature.

While I had not been centrally interested in the teaching of German as a language, I became aware, through the self-confident work of the Division of Modern Languages, of the new methods in descriptive linguistics, on which the instruction in learning all manner of foreign language was now based. Whether pragmatically in teaching—during the memorable war years of the Army's "Specialized Training Program"—large numbers of basically unprepared soldiers a modicum of spoken language, or in the more philosophical systematic explorations of approaches to the structure of language, largely indifferent to historical or philological premises, the topic of language moved for a while into the center of interest. The irresistible variation, either sociological or psychological, of linguistic propositions that students found in Wittgenstein, and later in the writings of Lacan or Foucault, was first systematized in Ferdinand de Saussure's *Course in General Linguistics*, and given its first general methodological application in the work of American linguists. It should not have surprised me that in a guest seminar by Leonard Bloomfield, one of the early masters of the "new" science, he puzzled his traditionally trained audience by a curt reply to a student's question, why in the Ojibway language there should be three genders for the word "strawberry"? "Linguists," Bloomfield, somewhat impatiently answered, "describe but do not ask for reasons."

Such views, troublesome enough to those like me who held to their "historical" beliefs, soon began to crystallize in an increasing concern with the character and consequence of the term "theory." The aggressive emphasis upon the relevance of this concept for the pursuit of literary studies was bound, especially in its most subtle defenders, to lead, twenty years later, to a denial of the presumed coherence of a given work, and the problematical nature—indeed the feasibility—of "interpretation." But these conclusions were still only tentatively discussed when in 1957 I left Cornell after twenty stimulating years of teaching, to go to Princeton.

What seems to me the most memorable feature of the Cornell experience was the firmly defended, if at times willful and polemical sense of a common humanistic faith: from the willingness of several administrations to encourage experiments, to the evident eagerness of the students to participate in the classical as well as the progressive aspects of teaching and learning. The temper of the campus was—until the devastating changes in mood and purpose of the late sixties—one of exceptional alertness and imaginative mobility.

The mood and intellectual disposition cultivated and practiced at Princeton differed surprisingly in faculty and students from what I had experienced at Cornell. The urbanity of a new, young president, Robert F. Goheen, was reflected in the quietly disciplined self-confidence of a faculty that sought continuous commitment to the tradition of a belief in firmly held humanistic values. As against the social and cultural convictions shared by the large community of Canadian life and represented by the University of Toronto, Princeton had for many decades offered in a diffusely structured America a model community of superior and exemplary social vision. If its Department of Modern Languages was the largest in the university, this confirmed the cosmopolitan spirit of the institution and its participants. "New" methods, whether linguistic or literary, new organizational structures, whether administrative or pedagogical, required arguments and defenses that were not readily accepted.

If a challenge by Woodrow Wilson, a conspicuous previous president of the University, put "Princeton in the Nation's Service," this presupposed a claim, maintained to the present, that its humanistic creed was not a parochial privilege but a genuine commitment to public service. It was obvious to the newcomer that this fundamental conviction required a faculty and a student body of quietly asserted continuity. It also assumed an ideological view of the unity of "culture" that had during the previous decade in many other institutions been put under vigorous and well-founded scholarly scrutiny. The English and Modern Language Departments sought, in various programs, to reinforce in the well-prepared students their particular ingredients in the shared canon of culture.

The "interdepartmental" vibration that at Cornell had at times led to a discourse of open challenge and tension, was here contained in a mosaic of expert outlines of distinct cultural or historical achievements. A course such as the one I had given there with some success—and altogether in English translations—had been summarily entitled "Masters of European Literature" and had used a variety of critical approaches. During my first year as Professor of German Literature at Princeton such a course was suspected of inexpertness and of transgressing departmental borderlines. When the reluctantly recognized field of German studies was given independent status it enlarged and liberalized its offerings both in the direction of modern linguistics and of literary criticism and history.

One of the most remarkable Princeton enterprises was the "Gauss-Seminars," inspired and conducted with Foundation support by the unforgettable critic Richard Blackmur (*Language and Gesture* 1952, and *The Lion and the Honeycomb: Essays in Solicitude and Critique*, 1955.) Under his learned, wise, and genial, if at times impenetrable, guidance, Blackmur brought to Princeton before an invited audience, including a select number of students, nearly all European and American men of letters—from Maritain, Auden, T. S. Eliot, Starobinski, and Ricoeur to Tate, Berryman, Bonnefoy and Amis. The effect of these seminars with their lively debates and their subsequent social encounters seemed to me of incalculable importance not merely for the Princeton community and its distinguished visitors but for the growing awareness of the mood of contemporary letters. The "Gauss-Seminars" were in turn the most significant evidence of the growing role of Princeton—however discreet—before and during the Vietnam War, in the widening discourse of contemporary literary criticism.

While in Germany the social and political uncertainties produced in the "Frankfurt School" such critically idealistic scholars as Theodore Adorno (*Negative Dialectics*, 1966), who, in a mannered and widely imitated style pronounced, in unison with the prewar writings of Walter Benjamin, his strong distrust of the reliability of speech, American students were as yet skeptical of such radical doubt about the deceptive transparency of literary and political statements. "Marxist" criticism, intelligently practiced in an academic context by Fredric Jameson (*The Politically Unconscious*, 1981), had, during the decades of its greatest vitality in Europe, among American students a far less compelling appeal than in Germany or France.

In 1967 I invited more than one hundred associates of the German "Gruppe 47," poets, dramatists, critics, film makers and journalists, to hold one of their periodic meetings—nearly the last, as it turned out—in Princeton. It was since its founding a "closed" group that—in camera—read and vigorously criticized the productions of its members. Princeton students from the several literary departments were invited to listen to the fascinating performances and, especially, the impulses and points of view that galvanized the critical responses. On that occasion the young Peter Handke protested, applauded by the German press, against the fashionable style of a literature of emaciated description or reporting

Colleagues throughout America managed to attend the sessions and heard the voices of fiction, poetry, and criticism that were then active in Germany. Princeton historians and philosophers such as Stuart Hampshire and Richard Rorty contributed to a large and frequently combative gathering—at the final symposium of nearly a thousand American and European writers.

The Princeton meeting was an indication of the widening horizon of the critical debate. Political and literary perspectives could no longer be distinguished; an extraordinary range of European philosophical and historical antecedents were drawn upon to lend argument and vocabulary to an incomparably lively critical discourse. French critics gave to aspects of their systems new historical justification. Sociologists, psychologists, and philosophers drew the magisterial German figures of Kant, Hegel, Schleiermacher, Nietzsche, and Husserl into the critical debate. The chain of contemporary German thinkers from Lukács to Heidegger and Habermas (*Strukturwandel der Öffentlichkeit*, 1962) shared with their liveliest French masters, with Barthes, Foucault, Lacan or Lyotard, in a debate that was soon afterward to change the purposes and methods of literary theory altogether. The impact (less upon European than American faculties and students) was widespread and intense. Beyond the conventional departmental organizations, students sought information and satisfaction of their curiosity from younger instructors whatever their ostensible specialty. An interest in "narratology," articulated long after Lukács's *Theory of the Novel* (1920) by W. Iser's *The Act of Reading* (1979) and M. Bakhtin's *The Dialogic Imagination* (1981), has remained singularly appealing among all attempts to define the relationship between fiction and the reader.

Paul de Man's *Allegories of Reading* and *Blindness and Insight* formulated ten years later, in 1979 and 1983, the conceptual tenets of "deconstruction," which Jacques Derrida's *Writing and Difference* and *Of Grammatology* (1967) developed into that extraordinary sensitive and fascinating system that dominated the critical debate of the eighties and early nineties.

The years after my retirement from active teaching at Princeton (though with continuing and stimulating teaching responsibilities in Berlin and elsewhere in this country and abroad), before the resolute disintegration of the unity of the literary text in anticipation of a synthetic postmodernism, deepened the interplay—far from a reality in my earliest years in Canada—of European and American intellectual constellations. Indeed, if a sum of fifty years of teaching can be drawn it would stress the double focus in which the body of literature and criticism was seen in the context and interaction of continental and American practice. I have suggested the all-encompassing, perhaps historically singular, changes in the intellectual and formal conditions of the writing and reading of literature, the centrality of semiotic perspectives and the motives for the fundamental questioning of "logocentricity," the very foundation of the European historical self-consciousness. What has remained the attempt at elucidating the variety of impulses of a common social and intellectual life can no longer be achieved without being at all times and in all directions aware of the experiences and experiments I have attempted to describe.

4

Versions of a Discipline

Thomas M. Greene

Comparative Literature profits from the handicap, or suffers from the blessing, of its radical indeterminacy. A generation from now its students may well be trying to define it for themselves as ours are doing. It has already assumed more than one guise since its effective inception in the United States shortly after World War II. I take it that the protean volatility of the discipline accounts in part for the existence of a volume like this one. A scholar who has tried to make his way through a series of theoretical and methodological shifts since the fifties might best begin to record his negotiations with them by means of personal reminiscence, adding whatever reflections on the wider scene seem appropriate. Thus the retrospective account that follows begins with the private and anecdotal, touching on ulterior concerns within the framework of a sketchy autobiography.

My early *curriculum vitae* falls into neat segments of two-year stints. There was a period at a small sectarian college in the middle west (Principia College at Elsah, Illinois, 1943–45), then service in the army (1945–47), then the completion of my B.A. as a civilian English major in Yale College (1947–49), then two years in Paris writing an abortive thesis on Lautréamont for a degree I failed to receive (1949–51). The study in France was followed by a three-year stint at the Yale graduate school in Comparative Literature. In 1954 I submitted a doctoral dissertation and began full-time teaching, at first in the Yale English department, later with a joint appointment in English and Comparative Literature. It would seem that the definitive moment arrived after my basic infantry training, when the wise men who control the destiny of soldiers chose to send me to New Haven to study spoken Japanese for nine months. I might have gone to any of five other institutions, or I might have become an office clerk. I arrived at Yale in the middle of the night in a G.I. truck, little guessing how long, for better or worse, I would remain. After service in the occupation of Korea, where I could *not* prudently use the Japanese I had learned, Yale accepted me back with other returning veterans, including all those who had studied there in a variety of training programs during and after the war. It would seem today that chance played a not inconsiderable role in fixing the locus of my academic career.

From the vantage of the present, I'm inclined to see almost all the developments in my academic biography finding their context within the walls of a single university, since at any given moment it has never seemed advisable to leave Yale. I say "almost all" because my serious education really began at Principia, where I fell under the influence of a man who had no reputation but was a master teacher. I want to record my debt to him because he must have had many counterparts in our country, men and women who have remained as obscure as he was, impassioned teachers working in little-known colleges for uncertain rewards. The man who influenced me so deeply had been trained primarily in ballet. He had even had a tour dancing opposite Pavlova, and—as he once hinted—had fallen in love with her. At Principia he ostensibly taught the history of the fine arts, but he actually taught the wonder of civilization. He was an elegant, subtle, lonely man who pronounced with ardor luminous unfamiliar names: Piero della Francesca, Isadora Duncan, Henri Matisse, Virginia Woolf, Martha Graham. From him I first learned to love a city I had not yet seen—Paris, and I also learned whatever skill has remained with me for looking at works of visual art. I set his name down here with posthumous piety: Frank Parker.

This was the first in a series of teachers who marked me with their minds and sensibilities. But the names of Parker's successors are anything but obscure. When I began study at Yale as a junior in 1947, the man whose course counted most in my life was a great rumpled giant who taught the history of theory, William K. Wimsatt, Jr. For some members of my generation, the discovery of theory has been a progressive acquisition of a largely postwar corpus. In my case, under Wimsatt and later René Wellek, it was in the air from the beginning but it began with Plato and stopped, quite logically for the time, more or less with Richards. Fortunately for his students of the forties, Wimsatt had not yet resolved the critical problems that obsessed him, so that twice a week for a year we had the privilege of assisting at the terrific wrestling matches with himself he presented to our awed eyes. He was a gentle and lovable but terrifying man who went over student papers with a daunting rage for order. He taught theoretical texts with exactitude, but he also taught the perennial theoretical problem posed by each major text. He believed deeply in the unity of literary theory across the millennia, and I have sometimes wondered if this belief would have survived had he lived another fiteen years. He referred once neutrally toward the end of his life to the theoretical "Copernican revolution" (his expression). The last thing he wrote, to my knowledge, was a review of Jonathan Culler's *Structuralist Poetics*. The review was a careful summary, chapter by chapter, which punctiliously and uncharacteristically refrained from any normative judgment. I took Wimsatt's reticence to reflect his recognition of a rigor alien to his own.

The force of Wimsatt's mind was a discovery made after my arrival at Yale. I already knew some of the work of Cleanth Brooks and greatly admired it. Brooks arrived here my first civilian year with great eclat and some controversy; it was inevitable that I take his course in modern poetry. He presided over our class with urbane poise and courteous detachment, calling upon each student in alphabetical order to comment on a poem in our anthology. The comment expected was by no means random; what Brooks typically asked for was a verdict as to whether the poem "came to terms with itself," whether it dealt satisfactorily with the problems it raised and achieved adequate closure. These were questions little in our training had prepared us for, and to Brooks's credit the "right" answers were not always predictable. Thus a given poem by Carl Sandburg, say, might be perceived to succeed whereas a poem by, say, Tate might not. Brooks's view of the right answer was always made clear, sooner or later, and always in terms of the specific structural elements supplied by the poem. This attentiveness to the poem's own governing structures, and the resourcefulness in analyzing their dynamics, were to me the man's most impressive qualities. The classroom atmosphere was far cooler than Wimsatt's, and the teacher's personal investment less visible, but I did in fact absorb in this ambience of southern gentility assumptions that I still hold. Brooks taught as critic and professor that reading means primarily the analysis of a detached verbal structure, and that evaluation is inseparable from reading. It went without saying that certain texts belonged to a category recognized as literary and thus required responses different from others.

The New Criticism as a movement suffers today from misunderstanding; it is sometimes assumed to have lacked a theory of poetry, which it did not, and it is assumed to have ignored history, which as a movement it decidedly did not, even if the history, assuming as it did a dissociation of sensibility, tended to be lapsarian. Brooks as a graduate teacher would be more open about his perception of the contemporary historical moment than in the college classroom; deeply conscious as he was of the breakdown of systems of traditional belief, he would refer to "the modern nightmare." Such attitudes were muted for his undergraduates, struggling with the organic structures of complex poems. Since my exposure to Cleanth Brooks, influences from other directions have modified my own work, but I do not wish to conceal from myself that I began as a child of the New Criticism. This is scarcely surprising; I studied with a man who, more than any other American, has influenced the teaching of literature in our century.

The two years of study in France, beginning with a Fulbright fellowship, confronted me with an immeasurably rich literature and a seductive culture. I absorbed as much as I could. Although I read a little Valéry and Blanchot,

I'm not aware that my thinking about literature as literature altered greatly in this time. I was too occupied reading primary tests in a gulping, unsystematic way to reflect on what I was doing—occupied also in coping with a French academic bureaucracy that finally defeated me. A fresh chapter opened with my return to Yale as a doctoral student in Comparative Literature. (Yale had made the most generous fellowship offer, and accompanied as I now was by a growing family, the generosity mattered.)

Comparative Literature as a discipline was still young in 1951, but it was perceived as up and coming. Only two years earlier it had acquired its own journal, and it was also organizing its own scholarly society, the American Comparative Literature Association. At Yale it was incarnated by René Wellek, appointed as chair of the new program in 1946 and thus far its only member. Wellek's authority and prestige sufficed to invest it immediately with respectability and to draw interested students. I must add however, that during my one year of graduate classes Wellek happened to be on leave, so that I never actually had a course with a man who would, in the nature of things, become my mentor. During the absence of the regular chairman, the program was directed by Henri Peyre, a critic I would only slowly come to admire as he deserved. Peyre in my young eyes read too fast, talked too fast, wrote too much; he successfully veiled under a pose of insouciance the profound generosity of spirit I would gradually come to measure.

The major discovery of that first graduate year was rather Erich Auerbach, an ineffective teacher but an unforgettable presence, avuncular, patient, and kindly. Auerbach embodied the best traditions of European historicism, their appeal intensified by the publication of *Mimesis* two years after I began study with him. Literary history was scarcely a novelty for me when I met Auerbach, but in him one encountered its depth, its mystery, its scope, its opacity, its charm. He represented a new force in my developing sense of literary study, a force whose impact was more or less equivalent to Brooks's textual scrupulosity. Textuality and historicity are not necessarily binary opposites, as Auerbach's own work showed, but they are the two foci about which my personal development has circled.

Auerbach, Wimsatt, and Peyre were all essentially comparatists, but the one Professor of Comparative Literature at Yale, Wellek, was the last in the remarkable Pléiade I came into contact with. In my second year of graduate study, I listened to him as an auditor read chapters from his forthcoming volume on romantic criticism, and in my final year he directed my dissertation on the epithalamion in the Renaissance. For a decade and a half Wellek directed *all* comparative dissertations at Yale, regardless of their subject and field, and directed them with authority. I suppose that one never quite learns from a professor what he or she expects one to learn; the most important lessons are transmitted involuntarily. What I learned from Wellek intensified an impression gained from Auerbach—namely, the inexhaustibility of all that there is to read, along with its unquestionable intrinsic interest. *Of course* you want to read everything, because you are curious, because it is there, because it enriches. The canon Wellek and my other teachers accepted as definitive has since been exposed to salutary criticism, as every canon must be. What I remember, however, is the spaciousness of that canon, and the exhilaration of its (apparent) limitlessness. We were not yet alert in 1951 to the potentialities of a planetary canon which would embrace literature as a universal human activity. As those potentialities are mined by a future discipline of Comparative Literature, I would wish for our successors a textual world felt to be as vast as the merely Eurocentric world I grew up with. That world I learned from Wellek, as I learned or tried to learn a judicious even-mindedness, an aversion to dogma, an Olympian detachment from faction. No one in my experience has embodied those virtues more admirably than the Wellek I remember from my student years.

It would not be easy for me to say today why I chose the Renaissance as the period in which I would concentrate. My first published article, written as an undergraduate, was on Lawrence, and the second, salvaged from the Sorbonne debacle, on Lautréamont. The modernist masters of the twentieth century, especially Yeats, Joyce, and Eliot, exerted a strong appeal. Yet I opted without great hesitation for what is now called the early modern period. Doubtless that decision had something to do with the teaching of still another distinguished scholar, Louis Martz, whose course on English Renaissance poetry complemented my discovery in France of Ronsard and Scève. It would be comfortable today to suggest that I was drawn by the values of Renaissance humanism, but I knew little of them when I began working on the epithalamion. All such decisions doubtless are both mysterious and overdetermined.

The choice of the subject of my first book, on the other hand, is easy to explain. During my first years of teaching I was assigned a section of a freshman course on epic and tragedy directed by the formidable Maynard Mack. The weekly staff sessions in Mack's office were democratic, free-wheeling, and exhilarating, livelier than any course I had taken and just as instructive. The choice of the Renaissance epic as the subject of a book came naturally, as did the Auerbachian method of beginning with a delimited passage from each successive work. The grandiose pretention of covering the classical and Renaissance epic from Homer to Milton was my own. The book that emerged in 1963, *The Descent from Heaven*, was finished just in time for a positive tenure decision; another three weeks would have done me in.

What seems to matter in retrospect about this book is its technique of approaching literary history by tracing a single topos through a series of various authors. The subtitle—"A Study in Epic Continuity"—pointed to the durability of generic convention as it worked against the eccentricities of each authorial sensibility and each cultural moment. An introductory chapter attempted to evoke what the epic became as a Renaissance construct without assigning it an inappropriate metaphysical necessity. The attention to historical particularity did, however, exact a price. My book had no organizing argument, no story to tell; it simply tried to register each successive epic voice within that voice's own terms. Writing it at any rate strengthened my engagement in the dramatic process of literary history; it also fortified my assumption that history and textual analysis needed each other. In the sixties this assumption ran counter to the powerful influence of Northrop Frye, whose *Anatomy of Criticism* I read with respect but no interest in emulating. At Yale his work provoked a flurry of discussion. Championed by Harold Bloom, attacked by Wimsatt, Frye's ahistorical stress on generic divisions engendered a few exciting undergraduate courses and was gradually absorbed.

When my first book appeared, I had begun to teach graduate students. The first, unsurprisingly, was devoted to the Renaissance epic, and among the few who took it the first year were A. Bartlett Giamatti and Jane Parry, now Jane Parry Tompkins, both strong Italianists and marvelous students of roughly equal ability. This was the first in a continuing series of graduate classes which I found drew more and more of my professional energy. The brilliance of my graduate students has constituted a challenge I feel I have never quite met but which has been a creative stimulus. Most of the writing I did during the later sixties and seventies, including a little book on Rabelais and various articles, tended to emerge from the graduate classroom. The really creative hours were those immediately preceding the seminar. The rewards were enormous; I was privileged, and still am, to work with exceptional students on the texts that matter to me. As a graduate teacher, despite the recurrent sense of inadequacy, I found the central project of my career. My eagerness to share texts with students whose insights extended my own contained doubtless an element of proselytism. I was long imbued with an opinion which now seems hopelessly obsolete: that the criticism of serious literature necessarily contains an element of praise. There was not much room in my classroom for the hermeneutic of suspicion. But that was not yet a perceived idiosyncrasy, and gifted young people turned up who tolerated it. I remain fiercely, egocentrically, proud of the colleagues with whom I once collaborated as a teacher.

During the sixties, the Yale program in Comparative Literature became a department and expanded beyond its only begetter. Lowry Nelson, one of the original program's first graduates, arrived in 1964 as a second tenured member and still others were added from the existing Yale faculty. In 1972, Wellek retired from the faculty to which he had.brought so much distinction, and I succeeded him as chair. At that time, there were six senior members, each, excepting Lowry, with joint appointments; Peter Demetz, Bart Giamatti, Geoffrey Hartman, Nelson, and the newly arrived Paul de Man in addition to myself. During the first year of my chairmanship, we reviewed the structure of the program and made a few changes, none of which affected its basic character. Meanwhile, a more or less independent undergraduate program, the Literature Major, had been organized in the college, placing heavy stress on theory and programmatically mingling subliterary texts with canonical. The Lit Major, which remains semiautonomous, continues to flourish, complemented today with a "Comparative Literature" option requiring more linguistic preparation and more literary history. The creation of the Lit Major by Peter Brooks, Michael Holquist, and Alvin Kernan, together with the arrival of de Man and the return of Hartman a few years earlier, would dramatically alter the climate of literary study at Yale during the seventies.

For myself, during the early years of that decade, I was less preoccupied by institutional change than by the focus and shape of my next book. This was slow in emerging and I passed through some dark moments before the glimmer of an organizing idea allowed me to hope for something substantial. Several obsessive motifs, each tantalizing but incomplete, teased my mind. One of these was the mingled history and metaphor of Renaissance archaeology, practice and trope enriching each other to form the central activity of the age as it explained itself to itself. Another motif was the heightened Renaissance awareness of anachronism, which is to say period style, an essential aspect of the era's mindset I first found underscored in a little book by Peter Burke. Still another motif was the engagement of verbal style and what might be called existential style in the minds of Renaissance humanists, that engagement reflected in Ben Jonson's remark—"language most shows a man: speak, that I may see thee." The product of this engagement, unique in every case, is what I would come to call "moral style" and to see as a defining property of the literary text—this in the age of the death of the author. A final motif that would focus my future book was the curious phenomenon of "originality" in the Renaissance, always inextricably connected with intertextuality. This last phenomenon would eventually become the nominal focus of my book on *imitatio*, for which I chose a title from the late Yeats's celebrations of tragic joy. *The Light in Troy* could not have been written if I had not shared to a considerable degree the textual, historical, and moral beliefs of Renaissance humanism. The humanists of course were scarcely unanimous about all things, but they did believe in the historicity of the text, a historicity traceable in its language through the new and dynamic discipline of philology. They believed in the value of texts and in the particularity of each authorial voice. They believed in the integrity of the text, its wholeness and its difference from others. They believed in a living continuity which was not self-destructively disseminative; that belief is enshrined in the title of a humanist masterwork, *De tradendis disciplinis*. These untimely assumptions underlay the book I began to write in 1974, recognizing progressively as I worked how anachronistic were my working principles in the age of deconstruction.

Deconstruction was indeed the dominant literary philosophy at Yale during the later seventies and early eighties, although doubtless never quite as hegemonic as it may have appeared from without. The extraordinary force of Paul de Man's mind was felt as soon as he arrived, first by students, then by colleagues, then, with the appearance of *Blindness and Insight*, by Anglo-Saxon readers everywhere. The impact of his cunning and redoubtable intelligence was heightened by an effortless personal charm which is hard to exaggerate. I personally found irresistible that subtle ironic spell for which in this case the word "charisma" is not too strong. De Man as teacher and colleague offered a fresh and disturbing theory of literature which was also a hermeneutic method; both the theory and method were supported by a radical philosophy articulated by Jacques Derrida, who presently added the weight of his presence to our Yale community. Both men, but particularly de Man, were tireless in working selflessly with the growing number of gifted students who flocked to sit at their feet. When, in 1968, de Man succeeded me as chair of Comparative Literature, his influence was easily institutionalized. This, I think, he desired. Because he truly believed that his "rhetorical" method of reading was superior and irrefutable, was indeed the only method philosophically respectable, he used his position as he used his pedagogic brilliance to establish its academic dominance.

One thing excluded from this new negative theology was history. A first-year student in Comparative Literature who wanted to study literary history was told that she was in the wrong department and promptly left it. For a historian like myself, this doctrine created problems. It is not surprising that the chapter of *Blindness and Insight* I most admired was "Literary History and Literary Modernity," even if it essentially dehistoricized its subject. In the classroom, during the late seventies, I found myself talking about the essential historicity of the signifier. And in the long book taking shape in my typewriter, the theme of history came increasingly to the fore. I began to drift toward a progressively radical historicism which in the opening chapter involved a polemic directed at Derridean dissemination. That chapter not only asserted the uniqueness of the *mundus significans* belonging to each cultural moment; it also argued for the uniqueness of the copula, explicit or implicit, in the metaphors of every *mundus* and even every single metaphoric usage. The copula in this formulation constituted the intuited possibilities of relationship a given culture made available.

This chapter dealt as well with a problem brought home to me by the work of Derrida, a problem I had not really confronted earlier although it was familiar enough in the Renaissance, namely linguistic instability through history. In order to understand *imitatio*, it was important to face that instability but it was also important to describe the ways cultures respond creatively to the threat of linguistic and textual deliquescence. The saturation of the critical atmosphere by deconstructive ideas led me to react strenuously, both in this book and in a cluster of essays later gathered in a collection. I am inclined to think that because of the vogue of deconstruction, my historicism became less bland, more self-conscious, and more extreme. In trying to work out my own position, I turned with interest to Hans-Georg Gadamer's *Truth and Method*, which treated some of the issues that preoccupied me with admirable rigor. But despite the esteem and sympathy Gadamer's thought elicited, I ultimately found his version of hermeneutics unsatisfactory, postulating as it does a clear and steady stream of interpretive tradition which enables a blending of horizons between reader and text. Gadamer fails to face the possibility that that stream might contain pollution, and the concept of *Horizontverschmelzung* leaves an awkward asymmetry between the remote text and the reader enlightened by tradition. In an essay which begins with a single sonnet by Shakespeare, I tried to define my differences with Gadamer through a theory of inevitable textual estrangement which still avoids the temptations of hermeneutic narcissism. Other essays which were written as by-products of *The Light in Troy* envisioned a remote text determined by its trauma of birth, always vulnerable to historical loss and misunderstanding but maintaining nonetheless a precarious integrity.

I'm not aware that these views affected the thinking of many others, nationally or locally. The Yale department of Comparative Literature, at any rate, has been transformed from a group perceived as a homogeneous school to a larger group notable for its catholicity, open to history as to a smorgasbord of methodologies. In the nation as a whole, at the present writing, there is assuredly no grounds to regret the repression of history. The repression which concerned me ten years ago has given way to a flourishing historicism whose intellectual godfather is Foucault. It would be wrong to overestimate the unity of the so-called new historicism, which has grown, no doubt healthily, in several directions as its practitioners have multiplied. Perversely, the obsession with history which characterized my best-known work has waned with the vogue of new historical scholarship, as though I could only develop through the irritations of reaction-formations. And it is true that the enthusiasm with which I reviewed Stephen Greenblatt's *Renaissance Self-Fashioning* has yielded to occasional misgivings. Greenblatt's own work, to be sure, continues to be powerful and stimulating, ennobled as it is by a genuine moral passion not always found in his epigones. One may legitimately question the justice of Greenblatt's characteristic *turn* from nasty anecdote to literary text, a technique which tends to discredit the text despite the delicacy of the footwork during the turn. But the discrediting seems to stem from what I take to be a Utopian thrust in Greenblatt's mind, a yearning for political purity which surfaces on the last page of his *Shakespearean Negotiations* in the writer's failed effort to believe in an "untainted" Shakespeare. Measured by this Utopianism, every author will fall short and first of all Shakespeare, who surveyed the compromises of political action with a disabused awareness that in the essential business of statecraft nice guys finish last. What is admirable in Greenblatt and what has made him the intellectual force that he has become is not only the potent originality of his writing but his capacity for self-criticism and his stubborn loyalties even to tainted heroes.

This is not the place for a thorough judgment on the various and proliferating new historicisms. But since the matter of history has been a central theme in these reminiscences, I want to register at least an attitude of questioning toward some strands of this critical movement, an attitude which would require much more space to defend. Part of my uneasiness lies in the uncritical application of twentieth-century theories to eras when the theories are anachronistic. It is easy to understand the Foucauldian suspicion of power during our own century, and particularly power wielded by a single individual, although this suspicion did not curb Foucault's own admiration for the Ayatollah Khomeini. What is dangerous is the arrogance of a few contemporary scholars, unburdened with political experience, in arrogating to themselves the right to pass judgments on the conduct of early modern monarchs. To consider the political institutions of the past as evil by definition, as offensively manipulative misuses of power, is to succumb to a naive and knee-jerk virtue which betrays history and vitiates criticism. Critics of Elizabeth I's cunning as queen forget that the men and women she ruled rightly feared one thing far more than power, the new historicist shibboleth, and this was the vacuum of power, the kind of vacuum caused by the sudden death of the French king Henri II. No early modern ruler had the technological means to impose suffering commensurate with the unspeakable misery produced by the endless religious wars in France, a misery of which the unprivileged folk suffered more than their share. Anarchy in the sixteenth century was infinitely more terrifying than power, however manipulated. The new historicist opposition of power and the Bakhtinian carnivalesque, misinterpreted as subversive by definition, suppresses the facts of social history. In David Underdown's impeccably researched *Revel, Riot, and Rebellion*, revel and rebellion most often stand opposed.

Despite what I find to be the intermittent naiveté of some new historicist scholarship, I have learned from it and welcome in principle the breakdown of the intolerable barriers between academic disciplines. The crucial question posed by the politicization of literary studies is whether a political reading must necessarily be a reductive reading. The jury is still out on that question, but it remains to overshadow not only the new historicism but all criticism which speaks in the name of previously marginalized groups, including women. We need the challenges to the traditional canon these groups can make, although it is erroneous to suppose that additions of names to the canon do not entail, in the nature of academic institutions, the dimming of other names. More attention to, say, H.D. will mean less attention to, say, Sir Thomas Browne, and it would be a wise scholar indeed who would pretend to adjudicate the balance of gain and loss in such shifts. What concerns me more than these delicate balances is the potential loss of textual understanding which might result from increased perceptions of ideological orientation. We have profited from impressive examples of politically aware interpretation, but we have also been exposed to instances of slack formularization. Anger is tolerant of kindred angers, and its cleansing force may sometimes blur the kind of critical discrimination necessary to any discipline. Anger can clear the air of cant, but it is not in itself the firmest basis for the leap of historical apprehension.

The work that has occupied me since the early eighties has taken its own, very different interdisciplinary turn. For some years I became interested in the shifting role of ritual, sacred and secular, in the early modern period, and its consequent shifting relations with the literary text. The term "ceremony" and its cognates in all the modern languages began to acquire negative connotations around the turn of the sixteenth century. The suspicion of the ceremonial occasion reflected in that linguistic change was complemented and intensified by the antisacramental attacks of the reformers. Rituals continued to be performed, but they had been called into question more openly and vigorously than ever before perhaps in the history of the west. This social, religious, political change was also a semiotic change; it challenged the authority of the symbolic performative signifier. I thought about writing a book which would trace the literary fallout of this momentous *mise en question*. Although I still believe in the distinctiveness of the literary text, I think that the Comparative Literature of the future will have to find its place in the study of such transliterary developments. We need badly a metadiscipline of historical semiotics to which Comparative Literature could contribute and from which it could grow.

The project on ritual seemed promising, but before I began it, I found myself obliged to reflect further on its semiotic bases, and that reflection led to a tangential line of research which occupies me now as I anticipate the leisure of partial retirement. What struck me about the structure of rituals was the core element of magic in each, magic being defined roughly as the use of reified signs in order to bring about what they represent. Thus in the sacrament of baptism, water is used, together with language and gesture, as a means of inner purification; it becomes an efficacious sign. The recognition of this universal element in ritual led me to the study of magic as a dominant cultural phenomenon which modern culture has partially repressed or sublimated but never, by definition, successfully eliminated. Freud's conjecture in *Totem and Taboo* that all the arts have their origins in magical practices has been confirmed by evidence of many sorts, and notably in the case of lyric poetry. The project which now occupies me examines the relation of poetry to its putative roots in magical spells. "Magic" is a term I try to employ neutrally, contrary to common usage. Considered in the broadest possible perspective, it corresponds to that difficulty we experience as symbol-using animals in employing symbols transparently, without inserting a wish or a fiat into them and thus converting what is apparently communication into a claim upon the world. The study of poetry in the light of that difficulty, the study of poetic solutions to the vestigial presence of teleological pressures, involves large and difficult considerations and might ultimately involve a new theory of poetry. It would also carry implications for a theory of culture, since the structures of poems can serve in some respects as synecdoches or models for macrocosmic structures in society.

This is a vast area for reflection which invites a swerve away from history, since the object of study becomes the poem as poem, transcending diachronic particularities. But there may come a stage to return to them. A preliminary formulation of my thoughts on these matters came together in a series of lectures delivered in Paris, later published as a small book, *Poésie et magie*. But some theoretical questions remain to be resolved, as well as hermeneutic applications to be plotted, before a longer counterpart to the Paris version can appear in English.

This project on magic, whether or not I bring it off successfully, satisfies my sense of what Comparative Literature might be as we approach the end of the millennium. It crosses linguistic and cultural boundaries; it presupposes the mutual reinforcement of theory and interpretation; it transgresses disciplinary barriers without sacrificing the autonomy of the poetic text; it gestures toward the still inchoate field of historical semiotics. But this is only one path which our radically indeterminate discipline may take in the unpredictable years to come. What concerns me chiefly as I try to make out the alternative paths is an apparent boredom with poesis itself on the part of too many colleagues and students, including some of the most gifted. The growth of cultural studies, the growth of political methodologies, the hegemony of theory, are disturbing developments only if they betoken an indifference to the marvel of the text. My career as teacher and critic has found its energy in that one miraculous nexus of joy. Even if the text is subject to variable readings, even if it grows more inscrutable as it recedes in time, it retains an uncanny potency. Or at least it retained this potency through the generation of my masters, and as I work, they continue to peer over my shoulder. As I work, the tragic loss of an excitement still unspeakable seems an ever more likely eventuality, traceable in the coarseness of so much published exegesis. It is a time apparently for faith, and one places one's faith in the dynamism perennially stored in the text, perpetually available for reactualization. The study of literature, now progressively grasped as a human universal, will survive the sclerosis of reduction and the indifference of an electronic era if a few readers continue to respond to the words on the page with lively wonder and stubborn questioning. The passing on of disciplines, *tradendae disciplinae*, requires the virtue of gratitude mingled with the virtue of rigor. It may be, as my old friend Geoffrey Hartman has written, that the revolution begun by Renaissance humanism has run its course. But in the post-humanist future one hopes that the emergent disciplines will ultimately find their continuity still in some form of rigorous gratitude.

5

Am I a Comparatist?

Thomas G. Rosenmeyer

Let's not kid ourselves: I am not a comparatist. I am not even entirely sure what a comparatist is or does. Some years back—I believe it was in the early seventies—I organized a panel on comparing at the annual meeting of the American Philological Association, the classicists' trade union. I asked the members of the panel, which included Hugh Kenner, the critic *par excéllence,* and Eric Lenneberg, the remarkable biolinguist, to say something about what comparing meant to them. Kenner was appropriately witty and wise; Lenneberg—who was then, prior to his premature death, moving to a position close to that of Ernst Cassirer—offered some fascinating insights into the work of the brain. But if there is such a discipline as comparing, the panel's suggestions failed to set its conditions and limits, and I came away without guidance. I was, however, until my recent retirement, a half-member of a Department of Comparative Literature, and continue to pay my dues to the American Comparative Literature Association. Having associated with others who call themselves, or rather are publicly called, comparatists, I realize the term is something of a conundrum. Whatever it is that sets comparatists apart from other mortals, comparing, *sunkrisis,* contrastive analysis is a very small part of it, and where it flourishes the polarities inspected tend to be found within a single literary tradition. But, rubbing shoulders with my colleagues and learning from them, I am, I suppose, something more than a classicist, which is what my training gives me a right to call myself in the first instance. Allow me, then, to understand by the terms comparatist and comparative literature that surplus of interest and activity that gives me a chance to poach in forests more properly hunted by others. To the discovery of those forests I came very late. As I settle back to sketch the possible reasons for this lateness, I hope the slow amble will advertise my own uncertainty in the matter.

I was nine years old in my native city of Hamburg, Germany, when a quarrel between my parents—my mother arguing that I should attend a liberal educational institution, and my father insisting that a humanistic Gymnasium would be best for me—was resolved in compliance with my father's wishes. I entered the *Johanneum,* a four hundred-year-old school founded by Luther's friend Bugenhagen, and dedicated to the study of Latin and Greek, with English, French, Hebrew and the sciences occupying a somewhat smaller though still respectable place in the curriculum. The ethos of the school was good middle class and *deutsch-national,* which during the first three years of my attendance meant that Jewish boys were periodically chased across the schoolyard and stuck into garbage bins. After 1933, when Hitler came to power, the persecution ceased; the golden youths were embarrassed to find themselves doing what Hitler, *"der Prolet,"* was now officially recommending.

I continued to attend the *Johanneum* until 1938, when I graduated. Traditionally graduation came after nine years, but the authorities decided to lop off one year to get the officer corps ready for the coming war. During the last two or three years things were difficult; one after another my old friends fell silent and kept ther distance from me, partly out of fear of being seen talking to a Jew, partly seduced by the concrete benefits membership in the Hitler Youth conferred on them. Doctrinaire Nazis remained rare in this *haute bourgeoisie* setting. The teachers were a remarkably varied group. The few genuine Nazis kept being called away to head and purify other schools, including the liberal institution my mother preferred. A number of others were courageous enough to make no bones about their opposition to the regime, and their courage remains in my memory as a rousing paradigm of what teachers can do. Several of them had to leave, but unless my recollection deceives me they ended up, not in a concentration camp but, perversely, in a cinema-propaganda unit in Berlin started by the most gifted of the group. There were, of course, quite a few fellow travellers among the teachers, but typically one of them asked me, upon graduation, to visit him privately in his apartment so he could write me a recommendation, just in case I needed it some time in the future. Finally, the one member of the faculty who had been an SA-man ever since the early twenties, long before fellow travellers began to contemplate the possible advantages of putting on a brown shirt, set himself up as a protector of the Jewish students against any kind of violence or unfair treatment. He could afford to do this; his credentials were impeccable. Whether my school experience, with its surprises, helped to toughen me against a hasty moral (and aesthetic) reductionism I cannot tell.

When I left the school (one of the last group of Jewish students graduated from a public high school) I knew a fair amount of Latin and Greek, somewhat less English, and a decent amount of science, including spherical trigonometry and quite a bit of biology. The biology teacher, one of the courageous ones, had taught us that the children of mixed marriages were often the most talented and the most beautiful. I had not taken French or Hebrew; they were electives, taught at 7 in the morning, hence of no interest to me. Hebrew continued to be offered, primarily for those who intended to become Protestant ministers. I did take up Hebrew, that is, modern Hebrew, privately. Like so many other secular, presumably assimilated Jews of my generation, I decided when I was about fifteen that I should reestablish my identity as a Jew. I started to attend a Sephardic synagogue and went through a brief phase as a militant Zionist, a follower of Jabotinsky, aiming to conquer Palestine with a gun over my shoulder. For about two years I immersed myself in Hebrew. My disenchantment with Zionism came swiftly, and showed the flimsiness of my commitment. I had helped to earn money for the movement by participating in exhibition boxing bouts—to defend myself against Nazi goons, I had learned how to box. One day my usual opponent called in sick, and the promoters put me up against a man forty pounds heavier. I was beaten to a pulp, and my Jewish revisionism died an abrupt death.

Along with other members of my family, I had long been trying to leave Germany but, unless you had money, visas to host countries were virtually unobtainable. After graduation, however, I decided to learn crafts that might some day, when emigration became possible, help me to sustain myself. Apprehensively endorsing Brecht's view that one should pick up anything that might some day come in handy, I apprenticed myself, in succession, to two import-export firms; neither of them found me burning with the bright flame that augurs a great talent in business affairs. I also took a substantial course in window dressing, the non-figurative art of arranging the contents of display windows; and another in piano tuning. For years after I carried my tuning fork with me, in the vain hope that some day the collective pianos of my new community would be crying out for my services. None of the things I did to prepare myself for my impending life as an emigrant ever proved useful. But the forced approach to a low-level versatility was, perhaps, not without its later uses.

When finally, in April 1939, I was able to go to England, it was because the older males in my family had, along, with thousands of others caught in the *Kristallnacht,* been put in a concentration camp. Their release was made contingent upon foreign countries opening their borders, and Britain responded. I had also, through the help of a friend, obtained a fellowship at Swarthmore College, which in the end I was never able to take up. I continue to be grateful to Swarthmore for the moral boost it furnished in trying times. In England no work permit was available. By great good luck it was made possible for me to study in Cambridge. The question was: what should I study? The Classics seemed the path of least resistance, and indeed I continued to read widely in the two ancient languages (and even toyed with one of the quainter British idiosyncracies, writing Greek and Latin verse). Hebrew had fallen victim to ideological disenchantment, and was fast disappearing; I have never been a natural linguist. I was not yet sure I wanted to make the Greek and Latin learned under distressing circumstances my main concern. Yet one legacy hung on: my exposure to the ancient languages had been to them as languages. Though at the *Johanneum* we read a few literary texts, including Sophocles's *Antigone,* those texts were not experienced in the way an adolescent responds to Rilke and Schiller and Romain Rolland. They were not taught as literary documents which the adolescent could feel enriched his life and furnished food for vigorous discussion. They were texts exemplifying linguistic rules, with considerable emphasis on the analogies between the two languages. So it was almost natural that I decided to go for Sanskrit, which I studied at the London School of Oriental and African Studies, then evacuated to and temporarily housed in Jesus College, Cambridge. I took formal courses for about six months. In each of these courses I was the only attendant; the war had broken out, and the British students had left to serve their country in one capacity or another. I had three teachers in succession, all of them formidable scholars. I also joined an Indian conversation circle, in which the *Bhagavad-Gita* was the topic of discussion. I was proud of my Sanskrit, though of course I had barely begun to scratch the surface of the language and its vast treasures. Nor did I ever get to the point where I might ask myself what the special qualities of the Sanskrit tradition, both literary and otherwise, were. In the end, both Hebrew and Sanskrit remained relatively unprofitable way stations in the career of an itinerant *bricoleur.*

After the evacuation of British forces from Dunkirk in the spring of 1940 the British expected a German invasion and decided to intern all male German, Austrian, and Italian aliens. For a few weeks we found shelter in various improvised internment centers in Britain, including garages and vacation resorts. In the eyes of the public, all Germans were the enemy, and the Nazi invasion was imminent. I still remember the well-meaning British soldier in Liverpool who told me not to worry, my "friends" would be arriving in England in very little time. On the Isle of Man, our last and longest British prison camp experience, I began the next abortive study of a language: Arabic. My teacher was Emil Fackenheim, now a philosoher of the Holocaust, but then an up-and-coming medievalist and Hegelian. When finally we were shipped to Canada, the study of Arabic (and of Sanskrit) was continued on the Plains of Abraham and in the Eastern Townships, during a two-year internment which brought me together with a remarkable group of intellectuals gathered in what we called the battles of Cambridge and Oxford. The barbed-wire enclosure of the camp, isolating us from contact with society and a world at war, stood in curious contrast with the proliferation of intellectual landscapes flourishing within the confinement. Otto Demus and Johannes Wilde provided expert instruction in medieval and Renaissance art history; veteran communists gave us an inkling of what the social sciences could contribute; and the few books we had were endlessly and heatedly discussed. All this was, of course, much more interesting than the rote study of Arabic. Hebrew, Sanskrit, and Arabic meant much to me when I busied myself with them. Today they are totally forgotten, a distant memory of early, unfocused attempts to build up a linguistic armory in a vacuum.

When I was released, in the summer of 1942, I was twenty-two years old, the product of a solid but troubled formal education, a linguistic hobo, and bedevilled with the social and intellectual hangups a sustained sequestration might be expected to bring with it. My immediate post-internment years in Canada—the army would not have me—were a mixture of working for a living and going to school. The former got me acquainted with farming in southern Ontario and Saskatchewan; for two years I did night work as a slag shoveller in a steel plant in Hamilton and as a stock boy in a rubber plant in New Toronto. In Hamilton I earned a Classics B.A. from McMaster University, and in Toronto a Classics M.A. That is, when the opportunity was offered to me to continue with my studies, I yielded to cowardly momentum and reverted to the languages, and now also to the cultures, for which the *Johanneum* and the evening hours in Cambridge had obviously prepared me. I had no illusions about this cowardice; I sensed that I was withdrawing into my "native" shell, the persona authorized by an old-fashioned father and cultivated in a hateful but competent institution, turning my back upon the Eastern cruising which I felt had come to nothing. At McMaster, especially, under the benevolent tutelage of a number of broadly civilized instructors, I participated in various student activities and did a certain amount of writing, both prose and verse, that might have taken me beyond the confines of Cicero and Thucydides. But I was anxious to make my mark in the professional field I had chosen, and in any case my night work left me little time to experiment. I recall several sessions with a young lecturer who was writing a daring psychoanalytic analysis of Goethe's *Faust,* which brought home to me the narrowness of my field and of my resources, but failed to dislodge me from them. Typical term papers were on Roman coinage, Roman army standards, and (more challengingly) Epicurus.

In 1945, some months before the end of the war in Europe, I joined a team of three at the Canadian Broadcasting Corporation in Montreal, broadcasting in German to Germany and into the prisoner of war camps in Canada. All three of us severally wrote, produced, and spoke our programs, interviewed relevant visitors, and occasionally visited the camps to establish liaison with the prisoners: a curious experience for this ex-internee, to be acting on behalf of the government in a setting where I had been a inmate myself. Dissimulation was the key, but I suspected even then that the Germans saw through me. Role-playing, though indispensable in a university setting, was not easily achieved by a twenty-five year old who did not yet fully know where he was going.

My year in Montreal gave me my first exposure to things French. In those days Montreal was a marvelously vibrant double-agent. each cultural entity, from newspapers to theaters to symphony orchestras and much else, was accessible in a French version and an English version, both coexisting in a state of (then) rather amiable but vigorous high-class competition. I especially remember a young French dramatic corps, *Les Compagnons,* a communal group that put on extraordinarily progressive interpretations of the standard repertory. I began to read French books in addition to English and German ones; in retrospect I wish I had rented a room in a French-speaking family, so my spoken French might have gotten the impetus it never got. The year in Montreal was, in many ways, crucial; I rarely thought about the Classics, and was exposed to stimuli and influences that might well have taken me out of the academic fold altogether.

But the craving for security, for setting my own course with an assured degree of competence, was too strong. My father left our home when I was six; I was thirteen when Hitler came to power, but ten when I was mocked by my fellow students; I was nineteen when I left Germany with twenty marks in my pocket; I was twenty when I was interned. Canada was generous enough, after my release, to offer me the opportunities of its variety. But life was not easy, and I had a difficult time recovering a sense of belonging which I had never really known, except during perverse periods in a hostile Germany when I sought shelter in stillborn associations. The classics, I felt even in liberating Montreal, were my home, my ticket to a productive and independent future of whose coming I could be reasonably certain. And so I abondoned the fleshpots of an exciting but probably hazardous career in the media, and moved to Harvard University—now finally I could enter the United States where I had originally hoped to study—for a Ph.D. in Classics.

Because I yearned to become a bread-winner and establish my own productive identity I spent only one year in residence, the minimum requirement, before accepting my first teaching position. But at Harvard, as before in Toronto, I had the good luck to study with Eric Havelock, a British classicist who was ahead of his time in drawing upon anthropology and the social sciences. I had never taken a course in the social sciences; even if I had been aware of their importance, my tight schedule simply left me no time for them. Havelock's fresh perspectives, and particularly his ideas about the link between literacy and culture, were a revelation, as was his counter-establishment personality. A poet, and a practicing socialist who stood for election as a member of the Cooperative Commonwealth Federation in more than one Ontario riding, he was the kind of classicist who expanded the horizons of the discipline, and probably laid the basis for my later impatience with its limits. I must confess that in subsequent years I found it difficult to accept fully his specific arguments for a pervasive and lasting orality in ancient Greek culture. But there is no doubt in my mind that of all the men—unhappily but, at the time, not surprisingly there were no women—with whom I took classes he was the one I admired most, and to whom I owe most.

My first job was at the University of Iowa, where Gerald Else, the Aristotelian of his day, was setting up a small but superior department. Though one of my responsibilities was to teach the so-called core course entitled "The Greeks and the Bible," acquainting first year students with a mixture of classical and Biblical materials in English, the bulk of my teaching was in the department of Classics. But I was lucky; two advanced courses which I taught regularly, "Mythology" and "The Ancient Novel," were attended by members of Paul Engle's Writers' Workshop, and my association with some of them was a prime reason for happiness. A young instructor at a biggish American university is well-off for companionship; he will find friends in a variety of fields, both among colleagues and among graduate students. I fondly recall close links with men and women in assorted fields in the humanities and social sciences. But then Iowa City in the late forties, with the veterans descending upon it and raising the maturity level of the student body, was a very special place. The five years I spent there, writing my Harvard dissertation (strictly Classics), teaching an overload of courses at all levels, living in an apartment of my own for the first time in my life, learning about football and baseball from Nick Riasonovsky (now a colleague at Berkeley), and above all entering into many friendships that have lasted: they were the years that began to assure me that I had a present and a future, that I need not be afraid of people in uniform, and that the Bible Belt had significant values to offer.

But the Classics continued dominant. I don't believe I ever heard anyone mention the term Comparative Literature, and it did not occur to me that my objectives might some day accommodate some of the lessons I was learning from my friends in English, French, History, Philosophy, and Sociology. I was trained, if four years of formal university study could be called training, in Classics, and in nothing else; to think of trying to publish something that was not strictly Classics would have seemed presumptuous and risky. Everything else came under the heading of conversation, bull session, amusement, *unzünftige* leisure activities. To be sure, Norman Foerster and his new humanism, and Warren Austin with his version of the New Criticism, had readied Iowa City for the respectability of interdisciplinary work. William Heckscher, one of Panofsky's associates, was preaching the virtues of icon- ography and elegantly demonstrated the cohesiveness of the medieval world. But my classicist colleagues had little to say about how the Classics could fit into a larger picture, and my own search for an effective identity kept me tied to the classical yoke. A possible deviation was offered by a project I undertook after my thesis was finished: the translation of Bruno Snell's *Die Entdeckung des Geistes,* a book on classical texts, but filled with the cosmopolitan and humanist spirit of that *grand seigneur* and influential scholar whose opposition to the Nazis during the war years has become a legend in our time. Snell had been a distant family friend when I was an adolescent. Translating his work proved a mind-stretching exercise. A great many people outside the Classics came to regard the book as a crucial text cementing their relationship to the Classics. Perhaps its effect on me was symmetrical, in the opposite direction. I began to see how the Classics could be essential in an understanding of Corneille or Wordsworth or Nietzsche, and how a study of the later figures, in turn, could mould the apprehension of the ancients.

I left Iowa because the chairman felt that he needed an instructor more committed to the cause of elementary Latin. The three years I spent at Smith College were thoroughly enjoyable. Erich Auerbach came to talk about Cervantes, Phyllis Lehmann gave the most polished art history lectures one would wish to hear, and the whole academic community was versatile and giving. But as in Iowa City there was nobody in Northampton who might have been recognized as a literary comparatist, with one notable exception. Edgar Wind surely was, but he was much more than that, with his expertise in all periods of philosophy, art history, and literature, and would have been horrified to be so labeled. Above all, my special task of protecting the turf of the Classics against a president out of sympathy with it reinforced my unwillingness to expand beyond the borders of my terrain.

In 1955 my wife and I moved to Seattle, a move prompted partly by our wish to adopt a child, and by the knowledge that in Massachusetts we would have had to convert to Catholicism to be given one of the children then available for adoption. The University of Washington was, once again, a sizable state university, like the University of Iowa, but in an environment shaped by Scandinavians, and more vigorously responsive to the political challenges of the day, that is, the witch-hunting associated with the name of Senator McCarthy. Our arrival in the state of Washington was, I think, the fulfillment of the promise of liberation hoped for in my roving across the continent. The first sight of the cherry orchards of Wenatchee, rising miraculously out of the parched desert, struck us with the shock of revelation. The clear air of Seattle, then a conglomerate of parks spelled by neighborhoods, quickened the pulse. I arrived as an assistant professor, without the certainty of tenure. But for the first time in my career I had the sense that I was in a department that looked to me for what I might be willing to contribute, though I did not yet know myself precisely what that would be. The chairman, John McDiarmid, was putting together a new Classics program that enjoyed the support of allied disciplines. Comparative Literature as a focus of identification was still years in the future. For the time being we labored to make the weight of the Classics felt in the larger community, via public lectures, participation in symposia, visits to schools, and any other means that a tolerant environment made available to us. Is it possible that the very generosity of the community interested in what we had to say made us more keenly aware of the need to look at the Classics from an extrinsic or oblique vantage point?

Two towering personalities with whom my move to the west coast brought me in touch undoubtedly had something to do with my slow march beyond the confines of the Classics. One was Paul Friedländer, the German expatriate who was an emeritus at UCLA, and whose writings included work on Byzantine *ekphrasis,* Goethe's reception of antiquity, and much else that may be considered comparative, in addition to his more strictly classical publications, the best-known of which is his still invaluable *Plato.* I visited him in Los Angeles, where he was growing papyrus plants in the tiny backyard of his small house. His contribution to a global conception of the Humanities has not, I think, had the recognition it deserves. I met him only twice, but the contour of his beautiful face and the gentleness of his demeanor remain significant memories, as do the tales of how badly he was held back in his early days at UCLA by a chairman who was for a time a member of the Ku Klux Klan. The other giant was Hermann Fränkel, like Friedländer a refugee, more strictly a classicist, though equally given to seeing the ancient legacy within the larger compass of a European cultural history with which he was thoroughly familiar. He taught Classics at Stanford, and I admired him particularly for his work on Apllonius of Rhodes, the Hellenistic epic poet whom Fränkel almost single-handedly restored to public esteem. I was skeptical about Fränkel's radical emendations and stipulations of lacunae in the text, but I marveled at his incomparable erudition and at the streak of poetry in him which made his translations into testaments of passion and beauty. Fränkel also had the gift of squaring literature off against philosophy and arriving at insights which, though very much in the tradition of German *Geistesgeschichte,* seemed to me to illuminate the cohesiveness of Greek culture in its various stages, and the mutual enrichment of diverse codes.

Precisely when it was that I first became aware of the need for myself to venture decisively beyond the borders of the Classics I cannot recall. One of the authors in whom I became interested as I was working on Apollonius was Theocritus, our first pastoralist. By 1961, six years after my move to Seattle, I had gained sufficient control over the material to offer a course on the author in Athens, where I was a visiting professor at the American School of Classical Studies. Apparently the topic forced me to become interested in what happened to the pastoral after the Hellenistic age, and I began to think about a book on the subject. A year or two later Alain Renoir, the chairman of a revitalized Comparative Literature Department at Berkeley, was for a time a visitor in Seattle, and we began to talk. By 1964 I must have joined the International Comparative Literature Association, for in that summer I found myself at a meeting in Fribourg, giving a paper entitled "Theocritus and his Successors." In the summer of 1965 Renoir invited me to teach a summer course at Berkeley; soon after that I learned that I was going to be asked to accept a position in Classics and Comparative Literature at that institution. By this time I had woken up to the fact that the University of Washington too had a program in Comparative Literature, consisting of one person who shall remain nameless. The University was growing at a fast pace; I suggested several names to him

for a possible expansion of the program. His invariable answer was that as long
as he was in charge, there wouldn't be anybody else. I went to the dean and
tried to argue the case for bringing in additional comparatists. The dean was
unwilling to rock the boat, which remained a single scull. Only during my last
year in Seattle did Ernst Behler and Frank Warnke become active in the program.
If Comparative Literature had been given its rope earlier, with a participation
of the Classics in the program, I might still be in Seattle.

One more word about my year in Athens. Although my acquaintenance
with modern Greek, and modern Greek Literature, remained painfully limited,
I did become aware of the precarious balancing of that literature between a
variety of traditions and canons, from antiquity to the avant-garde movements
of the nineteenth and twentieth centuries. If Comparative Literature as a
discipline has any value, the tracing of the stimuli that have helped to shape
Greek poetry and prose and of the role of the native repertoire in the process
is its proper concern. Programs in Modern Greek Studies are rare at American
universities, for obvious reasons; a degree in the field is not widely marketable.
But the history of modern (including medieval and Renaissance) Greek literature
is an exhilarating paradigm of how a wide array of national cultures can become
absorbed by the body of a small literary community and produce something
valuable and new. So modern Greek studies have an importance of their own,
and where they *are* found they are best organized under the aegis of Comparative
Literature, where the significant links with Italian, French, British, and German
texts and genres can be explored. This is anticipating; at the time I was only
dimly aware of how the study of the symbolist and other European traces in
the living texture of Greek writing might be pursued. I was struck by its power,
and by its otherness, and I wondered about the nature of an indigenous stock
that could surrender its identity and lend itself to the fusion into something
new. But as an outsider I was also impressed by the frankness with which the
Greeks themselves assessed the debts their masterpieces owed to the cultures
that had brutalized them over the years.

Berkeley signified my arrival within the ranks of official Comparatists.
But the constitution of the Department there, and my own lateral entry into
the field, immunized me against raising questions about the nature of my
commitment and that of most of my colleagues. With few exceptions, they had
been plucked out of their various specialist departments for their prominence
in their fields and their competence in several languages, and for their
willingness to work with each other and examine students of widely differing
backgrounds and aims. Because of Renoir's passionate belief that the legacies
of which we were the certified transmitters came out of Greece and Rome,
the Classics were strongly represented and there was considerable emphasis
on the influence and afterlife of the ancients. One of the four languages required
for the Ph.D. had to be either Latin or Greek. For the first few years, then,
I found myself in an environment which made me feel at home, and which

did little to alert me to the fact that the comparative study of literature offered troubling challenges of doctrine and technique. Some of my colleagues were modernists; there were theorists of film, and others interested in the overlap between literature and the visual arts, and literature and music. But the bulk of the publications coming out of the department were studies of single works, or authors, or genres, or periods. To be sure, Philip Damon wrote about Sappho as well as Petrarch, and had read every word of Lévi-Strauss; and Robert Alter dazzled us with switchbacks from the picaresque to the biblical to the self-conscious. What this meant was that these and other members of the department each commanded more than one specialty, and that occasionally these specialties could be brought into close proximity. But there appeared to be no overriding sense of the need to convert the proximity into imbrication, and to inquire into the principles underlying such a course. Subsequent recruiting and the needs of our splendid students made a difference. But my initial experience in the Berkeley Department of Comparative Literature was scarcely tailored to launch me into an aggressive search for new ways of thinking about my texts.

I spent the year 1972-73 in Paris, principally to have our children learn French, but also to put the finishing touches on a book on Aeschylus which was, once again, straight Classics, though some benevolent reviewers claimed that they could see the benefits of a concern with other literatures in it. Two incidents in Paris brought home to me, in a thoroughly unattractive fashion, what lay beyond the Classics and what promised to be waves of the future. One was listening to a lecture, strongly recommended by a friend who said it was the chic thing to do that year in Paris: a lecture in the Faculty of Law by a vulgarian orator whose name was Lacan. I say "vulgarian" because it was apparent that the speaker was primarily interested in insulting the audience. A vaudeville magician, he barked commands at his assistants, who appeared to have no evident function save to suggest the fulness of an Ubu-roi court. I had not heard of Lacan before, and it was not at all clear to me from the lecture that this man's influence on literary studies was going to be enormous. Though I had read a certain amount of Freud, I could see no ready connection between what I had read and what I was hearing that day. In any case, my readings in psychoanalysis have never prompted me to modulate my critical work along psychoanalytic lines, though my students have taught me much about the value, for them, of Lacanian and post-Lacanian approaches.

The second incident happened at the Ecole Normale Supérieure. The man in charge of the public lectures there had been warned by a prominent member of the Classics establishment that if he invited a certain Classicist (with an interest in hermeneutics) to give a talk, she would withdraw from the Ecole. This was too tempting a challenge to resist, and the organizer immediately proceeded to extend an invitation to the Classical hermeneut, whose lecture was almost entirely given over to a spiteful tirade against various colleagues who did not think as he did. (The author of the défi resigned her position, and was promptly berthed in the Collège de France.) The arranger gave him a very elegant introduction, and that is how I first became aware of Derrida's elegance of speech. It was the second time I had heard the name Derrida; prior to that, on a visit to Johns Hopkins, I had become dimly aware that such a person existed. But once again, the power that Derrida's speaking and writing would soon exercise over academic circles in this country was at the time hardly conceivable. Soon after, I read the *Pharmacie*, not to mention some of the later writings, and was intrigued by their cleverness and by their virtuoso intransigence. But it was not until 1980, thirty-three years after I began teaching and fourteen years after I joined a department of Comparative Literature, that I wrote my first piece, "The Nouvelle Critique and the Classicist," on what theories triggered by Nietzsche and Heidegger have, and do not have, to offer in the study of literature and particularly of classical literature. The paper was largely polemical, even captious. Subsequently, especially in a monograph published in 1988, with the obscurantist title *Deina Ta Polla* (a flirtatious inversion of the first words of a Sophoclean choral ode, translatable as "Of many [theories] there is a dread"), I expressed myself with greater moderation. What had happened was not only that I had taken to reading widely if at random in the corpus of new theory, from semiotics to deconstruction, from feminism and gender theory to the new historicism. More important, other classicists had started to absorb the new perspectives into their thinking. Radical deconstruction is still a relative rarity in classical learning, but gender studies and the new historicism have become powerful currents in our discipline, especially as enunciated by *l'école de Paris*, the school of Jean-Pierre Vernant, Pierre Vidal-Naquet, and Marcel Détienne. I have reservations about the immediate usefulness of their work for the appreciation of specific literary texts. On the whole I remain an unreconstructed subscriber to a version of the old Petrarchan humanism, as revalidated in such a treatise as Stein Haugom Olsen's *The End of Literary Theory*. Because as a teacher I am old-fashioned enough to believe that an immersion in great literary documents is one essential (though hardly foolproof) way of inducing maturity and sophistication, in short, of humanizing, I cannot do without the critical assumptions of authorship, of intention, of interpretation and evaluation, whatever the hermeneutic channelling through which they are fed. This may or may not reveal the narrowness of my ideological mindset; it also documents the Marxist insistence on the near-identity of aesthetic and ideological propositions. An inquiry that proceeds without these assumptions I rank as the philosophy of communication, or as a scrutiny of the indeterminacies of language, divorced from the purposes of the crafters of the texts. As a presumptive teacher of Comparative Literature I do not feel they are my business. It goes without saying that, as the great New Critics knew, an acquaintance with the special features of rival canons and of institutional realia is likely to sharpen and make more interesting the interpretation of the text at hand. And there is no doubt that the school of Vernant, along with others, has enriched our understanding of the social and psychological reciprocities against which the literary work must establish its unique identity.

In my teaching in Comparative Literature, I have tried to pay attention to some of the perspectives made possible by the prominent initiatives in critical theory. But whether it was a course on the novel, or on the theory of drama, or on the concept of irony, or on the literature of violence, my old specialty has always insisted on securing its pound of flesh. The ancients come first, and the modern or postmodern experience is measured against the conventions and insights readied by that perilously tangible conglomerate, the tradition of the Classics. Yet I cannot deny that today I read the classical authors differently from the way I read them before I ventured across the borders of the discipline. To discover in Aeschylus a dramatic technique that has tortuous analogies with what is found in Beckett or Handke, or to trace in Aristotle a handling of metaphor that can usefully be set off against treatments by Donald Davidson or Ricoeur, is to me a special joy, a vindication of the thought that Classics has an enduring role to play in the ferment of criticism and theory, but also a recognition that *Reszeptionsgeschichte* and insights coming out of Kant's transcendental subject have irreparably changed our understanding of the classical texts themselves.

The instances I have cited come under the narrowest understanding of "Comparative Literature." Broader issues, less strictly comparative but considered appropriate to the departmental agenda, kept knocking at the door, inviting me to pay attention to them. The roll of the dice would have it that now and then I had to be chairman, or director of graduate studies, in the Department of Comparative Literature. My younger colleagues treated me well, and were careful not to let on that they thought of me as a very slow learner of the necessities of the intellectual life. Yet learn I did, to a degree, and I ended up seeing the need of what William Heckscher had recommended as the oblique or tangential approach to any object of study. I do not look upon Comparative Literature or Literary Theory as necessarily more liberal or liberating or politically attractive than the more specialized Classics. The contrast between Bruno Snell and Paul de Man is no more enlightening than the contrast between René Wellek and, say, Friedländer's chairman. But there is no doubt that poaching is an exhilarating business.

It is a saddening thought that the majority of today's academics who call themselves comparatists have only the faintest notion of the materials predating the eighteenth and nineteenth centuries, or even the twentieth. Baudelaire, Poe, Marx, Nietzsche, Saussure, Heidegger, Freud, not to mention Blanchot and Lacan and Foucault: these are some of the father figures, the "ancient" authorities upon whose pilings courses in Comparative Literature are constructed. I recall asking a prospective colleague whether she might ever be induced to go back to ancient materials, and she said, yes, she was fascinated by Rousseau. Minority aspirations, militant feminism, and gender studies have added their own momentum to the feeling that what happened before the 1700s is of little concern to one who tries to stake out a position in a frenetically competitive setting, and that the study of the Classics is irrelevant in a society whose values need to be framed anew. The tendency of the younger comparatists today to philosophize about and generalize from texts, or to use texts to vindicate preestablished theories, has made the loose and exhaustive study of the primary texts unfashionable. Classics has been put on the defensive, and Comparative Literature, in its latest guise as a laboratory for exploration at the margins, has dissociated itself from that defense. At Berkeley the requirement of a classical language has now been reinterpreted to allow the study of Yoruba. I cannot say that I am discontented; as a classicist I welcome the provocation that forces my tribe to reappraise our discipline in line with the pressures of a changing community and the cunning allurements of postmodernism. A department of Comparative Literature is, of course, the most convenient and congenial workshop in which to undertake such a reappraisal. At least I have found it so, and I consider myself a substantial beneficiary of membership in the Berkeley department. I cannot know for sure if I have found the niche for which I was looking during the earlier days of my career. But though, outside of institutional accident, I cannot call myself a comparatist, I am glad that, associating with others who may or may not be comparatists, I have tried to listen to the magic flutes and to walk through the fire and the water of lessons which some of my colleagues, and my students, most of all, have wanted me to learn.

6

Reminiscences of an Academic Maverick*

W. Wolfgang Holdheim

If Comparative Literature is the natural field of study for people who cannot make up their minds, I must have been the quintessential comparatist from the outset. In my undergraduate years (at UCLA) I was successively a student of Sociology, History, Philosophy, and finally French Literature. At that point, a Bachelor of Arts degree caught up with me, so that further immediate changes became too impractical even by my standards, and I miraculously adhered to my last pre-baccalaureate subject for my Master of Arts and even for my Doctorate (the latter at Yale).

I started out with a pronounced interest in Sociology, at a time—right after the Second World War—when that subject still had the charm of novelty. I had visions, though, of studying authors like Karl Mannheim and Max Weber. When I was confronted instead with a scientistic discipline that tried to thrive on statistics, I fled headlong into History. I forget why I did not persist in that new field of endeavor, for it still interests me vitally (as indeed do Weber and Mannheim); I probably felt that I needed something committed a little less to factuality and a little more to analysis and interpretation. This transplanted me into Philosophy for some time. Here, however, I butted up against a problem that was to pursue me for the rest of my professional life: the distinction, sometimes contrast, between an intellectual endeavor in its ideal purity and that same endeavor in its institutional reality. Ideally, philosophers are by definition "lovers of truth," and seekers after it; institutionally, they all too often turn into expert repositories of Truth, fully able to determine what it is and what form it must take in order to qualify for professional attention. The result is the well-known phenomenon that at any given period, only a strictly limited number of approaches to wisdom tend to be taken seriously by Departments of Philosophy. When I was a student, you had to be either a pragmatist or a logical positivist to qualify fully, and I simply could not picture myself as either

63

of the two. Besides, a benevolent young professor warned me that there were very few jobs in the field, especially for people who spoke with an accent. I therefore decided to make yet another switch; it was the only thoroughly careerist decision I ever took. I veered toward literature, where I saw greater possibilities to indulge my emerging creativity. It would have to be a national literature: Comparative Literature did not yet occur to me as a viable alternative. I rejected English because of my German accent, which was then even thicker than it is now. (I had previously renounced the idea of legal studies for similar reasons.) Remarkably enough, I refused to go into German literature because (so I argued—believe it or not!) after all I knew the language and was not totally unfamiliar with all of the literature. I wanted to learn, and felt that I should really study something important of which my knowledge was more minimal. I had only my very precarious school French, acquired in Holland, and was almost ignorant of French literature. It was therefore evident to me that I was ideally suited to become an expert in French.

This, at least, is the way things then presented themselves to my mind, to the best of my recollection. It is as though I literally bungled my way toward my "chosen" field of study. Could there have been a hidden logic in these vacillations? To put it differently: what brings us closer to the truth—an account of one's early *ad hoc* bunglings or a retrospective interpretation? I do not want to theorize on this basic question of all autobiography, biography, and history, but I now realize that I must have been impelled by more complex motivations than I could be aware of at the time. There can be little doubt, for example, that my choice of French was really dictated by the need to find a counterweight to, perhaps even a release from, a German heritage which was peculiarly potent in people of my particular background (briefly: the Berlin Jewish, or, as in my case, half-Jewish bourgeoisie). Understandably, this heritage had become somewhat problematic for one who came of age in 1947. On the positive side, I hope and believe that my choice also reflected a desire to expand my cultural horizon, or more precisely: to conquer and reconquer for myself that broad framework of Western culture and humanistic *Bildung* into which I had been born, within which I had been raised as long as rational education was still possible, but which had been thoroughly shattered (so it seemed) by the historical developments we know. It turned out (providentially or fortuitously?) that the Yale French Department was just the right place for me and others like me. Quite a few German émigrés of that generation went into French studies for reasons akin to mine, and it is remarkable how many of them were (very deliberately, as I now know) received with open arms at Yale, at a time when their particular cultural combination often tended to raise some suspicion at other places. In fact it is impossible to do full justice to the atmosphere of broad-minded liberality which was then radiated by the Yale French Department, under the chairmanship of Henri Peyre. It was not only an institution for training scholars, it was a veritable center of civilized discourse—an intellectual community free from all provincialism and sectarianism, national, ideological, or otherwise. One should record such moments: it is bad enough that they must pass, it would be even worse if they were to be forgotten. I certainly learned about French literature and could indulge my growing love for it. But there was nothing limited in my training, and it is typical that my graduate study even cured me of the one defensive, negative aspect of my tangled motivations. For Yale was hardly the place to get away from the German tradition. I encountered it at its best in Erich Auerbach, a "good European" from exactly the same background as myself, and a leading representative of a *Romanistik* that was truly "comparative" in its scope. I must here record one of the most telling experiences I have had. When I was writing my dissertation, *Gide and Nietzsche* (already a comparative and interdisciplinary subject!), one of the readers suggested that I write a methodological introduction justifying my comparison between a philosopher and a belletristic writer, in order to satisfy the precision-mindedness of a judge such as Auerbach. I did so, haltingly and very inexpertly: it was my first encounter with literary theory. Later I was anxious to see Auerbach's notations on my theoretical effort, and found that he considered it persuasive but self-evident and totally unnecessary, because all those questions had been authoritatively treated by German thinkers for the last fifty years. In my youthfully naive way, I had rediscovered a German philosophical tradition of which (consciously, at least) I knew next to nothing then. I still do not fully understand how this could have come about, but I finally realized that I could not turn my back on an intellectual tradition that had taken the lead in clarifying crucial issues, and for which I seemed to have a natural affinity. I accepted to become what I was: a German of sorts (perhaps a representative of the "other Germany," or a belated Weimar product) who had *nolens volens* been exposed to a number of international experiences, including a prolonged stay in the Netherlands, emigration to the United States, and ultimately study in France as well. Mindful of Goethe's injunction, I set about acquiring what I had inherited.

This task (since Goethe has now been mentioned) necessarily involved a strong commitment to *Weltliteratur.* Looking back, how could I really fail to become a comparatist? Once literature had become the focus of my preoccupations, I never was anything else—well before I came to formalize the fact in professional terms. That professional formalization took place gradually but irresistibly throughout my career—first at Brandeis, then at Washington University in St. Louis, and finally at Cornell. It went hand in hand with a growing trend toward the creation of Comparative Literature departments and programs in the United States. That development, partly an epiphenomenon of the general academic expansion during the 1960s, also reflected a reaction against a certain narrowness in the still dominant state of mind. The interest in national traditions in their infinite richness and diversity, as expressed in the various languages and literatures, had once been a veritable intellectual breakthrough—but, as so often happens in things human, a process of institutionalized sclerosis had left its mark. *Romanistik* such as practiced by Auerbach, Curtius, and Spitzer had retained much of that original energy, but it had been an exception (even in the German academy) for some time. National literature departments in the third quarter of the twentieth century showed but few traces of the romantic fervor that had once brought them into being. Notably the native national literature departments in the major countries often displayed an exacerbated provincialism—an attitude fostered in part by a century-long tradition of increasingly self-directed nationalism, and in part by the firm bureaucratic assumption that the biggest must needs be the most important and the best: how, for example, could the tenfold number of professors and lecturers in English fail to prove the superior distinction of this field? Even foreign literature departments, however, often aped this attitude on a minor scale and had a peculiar little national emphasis of their own. This was certainly the case in some French departments in the United States, which were far from practicing their subject in the spirit that characterized the Yale French Department forty years ago. For many here, French was a *Liebhaberfach* (we have the thing but not the term); they studied and taught it because it was (still is) considered terribly "in," irresistibly civilized to know the language and to read its writings. This has in many cases led to a stance of rapt admiration for everything literary and intellectual imported from France, much as some ladies of the provinces will uncritically wear all the sartorial products that come from the capital. I must confess that this factor gave some added impetus to my comparative instincts. Ultimately, my reasons for choosing an academic profession had been cognitive and critical rather than sartorial and mimetic. I can only hope that this attitude of mine (comparable to that of certain émigré art historians who refused to accept the equally *Liebhaber* status of their own discipline) is not viewed as abrasively German. I continue to be better versed in the literature of France than in any other, to love and admire it along with French thought and culture, but think that I can honor those subjects more fruitfully by viewing them in the broad perspective they deserve, and with the sympathetic critical detachment that befits an intellectual discipline.

The most pervasive lesson of my life as a professional has been the realization that there is a built-in paradox in the very concept of an academic career. We need institutes of higher learning, yet higher learning cannot be bureaucratized with total impunity. Intellectuality is one thing, institutionalization is quite another, and while they must try to go together, they will often inevitably be at odds. This inherent tension, therefore, should at all times be delicately balanced; heaven forbid that it should ever be totally suppressed! It is revealing that intellectuals (and I use the term existentially, not sociologically, to designate those individuals who truly live *sub specie intellectus*) are often such hopeless administrators. Is it necessary to make the opposite point as well? The problem may be mitigated by the fact that even in a university, many (perhaps even a majority?) are not really "intellectuals" in this sense. Unfortunately, this mitigating circumstance has its risks. They are risks that I personally, for better or for worse, can hardly claim to have enhanced. Necessity constrained me for a lengthy period to contend with the scholar's nemesis: a chairmanship, despite my native distaste for many of its tasks. I am constitutionally unable, for example, to remember a bureaucratic rule from one day to the next. Impelled by an uncomfortable Prussian sense of responsibility, I nevertheless forced myself to cope without major disasters, but the experience cost me much more time and effort than it should have.

What helped me, superficially, was the diminutive dimension of a Comparative Literature department, which made administrative problems more manageable, at least in a quantitative sense. In other ways, however, this very smallness brought out the basic academic paradox with greater force. Lack of mass, as I found out very quickly, is not what impresses institutional mentalities. One of my deans repeatedly enquired why a Comparative Literature department was needed, given the fact that we already had departments of English, French, German, and the rest. Once it was seriously suggested that we be deprived of our modest but centrally located departmental office, since we did not really need "something quite so sumptuous"; the intended beneficiary of this sumptuosity was a lone (though secretary-provided) minority member of a large department. In sudden flashes, such episodes revealed the prevailing order of importance. We kept our department intact and did not vacate our office, and on the whole did rather well—but only at the price of a tiresome ongoing effort, dictating decisions and compromises that often owed little to academic considerations. Thus the additions of joint appointments to the department, designed in principle to enrich the department's intellectual fabric, was also motivated by the need to enhance its institutional stability: the (sometimes nominal) presence of senior colleagues from the outside might help to preserve us from extinction. And the creation of a regular undergraduate major in Comparative Literature was another move to bolster our quantitative impact. (Ideally, I rather tend to believe that Comparative Literature, except in certain select cases, should be a predominantly graduate field.)

In later years, of course, when Comparative Literature programs and departments proliferated throughout the country, our existence was no longer questioned. There has been a marked change in the prevailing attitude toward our discipline. Whereas in the old days we were often but barely accepted by serious-minded scholars, we now sometimes get the feeling that we have been transported into a world where everybody is (or at least deems himself to be) a comparatist. In a sense, we have become the victims of our own success. Again the institutional reactions bear this out. Comparative Literature departments must guard against becoming catch-alls, dumping grounds for ill-defined appointments. Frequently they are called upon to serve as props for job offers made by other departments, when the latter try to attract candidates who happen to desire a comparative association. Underlying an undisputed turnabout in atmosphere, then, there persists the danger of not being taken seriously.

Undeniably, such attitudes are favored by a certain elusive quality in the makeup of the discipline. The very term "comparative literature" is misleading. It goes back to those early days when the field, paradoxically, was an epiphenomenon of nationalism, betokening the study of influences and interconnections between more or less autonomous national literatures. It is characteristic that despite the change in spirit, no other name for the field has since been found. We know how the loss of their nationalistic, positivistic moorings has precipitated many comparatists into a downright self-tormenting quest for the essence of their field of study—and of themselves. Like T. S. Eliot's cat, they assiduously seek the Platonic idea of their name, sharing this unhappy passion for self-identification with two other insecure groups: the Germans and the Jews. In fact, it has occurred to me that in my quality of a German Jewish (better: half-Jewish) comparatist, I was peculiarly suited to what should have been my feline task. This, however, was not true in practice, because I have never been bothered at all by my doubtful status. I felt no compulsion whatsoever to define my discipline in either essentialist or methodological terms, and was quite satisfied by the conviction that I was quite simply engaged in the study of Literature, pushed to its final point. When my above-mentioned dean asked me to justify my (our) departmental existence, I no doubt came up with appropriate arguments, but this was only for the sake of the cause. After all, I could not tell him my real opinion: that "Comparative Literature" as an independent department was needed principally to confront the traditional departments with a counterforce. What was it that endowed the latter with their unassailed security? Over and above historical tradition, it was the fact that they were grounded in a particular language. Languages, of course, are complex things with spiritual implications: they are nothing less than world views (as Humboldt taught us), and they carry genuine national traditions of literature. But there is an equally genuine Western tradition as well, and an Asian one, and many others, including one of *Weltliteratur.* Those spiritual factors are not really what counts in constituting a clearcut institutional identity. What counts is the simple rock-bottom foundation of a language that is clearly unlike others. English is English and French is French: such are the indubitable and positive facts that an administrative mind will recognize. Let me be clear: I do not impugn the existence and justification of national literature departments. They have proved their worth, although it has been less in the context of that underlying positive factuality than in that of the elusive "spiritual implications." Universities do need criteria to organize the profusion of phenomena, and the national approach to literature is a better criterion than most others; as an educational experience, it is most valuable as an initial stage. But institutions tend to become bureaucratized, narrow, sectarian. How to counteract that process of reification and contraction? In a world of institutions, it can only be through a counter-institution, This, for me, has always been the "organizational" role of Comparative Literature. I view it, as it were, as an ironic institutionality that counterbalances the risks inherent in institutions; a departmental antidote to departmentality; a solvent that helps to melt down what is frozen, and to transcend all provincial narrowness.

Some might consider these as maverick opinions. I gladly accept this appellation; I would merely object to the implicit conformist suggestion that this is a phenomenon so far out of the ordinary that it can be safely marginalized and ignored. On the contrary, I contend that a maverick (a Kierkegaardian "individual") is exactly what the responsible intellectual should be. And it would be mistaken to charge that he is embarked on a purely negative course; this is so, again, exclusively from a conformist institutional viewpoint. Intellectuality needs a critical dimension to clear the way for its actual endeavor; did not Francis Bacon have to start out by identifying and impugning the oppressive *idola*? The *positive* aim of the comparatist is the acquisition of a broad and ever-widening perspective. This is by no means equivalent with extensive knowledge, although such knowledge (transnational, even interdisciplinary) is a valuable help and a necessary precondition. What is sought is (much more impalpably) a world view, an orientation in terms of which knowledge is evaluated, a horizon within which it is placed and can develop. The broadness we need does not lie in the subject matter. This is vividly and sometimes comically illustrated by a contemporary trend in literary studies that seemingly pushes expansion beyond all previous limits, drawing all ages and traditions (and all fields, such as philosophy, psychology, sociology, anthropology, linguistics, and many more) into the charmed circle of its preoccupations—only to amalgamate all this into a homogeneous pap in which each text becomes ultimately indistinguishable from any other. Conversely, there can be a truly "comparative" analysis of one particular writer, work, or even passage. How to acquire a quality that is so elusive that it cannot be defined but only recognized in the act? Needless to say, there can be no hard-and-fast prescriptions. It is an ongoing process of growth that is ultimately the responsibility of the individual alone. An academic department can further it most effectively by exemplifying a spirit of broad liberality. Rules, and even some requirements, are no doubt indispensable to give some shape to the process of education, to ensure that it not be abused and that some standards are maintained. Times and situations continually change, and the rules should be adjusted to those changes—but most emphatically, this does not mean that they should always strive to express prevailing interests as they unfold from year to year. There is a school of thought that thinks they should. Clearly, we are here dealing with an avant garde version of the ancient myth of progress. We see every day what this "activism" leads to: nothing more than a Disneyland conception of education, in which universities become uncritical reflectors of topicality, guided not by substance but by marketable fashion. Academic requirements should, quite on the contrary, be guided by a Nietzschean ideal of non-topicality; they should emphasize precisely the *gaps* left by modish concerns, and foster an attitude of critical distance from what happens to be in the air.

Comparative Literature has yet another dimension, it is the sphere not only of breadth but also of depth—the natural locus for what is now called "literary theory." We know to what degree this endeavor has moved to the foreground during the last few years, even in national literature departments. My natural affinity for theoretical analyses, together with my peculiar background and training, made it both easy and pleasant for me to reactivate my early philosophical interests. Unfortunately, they also made it painfully obvious that something was wrong with much of the theorizing to which we were being exposed. Already Bakhtin, himself a major theorist, warned against the dangers of the frame of mind which he called "theoritism": it loses touch with all reality, all particularity, all concreteness, and therefore with life's ethical dimension; it plunges out into a stratosphere of autotelic universal abstractions that tend to coagulate into oppressive norms.[1] Many recent developments in the academy have certainly borne out Bakhtin's warnings, successfully transposing Gresham's law (bad money drives out good money) from the domain of finances to that of reflectivity. In fact they have moved from theory via theoretism to theoritis, which goes even one step further, projecting theory into a never-never land of neo-nonsensicality. Here, critical thinking turns effectively into its opposite: into the aping of fashionable slogans, a veritable carnival of marketable jargon—in short: a pseudo-intellectual version of Disneyland. The slogans (remember Bakhtin!) have shown a tendency to harden into norms and rules that claim exclusive validity. Paradoxically so, since this theorizing has generally claimed to be skeptical in nature—but already Hegel knew that extreme skepticism is but one step removed from total dogmatism. For example, it has been discovered (and this is not a very novel discovery in the eyes of someone with a philosophical background) that knowledge is never totally neutral and "objective." But instead of leading to an attitude of prudent autocritical vigilance, as it should, this insight has been used as an epistemological license for a power-oriented dogmatism: since all cognition is inescapably "ideological" (all perspectivism is simplistically and self-servingly viewed as ideological), we have an absolute right to ideologize away.

Upon perusing a list of new scholarly book titles, one is narcotically affected by their aura of inexorable sameness. It is becoming as difficult to distinguish between the titles of scholarly works as between those of popular detective stories. (At this particular juncture, the noun "gender" occurs as frequently in the former as "death" or "murder" does in the latter; soon, no doubt, another term will play that role). This is part of the relentless homogenization mentioned earlier. All texts are ultimately the same, since all are conceived as self-directed enactments of the identical theoretical premises. Theoritis is a potent homogenizer. There have been suggestions to reorganize departments and programs (Comparative Literature above all) according to theoretical criteria. Such a reorganization would lead to a more oppressive uniformity, and a more intense provincialism, than any national approach could ever engender at its worst. The novice would have to overcome the initial obstacle of familiarizing himself with the correct terminology, much as the student of Russian has to start out by learning the Cyrillic alphabet. But once that surface difficulty is overcome, Comparative Literature (unlike the Russian language) would prove to be extremely easy. It is not the least important task of the comparatist to see to it that his field remains appropriately difficult.

The comparatist should, however, maintain a constructive attitude toward literary theory. Many literary scholars are hostile to theorizing as such. Despite the temporary abuses of the activity, such gut reactions simply will not do. Gut reactions are inherently suspect, and this particular one is an example of the attitude that made the abuses possible in the first place. Perhaps an invasion of irresponsible theorizing and heavy-handed ideologizing was inevitable, sooner or later, in an overly pragmatic tradition, where too many students have not been vaccinated with the philosophical antibodies that may permit one to evaluate the speculative urge (one's own and that of others) in a critical spirit. The truth is that theorizing as well requires breadth. Mono-theory is nothing but a kind of horizonless monomania; one needs perspective in order to refine one's thought, to learn to think sanely and substantively. And here again, the comparatist's task *par excellence* should be expanding the horizon. He should do his best to clarify theoretical issues, to place theories in their proper (historical and systematic) contexts and to judge them by their merits. This does not mean that he must pretend to be neutral and uncommitted—but commitment should not turn into a brainwashing campaign, and proselytizing is an activity that should be resolutely rejected. Intellectual groupishness is not only a contradiction in terms, it is the ultimate sin against the spirit. Gresham's law implies that there is also such a thing as good money; what we should strive for, then, is a currency reform. Naturally, the theorizing of the last few years has not been all bad, much of it is useful, and its profusion (however inflationary) has at least forced us to grapple with genuine theoretical questions. We should meet the challenge of practicing theory as an ongoing self-reflection of literature, grounded in concreteness and guided by the ethical postulate of clarification. And we should try to induce our students to do so on their own.

All this, though, is more easily said than done. In the field of literary studies, the comparatist should be the intellectual *par excellence*; the question is to what degree this mode of existence is still viable. I am most reluctant to say that we are in a period of crisis. Every generation sees itself in the grips of some "crisis," and an inflated crisological rhetoric is notably one of those contemporary habits I would rather avoid. Without indulging in a terminology thus trivialized, then, let us look at the present state of the academy in our field. No doubt there have always been phenomena in our institutes of higher learning that ill accorded with the latters' ideal function. One made allowances for those trends, since one was not naive and knew the world to be an imperfect place. We are back to the academic paradox, previously described: the balance between intellectuality and institutionality, individualism and conformism, the ideal and the real, the "ought" and the "is." Such a balance, however precarious, had always existed—at least as far as I can remember. When unsuitable procedures were practiced, it was more or less covertly or at least with something of a bad conscience, hypocrisy (as La Rochefoucault put it) being the compliment that vice pays to virtue. The trouble is that such compliments are becoming rarer for the wrong reason: not because honesty is spreading, not even because cynicism is expanding, but because of a growing inability to perceive what one should be hypocritical about. There appears to be a diminishing sense of what our function properly requires. The tension between the poles is weakening, the precious balance tends to fade away—in a move toward terrible simplification that is more "naive" than any starry-eyed idealism could ever be. At the not-so-ideal limit, there looms a universitas that has ceased to be anything but an institution, and where the intellectual's status will be nothing but a career—and a very mediocre one, judged by those standards, for no doubt one will continue to be severely underpaid. It would be simplistic to blame university administrators alone for this state of affairs. They are there to do their jobs, in often difficult market conditions; the counterweight has to be furnished by the academics, and their actions, sometimes their very philosophies, too often undermine their *raison d'être* as intellectuals. One theoretical orientation in our field, as I have argued elsewhere,[2] has acquired prominence largely because it can function as an intricate, and therefore seemingly sophisticated, justification for academic careerism. (Has it been noticed, incidentally, what has happened to the term "sophistication"? It now tends to designate the programmatic application of rigorously prefabricated complexities—a reversal of meaning if ever there was one!). Theoretism and careerism are secret sharers, for both are successfully able to ignore the ethical dimension. Conformism and clubbishness are rife, and cronyism is quite naively equated with the virtue of loyalty. The quest for truth and clarification is summarily discounted, and criticism becomes a largely performative exercise. All this can only serve to justify the circus procedures indulged in by certain university administrations, their uninhibited quest for "stars"—in total unawareness of the very term's histrionic origin.

Of course there is always the future. Things ceaselessly change and develop—but will it be for the better, and can one really exert a salutary influence on the process? Fashions are inherently short-lived, but who can ensure that they will not simply be followed by others, similarly insubstantial? The principle of cognitive responsibility, and with it the intellectual pole of the academic equation in the Humanities, has been systematically undermined. Its weakening can only give free rein to the unfettered careerist impulse, and to a certain endemic infantilism that has long been lovingly nurtured in large areas of the academy, amongst students and faculty alike. The net result, at the zero point, risks to be a carnivalesque dynamics that is an inferior imitation of development in time.

This worst-case scenario is a warning, not a prediction. The future is eternally uncertain; only the past is known. Looking back into my own past, I must admit that I am on the whole quite satisfied. I have actually had a "career" of some import without any undue concessions to modishness, without any compromises on matters of intellectual principle. Such things used to be possible, and one can hardly ask for more. Will they continue to be possible in the future? Again, I do not know. I am only impelled once more to quote Goethe, most unfashionably: "Mach's einer nach und breche nicht den Hals."

NOTES

   * A briefer version of some sections of this essay appeared under the title "Curriculum Vitae" in *Arcadia: Zeitschrift für Vergleichende Literaturwissenschaft*, Sonderheft für Horst Rüdiger zum fünfundsiebzigsten Geburtstag (1983):39–42.
   1. On "theoretism" in Bakhtin, see Gary Saul Morson and Caryl Emerson, eds. *Rethinking Bakhtin: Extensions and Challenges* (Evanston, Ill.: Northwestern University Press, 1989), esp. pp. 7–10, 29–30.
   2. See W. Wolfgang Holdheim, "Idola Fori Academici," in *Stanford Literature Review* Vol. 4 (Spring 1987), no. 3, 7–21.

7

How and Why I Became a Comparatist

Anna Balakian

I was born in Constantinople. It was a polyglot metropolis, a landmark of the Byzantine Empire which fell at the peak of its glory into the hands of the Tatars coming from the hinterland of the Orient. Today it is known as Istanbul, a very important Turkish city at the junction of Europe and Asia Minor, of predominantly Turkish tongue and reflecting a gradual assimilation of its ethnic differentials into the commercial sameness of modes and manners that characterize urban communities everywhere even while their archeological and historical distinctions are retained and given "landmark" status.

But I managed to be born just before Constantinople turned into Istanbul, and when at age six I joined my family in its peregrinations across Europe, I carried away with me images of multiculturalism and the sounds of many languages. In the core of the Babel was an Armenian tongue in its purely oral form, and I clung to a French book I had taken away with me as a token of the early childhood education to which I had been exposed in a French kindergarten.

In the years that followed, I was bandied about from one European country to another, from one national education system to another. When finally our movements came to rest in America, I had by age ten developed a deep sense, through personal experience, of the distinctions between international, national, and multicultural relationships. In America we had first landed in a place where the ethnicity was so thick and isolationist that I recuperated the German I had learned in a German speaking school in Vienna and then forgotten when my family took up a two-year residence in the French Alps. German in a German-speaking city was a national experience; German in New Britain, Connecticut, USA was an ethnic, ghetto phenomenon.

It took a subsequent move of the family to New York to restore for me the polyglot quality of an international city. The New York of the 1930s was quite different from the New York we know now and the multicultural tensions it was to experience in the last decades of the twentieth century. At that time the immigrant's urgent priority was to get on with the learning of English, to lose his foreign accent, to become and pass for American, forsaking and forgetting past allegiances.

But I could not forget my love of French. It had coincided with the mind's awakening, which is surely more significant than physical birth. When my mind opened up to the printed word and to the transfers of meaning through language it was by means of French that it had happened; and the Armenian roots and the subsequent German and Anglo-American layers had not altered the Frenchness of my basic means of communication. That is why, while grappling to become an American, I gravitated toward a French education in the heart of the American public college curriculum of an institution which employed a long array of native French teachers and college professors. I graduated from Hunter College with a major in French, intending to teach French for the rest of my life. In the thirties and forties career goals existed for young women but within a limited range. An M.A. from Columbia (the Yale of that era) and a tenured appointment in a reputable public high school was considered a sufficiently serious career goal. How was I to know that I would encounter the literary presence of Baudelaire (who had not even been on the undergraduate syllabus) and that simultaneously I would come into living contact with an eighteenth-century scholar, who with his limitless frame of reference would open wide my intellectual horizons! Baudelaire showed me that you could be French and yet focus on the plight of everyman. Paul Hazard, a Comparatist who, while conducting his courses in French, absorbed into them many non-French writers, demonstrated in his superb power of integration the invasive character of the Enlightenment. He revealed how the mind can be empowered without the use of military weapons but with ideas that bring together into a single focus what in its natural state would be a collage of confrontational diversities. This spokesman for the Age of Reason combined the rational with the sensitive and loved Baudelaire as much as Voltaire. He cleared a path for me beyond the M.A. and toward a literature—surrealism—which had at first expressed itself purely in French, but was beginning to touch many other nations and was in need of serious exploration. Since my parents had already harbored a secret hope that I might prolong my studies beyond the M.A. toward that impossible dream, the Ph.D., I continued in that direction with the support of other Columbia professors. I tackled surrealism and its sources and repercussions and attained the Ph.D. in French while teaching French language and literature full time at Hunter College High School. There were at that time no fellowships to give you release from other occupations, but the degree cost me in monetary terms only $400. (I found the bill recently in a drawer I was cleaning out.) Upon completion of the degree in the latter part of World War II, I got appointed as an instructor in French (with the Ph.D. in hand, I had to wait three more years for the Assistant Professorship) at Syracuse University where I taught the gamut from *The Chanson de Roland* to Jean-Paul Sartre, including my beloved Baudelaire, Rimbaud, Mallarmé, bypassing Anatole France and Pierre Loti, and begrudgingly including Albert Camus, for it was *de rigueur* that every freshman taking *Introduction to French Literature* be made aware of that strange Algerian antihero who did not cry at his mother's funeral.

But one day in 1957 a letter came, signed by Professor Werner Friederich of Chapel Hill, informing me that the first official encounter of Comparatists in America with their non-American counterparts was to take place at Chapel Hill in 1958 and I was being invited to participate in that momentous event.

I had to take stock of myself. I felt like that Frenchman in Montesquieu's *Les Lettres Persanes* who exclaims, "But how can one be a Persian?". Indeed how can one be a Comparatist? I had become a specialist in modern French literature, and was performing for the time being as a generalist in the field until space opened in my area of specialization. But was I a Comparatist? In fact what was a Comparatist? It was a man (I did not know of any women in the field) of infinite knowledge of literature and philosophy, like the late Paul Hazard, and an expert in several languages, with a refined and developed *Weltanschauung* and wisdom acquired through a life devoted to reading and scholarly probing. I still had so much to learn in French literature, my German was weak, my Spanish nil, Italian was for me a passive guessing game fortified by intuition, my Armenian a purely oral skill. Could I call myself a Comparatist just because I had wandered across Europe at an early age?

I thought of consulting a few mentors and colleagues. What really prompted me to explore my potential as a Comparatist was the fact that I had been nurturing a deep-seated pacifism—as I write the word I realize it is no longer in fashion—during my growing years between the two world wars. It consisted of a revulsion against all national confrontations and ethnic antagonisms. My valedictory address at high school commencement had been entitled "Aristide Briand, the Apostle of Peace," and although I adored French literature I was developing a certain disappointment with French chauvinism and agreed with Augustin Thierry that even the *Histoire de France* was really the History of Ile de France. In my mind there was a link between that wise, serene humanist, Paul Hazard, and vast international connections and kinships, whereas chauvinism of any sort and national rivalries were associable with the Hitler phenomenon. Naively perhaps and with the idealism of youth, I thought of Comparative Literature as an antidote to excessive nationalism, and surrealism was the one literature that was reacting against national divisions and even overcoming the barriers between the arts. I thought, innocently, that with the perspectives of Comparative Literature and the dissemination of the principles of surrealism we could change the world.

So I let colleagues who were acquainted with my early work and had observed my professional behavior convince me that if indeed my heart belonged to French, my mind should explore the promises of Comparative Literature. In my first book, *Literary Origins of Surrealism*, had I not already given signals of interest in the cross-references of literature with the plastic arts, with philosophy, with esoteric religions? Had I not discovered the mistranslation in an Achim von Arnim text that had distorted the original meaning to become unwittingly the basis of Breton's claim that the German writer of bizarre tales was a precursor of the surrealists' mingling of the rational with the dream? I was encouraged by friends and by the nostalgic image of the teacher who had inspired me and who had so fast disappeared from my life during the last year of the war. He had died in a poorly heated apartment in Paris from pneumonia and grief over the hostility among the four great nations France, Germany, England, and Italy, which constituted for him what he had defined as the "European mind." In fact, at that time Western Europe and its extension into the USA were the fundamental boundaries of the modern civilized world and the family of connected minds of which I wanted to be part and whose bonds I wanted to strengthen. So I bought a ticket and made a small financial investment that was to shape the rest of my life. I joined the contingent of the burgeoning American Comparative Literature group on the docks of New York City where we greeted the Europeans who landed by ship. They were the happy recipients of a Ford Foundation grant which made it possible for them to join us on our way together to Chapel Hill, there to convene as a single group and organize the official International Literature Association. (There had been one previous gathering mostly of Europeans in Venice but the historical counting of the years was to begin with Chapel Hill.)

The voyage to Chapel Hill had an ingenious plan. We were to travel by bus to make the ride as long as possible so that we would get to know each other. We first headed for Washington, D.C., for some sightseeing, viewing national monuments and the White House, then we proceeded to Jefferson's home, went on into the Blue Ridge Mountains, stayed overnight at the border of an Indian reservation, and finally on the third day arrived in Chapel Hill. We were a caravan of pioneers, mostly young, and practicing brotherhood. A nationally diverse collection of scholars being transformed into a tightly knit fraternity, thereafter for at least thirty years irrevocably bound to each other in collegiality. The relationship was to be reinforced by a cavalcade of triennials to follow, by collaborative efforts and achievements in group research, and the establishment of workable policies to produce an active and dynamic discipline. As I look back, the most dramatic manifestation of cohesion I remember was that of the Japanese contingent. The first night of the adventure they had acted aloof and diffident. There were no smiles on their faces. The hostilities of World War II were still very fresh. But by the third morning, the sun burst through the clouds; they had become part and parcel of the family as lingering memories of Pearl Harbor and our status as enemies had dissipated without any need to persuade.

The years that followed our momentous meeting in Chapel Hill were an uphill struggle for the first one hundred and twenty members of Comparative Literature. I believe that no one at that time had an actual degree in Comparative Literature. Metaphorically speaking, we were a new gender carved out of Adam's rib. We had to make a long series of adjustments in our relation with the orthodox literature departments, modify curriculums, redesign existing courses, review bibliographies, shake and sometimes smash the canon, bring in neglected authors who had particularly catalytic writings that were conducive to comparative treatment, negotiate with chairmen, and sometimes go over their heads to deans to find small spaces in the basement or the attic of the Humanities structure to house Comparative Literature. Each of the subsequent triennials as well as the meetings of the American Comparative Association, which was constituted shortly thereafter, accelerated the growth of our membership and increased awareness of our presence in academia.

Ten years after Chapel Hill the first steps toward the organization of the Coordinating Committee took place for the long range goal of writing a Comparative History of Literature in European languages. That project was to bring new and wider associations among the avowed Comparatists. Meanwhile it was disturbing to note that the numbers were multiplying not in keeping with increasing enrollments in foreign language study but in reverse relation to registration in foreign languages, where a falling off endangered the basic principles of Comparative Literature, in its need for a multilingual approach to texts that were meant to be read in the original languages and not in translation. We had never meant to be an asylum for the study of literature in translation and could never become a substitute for direct access to literary writings.

For instance, in my own case, the day I learned that I had the opportunity to teach symbolism as an international literary movement I disappeared into the bowels of the basement of NYU, where the library was located before the construction of the Elmer Bobst library. To produce an integrated, balanced course took more sweat and tears and time than writing a dissertation.

In 1970 I discovered the rich and deep impact of surrealism on Latin-American poetry and that awareness resulted in hard years of upgrading my knowledge of the Spanish language. I am happy to say that a Chilean text, *Eva y la Fuga* by the late poet Rosamel del Valle, little known even in his own country, and which took me ten years, on and off, to translate, is already two years after publication having an impact on college students reading it as an illustration of the basic elements of surrealism. I am hoping that it will make its way into the undergraduate literary canon. It is a jewel of a work in poetic prose.

As I lost the friendship of some colleagues at my university, antagonized deans, and converted students, I began to feel like the chauvinist of antichauvinism, a champion of "one world" philosophy that made me shun the prominent nationalistic traits in any literature. In a fit of bravura I refused the Palmes

Académiques, although I deserved the honor as president of the Metropolitan Chapter of the American Association of Teachers of French and because of my many writings on French literature. In fact, could this be the same person who for three academic years during World War II had conducted weekly radio programs to promote the study of French in the city schools? Of course, I should have graciously accepted the recognition.

Now I had become an activist for another cause. Request after request for funds from the university administration turned me into the image of a "hustler." I was envious of the support that the French, German, Italian, Spanish, and even Greek governments or agencies were giving the departments of national literatures and deplored the fact that there was no country called "Comparative Literature."

I made a nuisance of myself but the fulfillment of my ambitions peaked when I was able to initiate the hosting in 1982 of the Tenth Triennial Congress of the ICLA at my home institution, NYU. Seven hundred delegates from fifty-six nations attended. It was a spiritual and intellectual success resulting in three substantial volumes of Comparative Literature studies, but through an "oversight" the event was not even mentioned in the Annual Report of the University.

I had accepted the Chairmanship of the Department when Professor Robert Clements had stepped down, and I had become President of the ACLA in 1977. Comparative Literature had not only absorbed my professional life but had also captured my family life. My sympathetic husband accompanied me to virtually every Congress I attended, and my daughter, who had many talents that she could have pursued professionally, created a self-service curriculum for Comparative Literature at Columbia at a time when Columbia, where she was doing her Ph.D. in "English," did not have a specifically "Comparative Literature" program to offer.

To describe the Comparative Literature program at NYU, in which I was active for twenty years and of which I assumed the leadership for eight years, would be purely an exercise in the writing of the department's history, for that program has little resemblance to its current reality. Moreover, Robert Clements has described it in detail in his own book on Comparative Literature published by the MLA. Instead, I will briefly comment on the principles rather than take inventory of the content of that department.

The program had been originally conceived informally by Professor Clements. He worked from his base in French and Italian as a Renaissance specialist, intrinsically grounded in interdisciplinary perspectives. He was a natural to establish such a program, for in Renaissance studies it is the national divisions and the separation of the arts that seem unnatural. The faculty Clements assembled was from in-house members of language departments who could give a comparative perspective to their national literature courses as I had done in my Symbolism course. A roster of outside guests coming in to teach single courses complemented the internal lend-lease procedure. He managed to gather into the slim Comparative Literature Department the most distinguished array of "adjuncts" that, to my mind, has ever existed in academe and for an unmentionably low expenditure of the university budget; the large extra-dividend for those who accepted the modest fees was quite simply love. It was a star-studded roster including the young Bart Giamatti, the not yet famous Erich Segal, the suave Maurice Valency, and in my time, after I became head of the department, virtually every leader in the discipline including the recent President of the MLA, Mario Valdés, the distinguished Yale treasure, Geoffrey Hartman, the ubiquitous Claudio Guillén, and a number of foreign visiting colleagues. In some cases the stipend hardly covered the carfare. Certainly the incentive was not financial nor prestige-seeking (in many cases the university from which these Comparatists came had more prestige than ours). How many letters I have written to deans pleading with them to lend such a one or other to enrich our meager resources and disadvantaged students. I have not yet figured how 90% of those whom I invited came. All commented on the unique quality of our students, which made it particularly challenging to teach them. They were very generous with their time in serving as consultants years later on the dissertations of such students. But, alas, I am not aware of many cases where our influential visitors had any role in procuring for these interesting students positions worthy of their talents.

In terms of basic principles Clements had felt that Comparative Literature was a graduate field, demanding prior specialization on the part of the student in a single national literature on the undergraduate level and a mastery of at least two foreign languages, with the stipulation that a third foreign language could be worked up during the Ph.D. candidacy. One of the many deans who successfully presided at NYU, ever suspiciously, over the development of Comparative Language from program to department, was George Winchester Stone, who made the keen observation that he would not consider anyone a Comparatist who was under the age of forty. He thought that to attain a truly Comparatist vision was a matter of time as well as of desire.

But as Comparative Literature thrived in a multicultural urban environment such as New York, we rolled back first to add the M.A. level and finally dipped into the undergraduate minor. The language factor was not as big a hurdle in New York as it might have been elsewhere because many of the applicants were born into several languages rather than trained in them. On all levels we were recruiting from the local multicultural population and on the graduate level from local high school and college instructors who were seeking to upgrade themselves in jobs they already had and were studying with us on a part-time basis. It was only about the time when the Chair was passed on to me (1978) that Fellowship money became available and we were able to recruit full time and resident students from out of town as graduate candidates.

Our undergraduate program was kept low-key in order not to raid foreign language departments and because the English department had priority rights on teaching "Great Books," which elsewhere has been the mainstay of budgets for undergraduate programs in Comparative Literature.

In terms of the graduate course offerings, the approach was historical. There was a year-long course on the History of Literary Theory and Criticism; courses on the main literary periods and movements, such as the Middle Ages, Renaissance, Neoclassicism, Romanticism, Realism, Symbolism, Surrealism, and the History of Modern Theater, were structured so as to give a sense of continuity and a broad scope from which to choose specializations and dissertation topics. There were also genre studies and thematic approaches, and archetypal courses such as those on Don Juan and Faust. The basic courses were given in two-year rotations, the rest at less regular intervals, and were interspersed with idiosyncratic offerings and through special perspectives such as those falling under the rubric of "Literature and the Other Arts" or special aspects of Modernism; or special relationships in two or more literatures were offered whenever there was a happy encounter of slot and space. There were also several workshops to which came, as guest lecturers, eminent scholars from all over the country and visitors from abroad.

The required and the eclectic mingled in the course of study including a large share of related courses from other departments. But the three major concerns in academia today claimed no special space in the curriculum: literature as a social study, black and women's studies, or gender concentrations. These concepts were far from being neglected but were intrinsically included in every course we gave. I notice for instance today Aimé Césaire being featured as a Caribbean poet. I used to teach his work regularly as that of a francophone surrealist who happened to be born in Martinique and the transformations he brought about in surrealist imagery and écriture were brilliant examples of the flexibility and growth of surrealism in general. The Latin-American novel was an element in the study of the novel as a genre. Women writers were not studied in terms of their gender but in terms of their literary worth and contributions to the genre in succeeding generations, and Mme de Stael ranked very high in several courses as did Georges Sand, the Brontës, and Jane Austen. The women writers of the eighteenth century fit naturally into a course on the Enlightenment, and the women poets were a major part of the galaxy of the Renaissance poets, but we did not count them to make sure there was a correct quota of them in the bibliography.

Some very interesting dissertations emerged in the course of the years that highlighted what we had integrated in the course work, and many of these were subsequently published; to name a few of these subjects: the literature of "droit de seigneur," oral African literature and its development into written form in anglophone and francophone Africa, the Bildungsroman as it reflected the feminine psyche, the Don Juan theme in a comparison of its popular and high literary forms, a first annotated translation of a neglected Aimé Césaire dramatic work, the literary connections between two Lesbian writers, Nathalie Barney and Renée Vivien in the symbolist ambience, the connection of the American woman poet known as H.D. with Symbolism, and so many others that it would not be fair to mention the names and exact titles of a few and neglect for lack of space the many. The point I want to illustrate is that we did not draft separate courses to cover ethnicities, gender, sexual orientations, and popular culture, but there was in the richness of the course offerings and their contents sufficient material and broad enough awareness both on the part of the instructor and the student to direct any student so motivated to take the initiative and to pursue these channels on an individual basis.

In my keynote speech at Chapel Hill in 1980 as I terminated my presidency of the ACLA, I singled out three events that would have an impact on the future of the discipline. The most important perhaps was our decision to meet more than once every three years. The once a year meeting has in fact provided increased opportunity to assess the new directions our research is taking. A second innovation which we owe to Professor Thomas Greene was to invite graduate students to membership and thus develop professionalism. The students first met at Yale University as a separate body; by now they have been totally absorbed into the parent group and give papers on a competitive basis with their professors.

The third event was the return of the original non-American members of the ICLA to Chapel Hill. It was made possible by a grant from the Rockefeller Foundation. The Tenth Triennial of the American Comparative Literature Association indeed made it possible for the original group to say "You *can* go home again." This important meeting took place under the direction of Professor Eugene Falk, successor to Professor Werner Eugene Friederich.

I remember making a few further remarks that loom significant today in the light of more recent trends. I had two complaints at the time that have been rectified. One was that there were not enough of our members among the movers and shakers of the academic commissions and award-making agencies in the humanities. That situation has been greatly corrected in the last decade. Several members of the Comparatist group have become presidents of the MLA, a number of us have been MacArthur nominators; we have yet to get a Comparatist on the selection board of the Guggenheim and on the National Humanities Council.

I had also observed a dearth of anthologies. I cannot complain any more about that; there is an overabundance. My only fear now is that, obsessed by quota concerns, the makers of anthologies are including,—perhaps against their better judgment—texts of little literary merit. And from the selection of texts chosen from among the vast body of unfamiliar literature are still missing masterpieces of the literature of many European countries whose participation in major literary movements in the last millennium make their landmark writings essential to the composite picture of European literature.

Another worry I had a decade ago has deepened. The majority of our Comparatists had a double identity, one in English or in one of the "foreign" languages, and the other as a Comparatist. As in the song "J'ai deux amours" many of our breed had two loves, a national literature and Comparative literature. When priorities were in order, the first loyalty was toward the national literature. In coming of age, Comparative Literature as a full-fledged discipline demands full loyalty and unflinching dedication.

But it is no longer a matter of two loves. The barriers have come down completely and there is total permissiveness in declaring oneself a Comparatist. Virtually every scholar specialized in a national literature has found it convenient to add "and Comparative Literature" to his/her designation and position. Every exercise in intertextuality, random comparison of works in a heterotopic juggling of texts and crossovers becomes a manifestation of Comparative Literature. Sometimes mere surface knowledge of an Oriental language or casual reading of a few non-European works gives claims to East/West Comparative expertise.

We have arrived on dangerous ground. We are threatened on the one hand with a host of scholars crossing over without union cards to participate through our discipline in the newer concepts of interpretation of literature and the study of sociocultural texts within the context of comparative relationships; on the other hand, our numbers are being depleted by the departure of some of our own respected constituents for adventures in the ranks of derivative theoreticians of semiotics, and like a new company of pied pipers of Hamelin they are leading our younger generation over the hills and far away.

To return to the first issue: I am not suggesting that newcomers to our discipline should be kept out or restricted, but they should realize that there is a certain amount of retooling to be done. Surely when a biologist decides to take over the functions of a chemist it is assumed that there would be a certain degree of reeducation. Innovations are what keeps a discipline vigorous and dynamic but each generation cannot reinvent Comparative Literature from scratch.

On the second issue, theoretical dialogue cannot be permitted to tip the balance between discovery of unfamiliar writings and the reinterpretation of generally familiar works. René Wellek's statement in Chapel Hill in 1958 is still valid: "In literary scholarship theory, criticism, and history collaborate to achieve its central task," he declared in "The Crisis of Comparative Literature." In literary criticism related to the national literatures there is more and more writing about less and less. There has occurred an arbitrary sanctification of certain writers to the exclusion of others just as worthy or more so. Authors like Flaubert, Richardson, Proust, Joyce, Sade, Brecht, and more recently Bataille seem to have been wrung dry, when yet another structuralist exegesis or mythopoetic deconstruction comes along. And when these overladen works are submitted to what is called "intertextuality" the resulting relationships are promiscuous and too often devoid of intellectual responsibility, for they make no effort to ascertain the historical, cultural, or even psychological validity of the juxtapositions. The theory of intertextuality is quite the opposite of comparative study in spite of the inclusion of some of these intertextual operations in Conference programs under the heading of Comparative Literature. In the theoretical writing of isolated analyses of immanent textual relationships, the process does not validate itself with fertile demonstrations of creative influences or anti-influences but is content with rapid name-droppings that reinforce the collage character of the juxtapositions. In opposition to the communicating vessels of Comparative Literature studies, eminent new theoreticians, situating themselves within the discipline of Comparative Literature, are committed to the structuralist principle which, according to Genette, distinguishes itself by its lack of consideration for sources and motives.

Many names have been given to our era; one of those I like best is Nathalie Sarraute's "L'Ere du Soupçon." Another fitting one might be "L'Ere du Collage." Collage is the breakdown of interrelationships on all levels, whether ethnic, familial or societal. In the view of the late Roland Barthes, literature is part of that collage. It has no corporal, historical continuity but is the complex graph of the practice of writing. That is the lesson he preached on his entry into the Collège de France. Caution, it appears, must be taken to avoid the detection of "source" or "influence," lest we fall into what Barthes has called "the myth of filiation." But without that sense of filiation we might as well forget Comparative Literature. These intertextual investigations result in a paradoxical situation: fragmentation of knowledge in the very process of searching for a *system*. A monotonous chiming of "how does it function" never seems to come to grips with its own methodology of mythopoetic viewing of literature. Because if indeed, as some would have us believe, literature is only a complicated form of mythology, the identification of a myth demands the study of interrelationships of events and ensuing works, preliminary to the establishment of the collective base of a typology. The distancing of authors held together by natural associations and the substitution of forced juxtapositions to demonstrate an *a priori* theory rob literature of its coordinated contents. Let us be reminded of the observation of Northrop Frye in his article, "Literature as Context: Milton's Lycidas," which appears in the proceedings of that first meeting of the ICLA in Chapel Hill in 1958: "Where there is comparison there must be some standard by which we can distinguish what is actually comparable from what is analogous. You cannot just lump together an octopus and a spider and a string quartet."

But the threat of intertextuality is not as grievous as the predominance in literary studies of a philosophy borrowed from cultural anthropologists that has a political basis when it is introduced into Comparative Literature. In the name of ethnocentrism and the suspicions of spiritual colonialism it has become politically risky to suggest relationships between works of different literatures when one of the arms of the comparison is the literature of so called developing countries. The Comparatist who may have studied some unfamiliar writings in the light of more universally known ones can be accused of forcing his/her ethnocentric optic on the alien work and polluting it with the marks of a comparison that defiles the ethnic originality of the target work. In fact, the thinking goes, the Comparatist may be speaking of the newly discovered work only to prove the superiority of some "decadent" piece of Western literature. His or her interest is probably motivated by a desire to engage in an imperialistic literary safari in unexplored cultural domains. There have been eminent expressions of this attitude in regard to Orientalism as well as in the handling of Latin-American literature. In reviewing a book which accuses European scholarship in Orientalism of possessing improper motivation, Victor Brombert gently asks: "Is the desire to know the Other necessarily a way of killing him?"

Our efforts as Comparatists to familiarize our readers with unfamiliar and neglected literatures are often misconstrued in this era of suspicion. If the fear of ethnocentrism were to be applied to past literary traditions, we would have to desist from recognizing the Greek and Roman bases of Western literatures, those very classical sources which in their turn owed certain debts to the Orient. What did the Western European tribes do? Did they derive their cultures from the Visigoths or the Druids? The only redemptive factor of political invasions has been the gift of the arts left behind or appropriated. The arts die in the devastation only to be reborn with new features reflective of the cross-fertilization. The transmission of literary heritages is even increased in some cases relating to developing countries because the creators of literature come from older cultures themselves and are only partially the recipients of the ethos of a geographical zone. The inhabitants of these developing countries are not a "developing" population. "Developing" often pertains only to a political and technological situation and not to a cultural one. This is particularly true of the writers of many of the Latin-American countries whose interesting blending of old world and new can only be enhanced by study of the complex character of the heritage blend. The accusation of ethnocentrism could easily be turned around to suggest that the accusers are themselves the real ethnocentrists in claiming that spontaneous and autonomous literary generation is possible.

Politically the Comparatist has moved in the opposite direction from severe ethnic self-consciousness. We are the product of that moment of hope between the two world wars when there emerged a genuine longing to seek international brotherhood and to make of this morseled earth a planet without a visa. Comparative Literature was born of that climate, short-lived, of international filiation.

If ethnocentrism or the fear of being accused of ethnocentrism invades the scholarly activities of Comparatists or if causal comparison becomes taboo, we may as well close up shop because you do not need Comparatists to play literary hopscotch. To contiguity we oppose continuity, to deconstruction we oppose recuperation, to difference we oppose the power to distinguish. The sites of our encounters are always familiar and familial because for internationally oriented persons, such as Comparatists, there is no land that is exotic, no culture that is alien. We belong to each other and fish in the common pond of that distilled human spirit that is expressed in literature. If the literary product of each national unit or zone was so distinctly unique there would be no need for the discipline of Comparative Literature.

Comparative Literature is headed toward a struggle with political correctness. If you try to be all things to all men and women you can easily end up being of no use to anyone. You have to have conviction and stand by it. There can be no real debate until men and women of conviction confront each other without being classified as conservative, radical, correct or incorrect. Such signifiers have long lost their signifieds. I did not choose Comparative Literature to show the differences among cultures but to discover how these differences are transcended by the creative imagination no matter on what piece of soil they were rooted, to reveal how they touch each other in respect to the great problems of life, survival, and mortality, or the basic emotions of what we call the heart (love, fear, hate, vengeance, jealousy, compassion, lust, etc.), and in respect to the physical forces we control or unleash (violence, dream, ecstasy, the unpredictabilities of nature). The transcendence of ethnic and gender differences is what creates the summits and depths of human consciousness as it is reflected in literature. That is why at a certain moment in my life, "forsaking all others," I espoused Comparative Literature as my life occupation. "The road to the absolute" (which I chose for the title of one of my books) is paved not with isolations but associations. Comparative Literature is one of the most effective ways to make contact with the universal psyche.

In the face of formidable pressures to dehistoricize and dismember literature, I hope that Comparatists will maintain the intrinsic meaning of the discipline: to establish contacts, connections, and continuity and to be the frontliners in the coming struggle for the survival and expansion of literary scholarship.

8

Comparative Literature, Modern Thought and Literature

Albert J. Guérard

In thinking about this article I have come to realize how much my father Albert L. Guérard influenced my approach to literary studies. He, not I, should be writing this article. He would have been witty, paradoxical, and irreverent. He wrote this in 1958 in an article entitled "Comparative Literature?": "Comparative Literature? I have been a comparatist all my academic life, under several different titles, and in four different departments; and in this faith I hope to die. My attachment to the *principle* of Comparative Literature gives me the right to express my opinion that the *term* Comparative Literature is useless, dangerous, and ought to be abolished."[1] He regretted that the term denotes "the foreign relations of national literatures" and therefore encourages the very chauvinistic concept of national literatures that it might seek to correct.

Literary studies and writing novels represent nine-tenths of my intellectual life. My father's was infinitely richer. His liberalism and scorn for jingoistic patriotism were formed by the Dreyfus Case and the Boer War. A distaste for all forms of nationalism led to his study of international languages (*A Short History of the International Language Movement*, 1921), to his work on the Committee to Frame a World Constitution chaired by Robert Hutchins,[2] and, as one of the motives, to his leaving a professorship and chair of French at Rice to become Professor of General and Comparative Literature at Stanford in 1925. It also determined his lifelong commitment to democratic, not dogmatic, socialism and to his advocacy of a united Europe (*Europe Free and United*, 1945). He remained in many ways very French, and the interpretation of French thought and French politics constitutes the large share of his writings.[3] All the while, for more than fifty years in America, he remained intensely Parisian. His work in city planning (*L'Avenir de Paris*, Paris, Payot, 1929) was a labor of love, as were his many articles published in *Urbanisme*, honored there in a memorial editorial: "Aucun de nos lecteurs n'a oublié tous ceux que nous avons publiés depuis vingt ans. Que de conseils judicieux, que de propos pertinents! Comme il était attentif à nos problemes, à la manière dont nous les abordions. . . . D'une magnifique écriture, pétillant d'esprit, éminemment constructif."[4]

A distaste for the excesses of Germanic scholarship and philology is the burden of one of his early articles, "L'Enseignement supérieur du français aux États-Unis."[5] He had been *agrégé* ranked first in French and English literature, and was distressed, when interviewed at the MLA, to be asked at which German university he had studied French literature. He noted that in one prestigious American university, not named, *all* the advanced courses in French were in Old French, in another six of seven, in another three of four. The library of one of the richest universities in the world, again unnamed, though "bien équipée pour la philologie romane. . . ne contcnait, l'année dernière, *rien* des auteurs suivants: Agrippa d'Aubigné, Regnier, Bossuet, Montesquieu, Taine, Renan, Michelet."[6] No doubt "the philological ring" (strong at Stanford when he was assistant professor there, 1907–13) were among the first words I heard at the breakfast table. The general inadequacy of French studies in America led to "une incompréhension de la France moderne inexcusable" and to "une indifférence presque incroyable pour notre meilleure littérature."[7] Amusingly he attributed the Germanic influence in part to population: "Dix millions d'Allemands ou de demi-Allemands aux États-Unis, qui ont germanisé l'enseignement supérieur, contre cent mille Français, dont beaucoup sont des excentriques, des ratés, des aventuriers. Et, il faut le dire aussi, la plus grande hospitalité des universités allemandes, leur vie corporative plus active et plus attrayante, leurs diplômes à la fois faciles et prestigieux."[8]

My father had long been restless in French departments (Williams, 1906–7, Stanford 1907–13, Rice 1913–24, UCLA 1924–25) and when invited back to Stanford in 1925 came as professor of General and Comparative Literature. As such he was attached to the English department, although each quarter teaching one course in Frcnch and from time to time advanced courses cross-listed in history: "Reflections on the Napoleonic Legend" and "The Spirit of '48." By "general literature" he meant what might be called applied theory: the study of all the social and other forces that affect literary creation, the classification of literary works, the concepts of period and genre, all the influences that transcend nationality. He developed new courses: a nominally elementary "The International Study of Literature" (with each student choosing the classics in translation he would read), a seminar on International Literature (language and national psychology, effects of polyglottism, problems of translation, etc.) and advanced courses on "Types of Criticism," "Art for Art's Sake," and "Literature and Society." Two of these led to books of theory (*Literature and Society* [1935], *Art for Art's Sake* [1936], and a basic and comprehensive *Preface to World Literature* [1940]).

These books, full of witty and (for American readers) often elusive allusion, lack the power, depth, and ultimate seriousness of his writings on French history and international relations, but they are rich in wide-ranging, skeptical, often paradoxical insights. They delight in advancing, then nimbly demolishing familiar categories and assumptions, and are far indeed from the deadly seriousness of much literary theory of the last twenty years. The study of ideas, he argued, was essential to a mature appreciation of literature, but informed unpedantic *love of literature* was the ultimate objective. A recent article by Sholhom J. Khan, "Albert Léon Guérard (1880–1959): The Styles of a Humanist," praises these books: "In terms of intellectual culture and excitement they seem almost like a lost Paradise, from which we have since departed—if not necessarily in all ways 'declined.' "[9] An early article by Margaret L. Hartley, "The Courageous Idiosyncrasy of Albert Guerard,"[10] assesses more general qualities of mind and usefully complements Khan's.

My father was a superb linguist (and tried to read each month a book in four or more languages, reviewing many of them for the New York Herald-Tribune Sunday *Books* or for *Books Abroad*). But he was a strong proponent of literature in translation. He preferred the term World Literature (the study of great books from whatever source) to Comparative Literature, but his ultimate preference was for the broadest possible term for literary studies: *Literature*. When David Packard endowed a Stanford chair in his honor it was given the title: "Albert L. Guérard Professor of Literature," with the understanding that it could float among literary departments.

My own story has several parallel chapters. Excessive philological requirements led me to return to Stanford for my Ph.D in English after a year's graduate study at Harvard (1934–35). In one option Harvard then demanded eight semester philological courses out of the total of sixteen required for the Ph.D. Only a semester of Old French was required, but the professor admitted only those who would sign up for the full year. Stanford required three out of eighteen quarters. The Stanford English Ph.D., moreover, permitted a full year's work in a "minor." Mine was French literature of the seventeenth and eighteenth centuries. (Later, as a faculty member and committee of instruction chairman at Harvard, I worked hard to reduce the amount of student time spent on Old English, and at Stanford to reduce the time spent on Old English and Middle English dialects. The resistance was far more intense at Stanford, and earned me a few enemies.) The Old English requirement at Stanford was finally removed in 1991.

The first course "of my own" at Harvard, the first one I created, was comparative and strongly emphasized the history of ideas: "The Intellectual Background of English Literature, 1750–1830," with the background largely continental. This was in 1942, and some thinkers, Herder and Fichte as well as Godwin, Burke, Condorcet, and Rousseau, were studied with the ongoing war and postwar planning in mind. I taught English romantic poetry several times and once gave a seminar on Fielding. But my literary courses more and more disregarded English tradition. Harry Levin, then working to build up Comparative Literature, asked me to take over his Proust, Joyce, and Mann course. I couldn't face three such difficult masters, not to mention the challenge of following Levin, and proposed instead Hardy, Conrad, and Gide. I did not allege influence among them, indeed there was very little, but examined certain antirealist impulses the three shared. In deference to Comparative Literature, as opposed to Literature period, I required a reading knowledge of French. I rather stupidly proposed the same passage for sight translation to each of a long line of applicants until one honest soul said he had the passage by heart while listening to the others. The course ultimately led to books on each of the three authors. I came away from my intensive study of Gide fascinated by the image of a writer for whom Conrad and Dostoevsky were as close and as well loved as Stendhal, and who had a wide culture extending from music to politics and science.

The reading for my graduate-undergraduate course "The Short Novel" could be done entirely in English, and I stressed both novelistic technique and the writers' psychological insight. I depended heavily on the one-volume collections of short novels by Dostoevsky, Melville, and James, and assigned individual works by Gide, Conrad, Fitzgerald, Edith Wharton, Nathanael West, Janet Lewis (*The Wife of Martin Guerre*), Josephine Johnson (*Wildwood*), and Glenway Wescott (*The Pilgrim Hawk*). An innovation then was to permit students to write part of a short novel in place of a critical term paper, and six of them ultimately became published novelists. Hillis Miller wrote an analysis of *The Double* for this course.

My very large undergraduate course, Comparative Literature 166, "Forms of the Modern Novel," once with over five hundred students, similarly moved at will among literatures, but was rather more comparative than I would make it now. At first it seemed important to distinguish the multiple meanings of realism and naturalism, and to compare, for instance, the naturalist practice of Stephen Crane and George Moore with the theories of Zola. But in time I simply chose to present individual great writers from Stendhal to the present, again with an emphasis on novelistic technique and novelistic psychology. To move so far from "The History of English literature in Outline," my first (and assigned) lecture course, and to attack so openly the idea of authorial intention, and to discover latent homosexuality in novels of Dostoevsky, Mann and Gide, was to seem gloriously subversive in those days. Among the writers read in more than one year: Stendhal, Flaubert, Gide, Camus, Dostoevsky, Mann, Hardy, Conrad, Joyce, Hemingway, Fitzgerald, Faulkner, Greene. Reading period options included contemporary writers, even my very recent student John Hawkes (*The Cannibal*, written in my fiction-writing course.)

I taught at Harvard from 1938 to 1961, and during that time was happy to swell the Comparative Literature course offering, but had no hand in the

Comparative Literature program itself, which was ably guided by Harry Levin and Renato Poggioli. I returned to Stanford in 1961 to find the undergraduate program in English structurally unchanged from 1934, when I took my B.A., and the Ph.D degree in one respect more limited than in 1938, since the practice of a minor had been virtually abandoned. Three courses in English philology were still required. I was particularly concerned that the modernist (concerned, say, with 1850 to the present) had no time to read great foreign writers, Proust and Mann for instance, or to read Freud, Nietzsche or any of the other "makers of the modern mind." The English Ph.D. could escape with zero knowledge of the main currents of European cultural history. I therefore proposed an alternative program within the English department: the "Ph.D. in English and Comparative Literature." This program, which still exists, emphasized English and American literature from 1350 to the present (with a very limited philological requirement and 1350 so as not to exclude Chaucer), with the time saved from philology and early literature devoted to the literature, history, and thought of a chosen period in a foreign culture. All in all, more (including an *advanced* knowledge of a foreign language) rather than less was required, and over the years the program has had few takers. But it may have given some encouragement to the later creation of the successful nondepartmental program in Comparative Literature, initially chaired by Herbert Lindenberger. And its aims were ultimately fulfilled by the non-departmental, interdisciplinary program in Modern Thought and Literature, which I was instrumental in creating.

I had no direct hand in the "building" of Comparative Literature at Stanford and have been a sympathetic observer of the program, not a participant. My missionary efforts to bring Modern Thought and Literature into being were strenuous and often painful, to me and to others, and may be of some interest to others working for academic innovation.

The English department gradually relaxed some of its traditional rigidities. But I remained convinced that the English Ph.D., far narrower in 1961 than now, offered inadequate preparation for the future professor of English in the modern field. I believed, moreover, that to write serious fiction or poetry, or even to practice some other art, enriched rather than corrupted the future professor of English, and should be an optional part of the student's program. My own fiction writing was largely responsible for many of the insights developed in my critical books on the novel. I also believed that graduate students in English, who often aspire to be writers, are harmed by the frustrating unspoken obligation to give up writing for four years or more.

Modern Thought and Literature was thus proposed as no less than an alternate nondepartmental degree in English, with the further subversive hope that some of its innovations would ultimately be imitated by the regular department. One of these was that the student should propose to the governing committee how to divide his time, and that he or she, not the committee, should establish the reading list for the preliminary examination. Moreover, some credit for creative writing or for practice in one of the arts would be allowed. The English department's foreign language requirement was intensified by the obligation to present an *advanced* knowledge of one foreign language. Students were to be responsible for an extensive knowledge of a single literature, normally English and American, with more emphasis on one of the two, from 1750 to the present, and for a year's work in one or more areas of modern thought. Candidates with an inadequate undergraduate preparation in earlier English literature could be asked to take appropriate additional courses. But there would be no requirement in English philology.

Inevitably the efforts to build this program were vigorously resisted. One of my first proposals, sponsored by a national "Committee on Innovation in the Humanities" that met monthly, chaired by Walter Ong, was to create at Stanford a pilot "Institute for Literary Studies," with good prospects of funding by the Office of Education. The Institute, bringing scholars and writers from other universities, would join Stanford faculty in considering ways to improve undergraduate instruction in the humanities. One way to improve undergraduate education was, we reasoned, to make Ph.D. programs more relevant to undergraduate teaching. The Institute could thus sponsor what would ultimately become the Ph.D in Modern Thought and Literature. Not surprisingly a strong minority in the English department considered the proposed Institute a threat, and the project had to be dropped. For the moment all that survived at Stanford of the national committee's proposals was an innovative Freshman English course, the "Voice Project," directed by John Hawkes, which brought a number of good writer-teachers to Stanford for a pilot year.[11]

The next step in the creation of Modern Thought and Literature was to call for discussion at an open meeting, then to create an unofficial committee of sympathetic colleagues and a few graduate students in the English and other departments. But to have an actual curricular base meant freeing some of my own time from departmental control, and here job offers from other universities were instrumental in the bargaining process. And it meant finding professors who had a sufficient power base to free a fragment of their own time. Thus among the first offerings were two courses in literature and psychology, one by Robert Sears, the dean of humanities, the other by Dr. Irvin Yalom from psychiatry. The members of the first administrative committee represented a distinguished cross section of the humanities, and that broad-based richness has continued to the present day. The final steps, too cumbersome to record here, meant getting the approval of the dean of graduate studies, then of the faculty Senate, and having full support graduate fellowships. In the first year this meant persuading four top graduate students to transfer from English, bringing their fellowships with them. Eventually the program received a regular allotment.

The Modern Thought and Literature program has brought some of Stanford's most interesting graduate students, and a number of these were attracted by the opportunity to spend at least some time in creative work. The program was and to some extent remains unique, but it no longer seems eccentric, given the wide proliferation of "cultural studies." Lewis Mayhew, the historian of education, thought we had a "nice program" but predicted that our students would not find jobs.[12] The employment record over the years has been somewhat better than that of English. In a down market the unusual student may have the inside track.

Inevitably there have been changing realities not immediately apparent in the relative fixities of college catalogs. In this program as elsewhere there has been an increased interest in theory and in the interdisciplinary component generally. Normally the program chairs have been drawn from English, but the two most recent chairs are distinguished professors from other departments: Mary Louise Pratt (Spanish and Portugese) and Ronald Berman (German). The possibility remains of opening the program to other students than those intending careers in English. A single sentence in the catalog leaves the future open: "Another literature taught at Stanford may be substituted."

A particularly welcome development has been the institution of an undergraduate major. I subjoin a brief summary of the Modern Thought and Literature requirements.

Graduate Program

1. An introductory seminar.

2. Forty-five units (one year full time) advanced work in literature of one language, at least thirty of these in post-1750 English and American literature.

3. Forty units of advanced work in a coherent interdisciplinary program. The program may include courses and readings in various areas of modern thought and culture, and individual creative work.

4. Student organizes a colloquium or submits a 25–30 page essay based on a term paper written during the year.

5. Qualifying examination (beginning of second year) demonstrating knowledge of major writers and movements in the chosen literature from 1750 to the present. The examination may be oral or may consist of a collection of critical commentaries. The student creates the qualifying reading list, to be based on an advisory list provided by the program.

6. Four quarters of supervised half-time teaching.

7. Reading knowledge of a foreign language and an advanced reading knowledge of a second foreign language.

8. Oral examination covering student's area of concentration.

9. Dissertation drawn from literature of specialization, from the area of non-literary studies, or from a combination of the two.

Undergraduate program

1. Completion of the Cultures, Ideas, and Values university requirement (fifteen units, freshman year).

2. Humanities 90. Introduction to the Humanities Honors program.

3. Two seminars drawn from the series Humanities 191–197, of which one must be Humanities 197 (Modernism and the Humanities).

4. Six courses in a national literature, read in the original language, and covering a wide range of periods and genres.

5. Three courses covering major movements in intellectual history since the Enlightenment.

6. One course in the history of modern science or technology.

7. One course in modern art or music.

8. One course addressing modernization from a historical or scientific perspective.

9. Completion of at least two years of college-level study of a modern language or demonstration of equivalent proficiency.

10. Honors essay on a literary topic treated in an interdisciplinary manner.

NOTES

1. *Yearbook of Comparative and General Literature No. 7,* Chapel Hill, North Carolina, 1958, 1–6. See also "The Quick and the Dead: 'English' or 'Literature'?" Supplement to The CEA Critic XIII (February 1951), No. 2, 1–8. "Beyond the limits of this vast Republic, we should take in, not merely English literature, but all literature in English, and all great literature wherever found. Our domain ignores political, racial, linguistic boundaries. It is not national, but human: *homo sum.* Art is that which enhances

the consciousness of life; and in literature, we recognize only two divisions, not the ancient and the modern, not the home-grown and the foreign, but the quick and the dead." *Op. cit.*, 2.

2. *Preliminary Draft of a World Constitution*, proposed and signed by Robert M. Hutchins, G. A. Borgese, Mortimer J. Adler, Stringfellow Barr, Albert Guérard, Harold A. Innis, Erich Kahler, Wilber G. Katz, Charles H. McIlwain, Robert Redfield, Rexford G.Tuxwell; in *Common Cause: A Monthly Report of the Committee to Frame a World Constitution*, Vol. 1 (March 1948), No. 9, 321–360.

3. To increase American understanding of France was the intention of hundreds of articles and reviews and at least a part of the intention of his eleven books on French history, from *French Prophets of Yesterday* (1913) to *France: A Modern History* (1959).

4. *Urbanisme: Revue Française*, 29e. Année, No. 66, unpaginated.

5. *Revue Internationale de L'Enseignement* (Paris 1908), 5–11.

6. *Op. cit.*, 7.

7. *Ibid.*

8. *Ibid.*

9. *Virginia Quarterly Review*, Vol. 65 (Summer 1989), no. 3, 454–472.

10. *Southwest Review* 45 (Autumn 1960) No. 8, unpaginated.

11. See John Hawkes, "The Voice Project: An Idea for Innovation in Teaching of Writing" in *Writers as Teachers/Teachers as Writers*, ed. Jonathan Baumbach (New York, 1970), 89–144.

12. In conversation.

9

Comparative Literature, CL, and I

Thomas R. Hart

My three years on active duty in the Naval Reserve in World War II were spent on college campuses. The Navy sent me to the University of Rochester, where I completed about half of an undergraduate major in German, and then to Notre Dame for Midshipman's School. I was commissioned an ensign in February 1945 and spent the next fourteen months studying Japanese in the Navy School of Oriental Languages, first at the University of Colorado in Boulder and then at Oklahoma A & M in Stillwater, where most of the Japanese section of the School was moved in the summer of 1945.

I was discharged from the Navy in the summer of 1946 and entered Yale as a junior in the fall, majoring in Spanish and Portuguese. My undergraduate literature classes consisted largely of conversation in Spanish or Portuguese about the works we read; we were not asked to analyze and interpret them nor were we taught anything about their social or intellectual background. I was happier with my French courses, in particular one on the nineteenth-century novel, which introduced me not only to Stendhal, Balzac, Flaubert, and the Goncourts, but also to the Impressionist painters.

I did not want to continue my studies in Spanish at Yale nor did I want to move to another university for graduate school; my wife had a job in New Haven, which, with the money I received under the GI Bill, gave us barely enough to live on. Norman Holmes Pearson, whose course on American literature I audited in my junior year, suggested that I talk with a new man who had come from the University of Iowa to create a program in Comparative Literature. I had no idea what Comparative Literature was but I followed Pearson's advice and went to see René Wellek.

I received my B.A. in June 1948 and began graduate work in Comparative Literature in the fall. My undergraduate work at Yale had been a disappointment; graduate school was a revelation. Cleanth Brook's course on twentieth-century

British and American literature brought me into direct contact with the New Criticism. Wellek's lectures on literary scholarship introduced me to the Russian Formalists and to German *Stilforschung;* I wrote a seminar paper on Leo Spitzer's *Linguistics and Literary History,* which had just appeared.

The only classes in Comparative Literature then given at Yale were Wellek's on literary scholarship and the history of literary criticism. Most of my graduate work was in French. I studied nineteenth- and twentieth-century literature with Henri Peyre and Jean Boorsch and took courses in Old French and stylistics with Charles Bruneau, who came from the Sorbonne for a semester. I did no further work in Spanish at Yale, though I audited graduate courses given by Dámaso Alonso and Rafael Lapesa as visiting professors. Erich Auerbach did not join the Yale faculty until after I had completed my course work. I did, however, audit his courses on Dante and on the Medieval Romance lyric and he was one of the readers of my dissertation. I often talked with him outside class and always found him cordial and helpful; he has influenced my work more than anyone else except René Wellek.

If I had been asked, I would have said that my special interest was literary theory, which then meant almost the exact opposite of what it means today. I learned that there is a clear distinction between literature and nonliterature. Novels belong to literature; history and autobiography do not. As a graduate student, I read poems, plays, and novels, and interpretations of them, plus a good deal of literary history. I did not read Freud or Marx, nor did I learn anything about philosophy or political science or sociology. Although I was keenly interested in linguistics and anthropology, and audited graduate courses in both, it never occurred to me that they had anything to do with my work as a student of Comparative Literature.

For my dissertation I first thought of studying the German Romantics' interest in the medieval romance literatures and prepared a seminar paper for Wellek on their studies of Spanish ballads (it was subsequently published in Spanish in *Clavileño,* thanks to Dámaso Alonso). Eventually I chose to write on the history of Spanish literary history, which seemed a natural complement to Wellek's *Rise of English Literary History* (Chapel Hill, 1941), with the difference that the early histories of Spanish literature I studied were by foreigners—Bouterwek, Sismondi, George Ticknor—who interpreted Spanish literature from the perspective of their own national literatures. Wellek was an ideal dissertation director; he was patient, tactful, and demanding while at the same time he left me plenty of room to pursue my own interests. My work with him produced a lasting interest in the history of literary scholarship and in the writings of poet-critics. His books have served as models for my own studies of scholars—Leo Spitzer, Erich Auerbach, and Roman Jakobson— and of the literary criticism of writers better known for their poetry or fiction such as Jorge Luis Borges, Mário de Andrade, Paul Valéry, and Fernando Pessoa.

A Fulbright scholarship to study Romance Philology at the University of Montpellier in 1950-51 gave me my first trip to Europe. In Montpellier I became interested in modern Provençal; my study of the nineteenth-century poet Frédéric Mistral, written forty years later as a fellow of the Camargo Foundation in Cassis, appeared in the *Journal of European Studies* in 1991.

I received my Ph.D. in Comparative Literature, the third granted by Yale, in June 1952. I did not, of course, expect to find a job as a comparatist; there were hardly any such jobs in the 1950s. I hoped to teach French but had to settle for an instructorship in Spanish at Amherst. After one year I moved to Harvard, where Auerbach had recommended me to the chairman, Herbert Dieckmann, whom he had known in Istanbul. I had been told that I would teach French and Portuguese at Harvard but a note from Diekmann in midsummer asked me to teach Spanish rather than French for the first year. Since it seemed possible that I might have to teach Spanish for some time, I thought it prudent to learn more about it; I audited a graduate course in Spanish literature every term that I was in Cambridge. I also attended some of the courses on linguistics and poetics given by Roman Jakobson, whose name I had heard frequently in Wellek's lectures at Yale.

The only tenured faculty member in Spanish at Harvard in 1953 was Raimundo Lida, who replaced Amado Alonso after the latter's death. To bridge the gap while the department was being rebuilt, Harvard brought in a series of distinguished visitors: Dámaso Alonso, whom I had known at Yale, Enrique Anderson Imbert, Carlos Clavería, María Rosa Lida de Malkiel, Angel Rosenblat, and Bruce Wardropper. I attended the classes of all of them and left Harvard with a solid preparation as a Hispanist. The most important for my future career was Bruce Wardropper's course on the Spanish theater of the Golden Age, at the Harvard summer school in 1954. Wardropper introduced me to the work of A. A. Parker and Edward Wilson, who had been his tutor at Cambridge. Later on I came to know both Parker and Wilson personally; I owe a great deal to them and to other British Hispanists, notably P. E. Russell and my close friend Alan Deyermond. A lecture tour to more than a dozen universities in England, Scotland, and Ireland in the spring of 1979, arranged by Keith Whinnom, and two sabbaticals spent in Oxford, the second in 1986 as Visiting Professor of Spanish and Visiting Senior Member of Linacre College, are among the happiest experiences of my academic life.

I left Harvard after two years to accept an assistant professorship at Johns Hopkins, where Wardropper was chairman of the department of Romance Languages. On the day I arrived in Baltmore I was surprised to learn that he was about to go to Ohio State; my family and I moved into the apartment he vacated. The Hopkins department had been reduced to a skeleton when I joined it in 1955. Charles Singleton had resigned to become professor of Italian at Harvard; Pedro Salinas, a fine poet and sensitive critic of Spanish literature, had died; and Leo Spitzer had retired from teaching, though he came every day to the office in Gilman Hall that he shared with his disciple Anna Granville Hatcher. The department was left with only two tenured faculty members, Miss Hatcher and Georges Poulet, who resigned the following year to become professor of French in Zurich. His successor as chairman was Nathan Edelman, a fine scholar and exemplary human being, who did an outstanding job of rebuilding Romance Languages at the Hopkins. In 1957, Charles Singleton returned from Harvard to become professor of Humanistic Studies. In 1957, too, René Girard came from Bryn Mawr, joined a year later by Lionel Gossman, who had just completed his doctorate at Oxford; in 1959 Wardropper returned after four years at Ohio State. Johns Hopkins had regained its preeminence in Romance studies.

At Johns Hopkins I had much more contact with senior scholars than I had had as a graduate student at Yale or as an instructor at Harvard. My colleagues taught me by example that self-discipline is essential to a scholar. Most of them were friendly and helpful but their erudition and the seriousness with which they pursued their research often made me wonder whether I had any reasonable hope of becoming like them.

In Baltimore I became acutely conscious of the gaps in my preparation, particularly my ignorance of the history of ideas; A. O. Lovejoy was still often seen on the Homewood campus and George Boas was a very active member of the faculty. John Freccero, as a student in my graduate course on sixteenth-century Spanish poetry and drama, introduced me to patristic exegesis. John's tutoring prepared the way for my study of Gil Vicente's *Auto de la sibila Casandra,* first presented as a talk to the Philological Association, a dreaded *rite de passage* for new members of the Hopkins faculty. Several of my colleagues warned me that Leo Spitzer would be sure to ask the first question after my paper and implied that I should be prepared for rough treatment. In fact, Spitzer's questions were probing but friendly; that afternoon he came to my office and spent more than an hour suggesting ways to improve both the content of my paper and my oral presentation of it. I found him always willing to talk about his work or my own, perhaps because he thought of me as a pupil of Auerbach, whom he had known in Germany. I remember his evident shock— "Er war noch jung!"—when I took him a clipping from the *New York Times* announcing Auerbach's death on October 13, 1957.

At Johns Hopkins there were no graduate courses in Spanish that I could attend. I turned instead to English literature, an excellent preparation for my later work as Editor of *Comparative Literature,* though of course I did not know it at the time. Daily conversations with Don Cameron Allen and Earl Wasserman over coffee in the Levering Hall cafeteria showed me how much I could learn from scholarship in English literature, incomparably richer than scholarship in Spanish. Don Allen generously gave me access to his superb collection of Renaissance books and taught me how to use them; he also did his best to guide me through the labyrinth of academic politics. I audited courses on Chaucer and Middle English literature given by Richard Hamilton Green, who came to Hopkins from Princeton with the gospel according to D. W. Robertson, Jr. My Robertsonian phase lasted only as long as my first book, *La alegoría en el "libro de buen amor,"* published in Madrid in 1959, but Northrop Frye's *Anatomy of Criticism*, to which Dick Green also introduced me, has remained important to me. Frye's later work on Romance has shaped much of my work on Gil Vicente and Cervantes.

In 1960, I left Johns Hopkins to become associate professor of Romance Languages at Emory, where for the first time I had an opportunity to offer courses in Comparative Literature. In Atlanta I worked closely with a remarkable polymath, Gregor Sebba, who, like his friend Nathan Edelman at Johns Hopkins, showed me that true scholarship is inimical to narrow professionalism. Gregor was responsible for my coming to the University of Oregon in 1964 by recommending me for a position that had been offered to him.

I taught Comparative Literature regularly throughout my twenty-six years at Oregon. In a three-term sequence on the Medieval Romance lyric I examined the Provençal troubadours and their successors in Portugal and Italy. A course on pastoral, repeated several times and offered in the summers of 1977 and 1979 as one of the Seminars for College Teachers sponsored by the National Endowment for the Humanities, gave me an opportunity to explore a wide variety of texts. They included, not always in the same year, Virgil's Eclogues; *The Faerie Queene* (book 6, canto 9); Montaigne's essay *Des cannibales*; *As You Like It* and *The Tempest*; several of Cervantes's *Novelas ejemplares*; *Lycidas*; Flora Thompson's wonderful evocation of her childhood, *Lark Rise*; Henry James's *The Europeans*; D. H. Lawrence's *Sea and Sardinia*; Alejo Carpentier's *Los pasos perdidos*; and Lévi-Strauss's *Tristes tropiques*. A seminar on *Orlando furioso* and *Don Quixote* became the basis of my undergraduate lectures on Cervantes at Oxford in 1986 and of my book *Cervantes and Ariosto: Renewing Fiction* (Princeton, 1989). Much of my teaching at Oregon was in Spanish or Portuguese literature; I became professor of Comparative Literature only in 1989, one year before my retirement from full-time teaching.

I came to Oregon with the tacit understanding that I would succeed Chandler Beall as Editor of *Comparative Literature* (hereafter *CL*). I edited the journal from 1972 until I retired in 1990; I still edit it during one quarter in each academic year and will do so until I am seventy, in 1995.

CL grew out of the efforts of a group of American scholars to establish a Comparative Literature section within the Modern Language Association and to create an American journal. After several attempts to interest other universities in a journal had come to nothing, Chandler Beall offered to approach the University of Oregon and made a formal proposal to its president, Harry K. Newburn, in September 1947. In a letter of November 13, President Newburn agreed to finance *CL* for a trial period of three years, stipulating that the University of Oregon would retain full ownership and direction, that there would be an editorial board representing the comparatists of the MLA, and that Chandler Beall would be the editor. The first members of the editorial board were appointed by President Newburn in February 1948. The names of three of the original five—René Wellek, Harry Levin, and Victor Lange—still appear on our masthead, though René Wellek's health no longer permits him to participate actively in the work of the board. The first issue appeared in the spring of 1949.

Only a handful of American universities offered programs in Comparative Literature in 1949. Many people, including some members of the editorial board, questioned whether enough good articles could be found to fill the pages of the new journal; Chandler Beall's correspondence with members of the editorial board shows that similar doubts continued to be expressed during the first several years of its existence.

One can trace the development of *CL*'s editorial policy in Chandler Beall's extensive correspondence with members of the editorial board, particularly René Wellek. Beall discussed many problems with them at the annual meetings of the Modern Language Association. He spent a great deal of time and energy in trying to smooth over differences between Werner Friederich and other members of the board, though he never hesitated to make his own position clear. In a letter to Friederich of September 12, 1952, he wrote,

> I appreciate your letter. . .and I share your dislike of squabbles. On the other hand, I disagree with you on the matter of criticism as a part of our field, and can't comprehend how we can profess interest in literature, comparative or otherwise, and not be intensely interested in criticism thereof. Even *RLC*, which is narrower than we are or want to be, reviews books of criticism and theory that are not strictly comparative in the narrow sense of "A influenced B". . .I'll [quote] Wellek's comment on [a] manuscript that you had noted was "not at all comparative." Wellek also votes to reject (as do I) but adds: "I don't agree with Mr. Friederich's main reason for rejection: that it is not comparative. I thought and still think that we include questions of general literature and theory within our scope." I think he has a point there.

The opposing views held by Friederich and Wellek became a subject of public debate in Wellek's paper, "The Crisis of Comparative Literature," presented at the second congress of the ICLA in Chapel Hill in 1958 and reprinted in his book *Concepts of Criticism* (New Haven, 1963).

CL has, of course, changed in the forty-three years since it was founded, just as the discipline itself has changed. It has been a long time since we published an *état présent* or *Forschungsbericht*, a frequent feature of the early volumes, as were articles on the reception of author A in country B. More of our articles now deal explicitly with questions of theory, though the kind of theory involved has changed enormously. Some significant developments have hardly been represented in *CL*. One is deconstruction, probably because it is hard to establish a relationship between two texts if one assumes, with Hillis Miller, that "the same text authorizes innumerable interpretations; there is no 'correct' interpretation." Another is the New Historicism; its practitioners have been concerned primarily with the relationship between a text and its context in a particular time and place, which may, of course, include other texts, rather than with the relationship between texts composed at different times or in different places, which we define as the domain of *CL*.

CL does not commission articles. The final decision about whether or not to accept a manuscript is made by two members of the editorial board. My role is limited to deciding which manuscripts I will send to the board and which members of the board I will ask to read them. I try to ensure that the manuscripts sent to an individual member of the board fall within the range of his or her interests and also that no one has to bear a disproportionate share of the burden of evaluating them, which sometimes conflicts with the first principle.

Many articles are rejected because they offer what Chandler Beall liked to call "comparison for comparison's sake," showing that one work is like another but failing to demonstrate that the comparison leads to a better understanding of either. Others are rejected simply because they belong in a different kind of journal, perhaps one devoted to philosophy or to political science. I usually return them within a couple of days, with a note saying that they are "not suitable" or "not comparative in our sense." An article on two authors who write in the same language will normally be excluded, even if the two are of different nationalities, like Hardy and Faulkner or Cervantes and García Márquez, since there are plenty of other journals to which it might be submitted; Chandler Beall used to say that the policy was determined by a need for the division of labor, rather than by a rigid conception of what Comparative Literature ought to be. An interpretation of a single work is also likely to be rejected unless it exemplifies a significant theoretical problem. The central issue is whether the article throws light on other works, though these need not be explicitly discussed.

I send about one in five of the manuscripts we receive to the editorial board; about a third of these are usually accepted for publication. I have no formula for deciding what percentage of manuscripts will be forwarded to the board; I try to judge each article on its own merits. If an article goes to the board, I can usually tell the author within two months whether or not it has been accepted, though we do not send out manuscripts between mid-June and Labor Day, because many board members are away from their academic addresses.

The members of the editorial board continue to play an important role in shaping *CL*'s editorial policy through their assessments of individual

manuscripts. Comparative Literature as an academic discipline owes them an
extraordinary debt of gratitude. Their work goes far beyond deciding which
articles will be accepted for publication. They offer suggestions for revising
many of the articles submitted to them, including many they do recommend
for publication. Occasionally one reader feels that an article should be rejected
while the other recommends acceptance subject to revision, but they are rarely
far apart in their assessment of it. In my twenty years as editor there have been
only two or three cases in which one member of the board enthusiastically
urged publication of an article that another judged totally unacceptable.

The evaluations by members of the editorial board suggest some
generalization about the qualities that make a manuscript publishable. Some
apply to *CL*; others are of more general application. Ideally, an article that
examines the work of two writers should be equally interesting to specialists
in either. In practice, an article on Chaucer and Ovid or Milton and Homer
is likely to appeal more to students of English literature than to classicists. The
writer needs nevertheless to have a clear notion of the needs of both. A specialist
in the eighteenth-century English novel who writes about Fielding and *Don
Quixote* must learn the sort of things *cervantistas* know, insofar as they have
a bearing on the subject at hand. In particular he or she needs to be familiar
with scholarship on Cervantes and not just with the small portion of it available
in English. Every article should make clear what kind of problem it is intended
to solve; I reject many manuscripts with a note saying that "so much has been
written about Goethe (or another major writer) that every new study addressed
to scholars must show how it compliments or modifies earlier treatments."
Finally, style is extremely important in scholarly writing, as it is in every other
kind. Many articles are rejected not because their subject is trivial, their
scholarship superficial, or their thesis unconvincing, but because they are so
badly written that few readers would have the time and patience to discover
their merits.

10

Born to Compare

Lilian R. Furst

It was not until I was about twenty-one that it dawned on me that there was any method other than the comparative. Born in Vienna to a father from Hungary and a mother from Poland, I had early on grown accustomed to hearing comparisons made, and all the more so after we moved to England in 1939, thereby adding another whole dimension to the repertoire: comparisons of school and university systems, of health care and religious practices, of manners and lifestyles. It was so natural in our family always to compare that it did not occur to me that people might think otherwise.

I had assumed that I would follow my parents into their profession, medicine. If the method of discussion was comparative, the dominant subject was medicine, whose quirks and constant challenges I found fascinating. So it was quite a blow when my school declared, when I was about twelve, that I had a gift for languages. I recall the acute embarrassment and palpable silence in the house at this upsetting discovery—almost as if it had transpired that I was into drugs or some other aberration. Tactfully, my parents reserved comment at the time, perhaps hoping that I would outgrow this tendency, as an adolescent outgrows acne, or perhaps simply regarding it as another unexpected stroke of fate, such as had beset our lives ever since the Nazis annexed Austria in 1938. Only much later did I learn the reasons for their doubts at this suggested career choice for me. They stemmed not from any ideological prejudices or preconceptions, but from bitter experience, which caused them practical anxieties for my future. How was I to earn a living with modern languages? Teaching was the obvious route; however, they had learned the hard way that a Jew should have an independent profession, and not be exposed to the humiliation of applying for a position and being rejected. There have been times in my life when I have thought back to their hesitations, and understood them better than I might have done then.

In the event, the decision made itself because I developed a long illness when I was fifteen, and while I could read books at will in bed, I could not continue the laboratory sciences. By then it had in any case become amply evident that I had little inclination for the sciences, and should follow my bent for languages. My interests in that direction had been stimulated between the ages of eleven and fifteen by a highly intelligent Hebrew teacher, who opened up the structure of the language in an exciting manner. Since I was learning Latin at the same time at school, I began to have an insight into the workings of languages as well as the possibilities of words in literary texts.

As an undergraduate I opted for the unusual dual major in Modern Languages, which took an extra year because in fact it compressed two complete three year honors courses into four years, creating a frighteningly heavy workload in the second and third years, when one was fully engaged in both fields. Undergraduate education in Great Britain, to indulge in a comparison, is rather different from its Liberal Arts counterpart in the United States. The major is chosen before entry to college so that specialization sets in much earlier. Only one or two subsidiary, complementary courses are taken in the freshman year, but in compensation for the absence of Anthropology, Psychology, or Economics 101, far wider and deeper coverage is possible in the major. In both German and French I was taught the history of the language, medieval as well as modern periods of literature, and some cultural history and history of ideas. Interestingly, the German department organized its curriculum along traditional historical lines, while the French department had switched to an approach by genre. Missing in both cases, however, was any conscious consideration of methods or theory.

As a result, no doubt, I went on comparing. According to its catalog, Manchester University offered a couple of comparative courses as one of the optional "Special Subjects" chosen by students in their senior year as an equivalent to the American capstone seminar. These comparative courses had been inaugurated and sponsored by the distinguished medievalist, Eugène Vinaver, for thirty-three years head of the French department. Himself born to compare, Vinaver had moved after the Russian revolution from St. Petersburg to Paris, where he had been educated before going to Oxford, and eventually Manchester. A humanist in the truest sense, Vinaver played a decisive formative part in turning me into a comparatist, and always remained an ideal for me, not least in the courtesy and consideration he extended to students. Many years later, I dedicated my first book to him. The German Department also was sympathetic to comparative work under the leadership of Ronald Peacock, whose primary field was modern European drama. I was certainly fortunate as an undergraduate to be taught by two such eminent scholars, both engaged in comparative studies. Nonetheless, the comparative courses, though listed, were not actually being offered. I was the nuisance student, beating the doors and asking for what was supposed to be available. In the best British style, a compromise was reached. I took modern French lyric poetry as my special subject, but was allowed to write my honors essay on Stefan George's translation of Baudelaire's *Fleurs du mal* under the direction of David Luke, who was in the German department, yet whose knowledge of French literature was equally extensive. His course on twentieth-century German literature was so cosmopolitan in its range of reference that it, too, animated my eagerness to compare. Altogether, as a closet comparatist, I was well served by my undergraduate education.

It was a very different story when I went on to Cambridge with the aim of doing a Ph.D. My choice of institution was arbitrary, to put it mildly. I had seen an announcement of graduate fellowships at Royal Holloway College, London, and when I went to ask Professor Vinaver for a letter of recommendation, he suggested I should apply to Oxford and Cambridge too. At Oxford I applied to Somerville College, but more or less wrote it off as a possibility as soon as I saw the application form because it asked about my religion. While I had not the slightest desire to conceal it, I objected on principle to an institution that would pose such a question. Girton College, Cambridge, on the other hand, wanted to know my mother's and my grandmother's maiden name, which made me chuckle and wish them good luck in tracing my matriarchal educational background. When Royal Holloway College summoned me for an interview, I found out that, though a constituent of London University, it was miles out in the country at Englefield Green, Surrey, in an ominous prison-like red-brick building that smelled of staleness and from which I fled in horror. Girton struck me as somewhat less forbidding and remote, and since I could have a room in College for the first term, solving the immediate housing problem, that was where I decided to go.

If I was irresolute about the whereabouts, I knew with surprising assurance what I wanted to do for the Ph.D. It was to be a continuation and expansion of my undergraduate project into a comparison of George and Rilke as translators from French. I had already assembled all the texts, started to develop a methodology, and was keen to get going. I was taken aback and terribly disappointed when I received a letter shortly before the end of the first term informing me that the Faculty Board of Medieval and Modern Languages had turned my topic down. The reason given was that I would have to have two directors, one expert in German and the other in French. Considering the difficulties I ultimately had in satisfying even one director, perhaps this would have been precarious. But in retrospect the motives for the rejection of my proposal strike me as not unconnected with the resistance to Comparative Literature. I was told that in order to take a Cambridge degree I had to choose one language, and since I was a native speaker, I opted for German and began a dissertation on the *Künstlerroman* 1890–1930, for which I never felt the genuine ardor I had for my comparative topic. I am still sorry that at twenty-one I had neither the experience nor the spunk to defy the opinion of the august Faculty

Board of Medieval and Modern Languages. I should, of course, have packed and left. The place to which I should have gone was Harvard, where I would have received a thorough grounding in Comparative Literature. Unfortunately, that was beyond my horizon at that time, to my great regret, even to this day. It was Harry Levin of Harvard, when I met him some fifteen years later, who was the first to endorse my original comparative topic as a promising one with unqualified enthusiasm.

My three years in Cambridge as a research student were the unhappiest in my life, partly, no doubt, because I was thwarted in my innate thrust toward thinking along comparative lines. In British universities there is no organized course work for the Ph.D. The attitude to graduate students is summarized in the phrase: "Throw them in, and let them sink or swim." I managed just about to stay afloat, working at my dissertation in a desultory fashion, drinking an inordinate amount of nasty coffee and strong tea in the university library's tearoom, which was the chief place to meet others in the same boat. Once a term I saw my dissertation director, who would make, literally, odd suggestions. At first I felt obliged to follow them up, but when I reported the outcome at our conference in the next term, he would ask: "Whatever made you do that?" I couldn't answer: "You!" In time, however, I learned to listen to his ideas politely, ignore them completely, and go my own way. On the whole, I regressed during those three years, and was at the end much more bewildered and discouraged, and much less prepared to teach than at the outset. Since I had not been an undergraduate at Cambridge (or Oxford), I was considered not to understand the system of teaching by tutorial supervision, and consequently was never given the opportunity to acquire any teaching experience. My main business in Cambridge seemed to be "keeping terms," i.e., sleeping fifty-nine nights (officially between 12 and 6 A.M.) between specified dates within five miles of the Church of Great St. Mary. My landlady had to certify in each of the nine terms that this had been duly done.

The Cambridge years were so bleak that I began to doubt whether I had made the right career choice. In exploring alternative possibilities, I went to the university placement office for women, where I was told bluntly that the only firm to which I could apply for a position was the department store chain, Marks & Spencer, because I was Jewish. Marks & Spencer turned me down as a sales management trainee on the grounds that I had too academic a training. Having satisfied the residency requirement by sleeping off the requisite number of nights within the prescribed orbit, I was stranded with a few chunks of a dissertation, in which I had largely lost heart. At the last moment, in late July, an assistant lectureship in German at the Queen's University of Belfast was advertised. I learned subsequently that the person appointed had backed out at short notice. When I flew to Belfast for the interview, I did lots of sightseeing, convinced that I would never be in Northern Ireland again. To my great astonishment, I was offered the position on the spot on a one-year renewable contract. I was to teach the freshman survey of German literature 1730–1870, an advanced class in twentieth century literature, a conversation group, and three sections of German prose translation, which involved grading sixty versions every week.

Like the proverbial man who came to dinner and stayed and stayed, I went to Belfast for one year and remained eleven. The political situation in Northern Ireland at that time was one of chronic tension, but not yet the open strife that was to erupt shortly after I left. The university was remarkably free of the religious animosities prevalent among the population at large. All instructors were required to sign an undertaking that we would not say anything that might offend anyone's religious susceptibilities. Actually, in that environment, to be Jewish was a positive advantage, for one was neutral. The story is told, probably authentic, of a Jew who was asked whether he was a Catholic Jew or a Protestant Jew! I, for my part, felt quite free. The atmosphere at Queen's University was friendly and egalitarian, in contrast to the hierarchical snobbery I had encountered in Cambridge.

My primary source of satisfaction in Belfast was the joy I discovered in teaching. Though I was woefully inept at the outset and would sometimes see the look of pity on the students' faces at my efforts, I loved it. I loved the power of the rhetoric, and as I learned to explain and communicate better, I was rewarded by seeing the dawn of understanding in at least some of the students. I surely learned more than they, especially from the survey course, in which I gradually grasped the developmental dynamics of German literature. It was a vast relief also to be reading and thinking about something other than the *Künstlerroman*. I was most fortunate, too, to have come into the department at a time of renewal and expansion not long after the appointment of a new, imaginative head, who expected the entire faculty to participate in the restructuring of the curriculum. I sometimes wondered later whether it was merely nostalgia for youth that made me look back later on this phase of my life as a particularly fulfilling one. But when the members of that department had a reunion in the summer of 1988, I found that we really did enjoy unusually cordial personal and professional relationships which matured into lasting friendships. We pulled together willingly and without jealousies in the common cause of building the department, trying communally to get a reasonable slice of a cake that was never large in British universities.

I knew that the price I had to pay for keeping my teaching position was to complete the dissertation, which I had been glad to shelve in favor of preparing classes. The pleasure of teaching, together with the encouragement of my department head, restored the self-confidence that had been eroded in Cambridge. During the following summer I took the wretched thing out again, consigned a considerable portion of it to the wastepaper basket, and finished it before classes began again in October. It took another six months to revise and polish it and get it typed so that I submitted it, deliberately, on 1 April, All Fool's Day. It turned out that the examination fees had been raised that very day, but as I hadn't been informed, I was forgiven. Another seven months elapsed before I was called to defend it; I was so seasick after a rough crossing of the Irish Channel that I just wished the world would stop moving. Two whole years after starting to teach, I finally got my Ph.D.

The degree (in American: Commencement) ceremony itself was the most peculiar ritual in which I have ever engaged. It was scheduled for 2 P.M., and the College graciously invited me to lunch beforehand. With memories of meals at Girton, which had not changed since Virginia Woolf's description of them as they were in 1928 in *A Room of One's Own* (except that in the meanwhile the closing biscuits and cheese had been eliminated), I ate the largest breakfast of my life, only to discover that out of term the Fellows ate in a small private dining-room, and what is more, they ate well there! The College's Praelector, one of whose functions was to present degree candidates, inspected the day's two candidates, and trained us for the ceremony: kneel before the Vice-Chancellor, put your closed hands up before your face so that he can put his around them in order to pronounce the sacred words; then take a large step backwards, and bow to him. The importance of the large step backwards was drilled into us so that we didn't, on bowing, put our heads in his lap! I had received written instructions to wear a black dress and black stockings and shoes, no make-up of any kind nor jewelry. I had to borrow a black dress from my mother, who was smaller and slighter than I, but assumed it would do under the cover of my long silk gown. It was, therefore, disconcerting to learn that I would have to kneel; I was afraid the dress might split. The reasons for this severely austere garb became apparent when we were presented as "hunc virum" ("this man"). Although women had been formally admitted to degrees at Cambridge since 1948, the fiction was still maintained that we were men, and an attempt was made to pass us off as such through our utterly unadorned appearance. We were to be admitted to the degree in the name of the Father, the Son, and the Holy Ghost, and for those with objections to this phrase, the other option was in the name of God. If this was your preference, a mark was made by your name beforehand, and as you came up to be admitted, an attendant whispered "alternative formula" in the Vice-Chancellor's ear. It was all very stagey, especially as we were given only a blank scroll that was immediately retrieved; the actual diplomas, which are understatedly small, were not ready, and arrived by mail some weeks later.

I was glad to get back to the less pretentious environment of Belfast. The tenure review comes sooner in the British system than in the American. I was able quite quickly to extract two articles from my dissertation, and to write another two on German topics. The department and the dean warmly endorsed my tenure, but I was turned down by the Board of Curators, which included prominent people from outside the university, on the grounds that there was no point in tenuring a woman since she would marry and have a family! This was in the late 1950s. The university president was so distressed at this decision that he proposed a different review structure in the next year, whereby the Board of Curators would be bypassed, and my work would be sent to leading Germanists for evaluation—a procedure more like that current in the USA nowadays. So at age twenty-eight I was tenured.

Tenure, to me, meant one thing: the liberty to work as I pleased without a director, a Faculty Board, or Curators to dictate what was fitting and what was not. In other words, it meant that I could attempt comparative work. After tenure, for seven years, small more or less automatic salary increases were given until the so-called Merit Bar, a serious review of the work accomplished during those years, at which point the salary increases might be stopped if the research was deemed unsatisfactory. With seven years ahead of me, I knew without hesitation what I wanted to do: a comparative study of the Romantic movements in England, France, and Germany in order to discriminate between them. The project had its origins in my undergraduate days, when I had taken courses on Romanticism in three different departments and was offered accounts that seemed to me heterogeneous. I had since read René Wellek's "The Concept of Romanticism in Literary History,"[1] in which he argues for the basic unity of all the Romantic movements. While I could see the similarities, I was just as strongly aware of the differences, and wanted to analyze and document this interplay of difference within similarity. Years later, after I had completed the project, several friends confessed to me that they had not wanted to tell me that they thought it was not feasible.

I had not the slightest idea how to set about this task, but with a youthful insouciance and innocence that I now envy, I went about satisfying my intellectual curiosity. For about five years I read, and there was plenty to read in both primary and secondary sources. Those were the years without immediate pressure when I laid the foundations for much of my subsequent writing. Academic life in Great Britain was far more tranquil than in the United States. I attended the annual conference of the Association of University Teachers of German, a pleasant, leisurely meeting at which the number of cups of coffee consumed per capita by far exceeded the number of papers delivered. I never dreamed of offering a paper myself, and being junior, I was not expected to do so. The entire pace was slower because courses met once a week throughout the academic year from October to May. There was less organizational busyness, and consequently more time for reading for both students and faculty.

After five years of reading, the quantity of my *fiches* reached such alarming proportions that I began to wonder how to arrange them into a coherent argument. Advice from my colleagues was well meant but not particularly pertinent. Eventually I hit on the idea of focusing on three central aspects of romanticism, namely, individualism, imagination, and feeling, to try to illustrate the innate patterns of difference in similarity. I spent days with my *fiches* spread all over the floor of my living room, sorting and resorting them into piles that were to become chapters. I asked a historian friend when to stop reading and start writing, and his answer was: "Now!" I still would have delayed had I not woken on 1 March 1964 to a snowstorm that immobilized Belfast. Stuck in my apartment, I had nothing other to do than to start writing. Perhaps that is when I first sensed the therapeutic value of scholarship, especially the wrestling with words that is at the heart of writing.

Once I started to write, I became engrossed in a way that I never had been in the dissertation. It had been an academic exercise, whereas in making comparisons I had something to say. The following year I crowded all my teaching into two and a half days midweek so as to leave five mornings to write. I had a stroke of luck when a representative from Macmillan came to Belfast, and invited me to submit my manuscript for their consideration. I sent the first three chapters, heard nothing for months, had the manuscript returned, and to my utter amazement received a letter offering me a contract. The book had no title yet; I always thought of it as "The Hydra" because it kept on growing new problems. Ultimately it became *Romanticism in Perspective*, which appeared in 1969.

By then I had moved back to Manchester to the only position in a department with the somewhat curious name, Comparative Literary Studies. The name caused much confusion: I would get mail addressed to Contemporary Literary Studies, Contemplative Literary Studies, and even Comparative Literacy Studies. Clearly, the concept of Comparative Literature was unfamiliar in Great Britain at that time. Manchester's was the first department in the field, the brainchild of Eugène Vinaver, who had endowed it with its unusual name on the grounds that there was English, French, Italian, Spanish, etc., literature, but no comparative literature.[2] To ensure its continued existence after his retirement, he pressed for an appointment. When I saw the post advertised, I grew terribly excited, immediately identifying it as "my" job. In support of my application I submitted half the manuscript of *Romanticism in Perspective*. I was overjoyed when I was offered the position. I saw the move as a homecoming, a return to my alma mater, and I had every intention of staying there for the rest of my career, doing my best to build a department. Admittedly, after a few days my delight gave way to panic as I realized that I had no idea what Comparative Literature was, and that I was unable to teach more than a single course in it, on the romantic movements. I turned for enlightenment to the various manuals of Comparative Literature, mostly French in origin. They agonized over the distinction between Comparative Literature and General Literature, over such matters as influence and transmission, and were altogether so drearily pedantic as to fill me with dismay. This was not at all how I envisaged Comparative Literature, which to me has to be rooted in the comparative analysis of texts.

My start in Manchester was not exactly easy. I had students from English and from the various language departments, which were very strong. My course on European Romanticism finally brought to reality the comparative listings in the catalog, which I had pursued as an undergraduate. The response was gratifyingly large. But for a while I had no office owing to the shortage of space. All I had was a piece of cardboard with my name and Comparative Literary Studies on it, and every day I would have to ask the French department secretary whose office I could borrow. It was the janitor who finally took pity on me, and confided to me that there was an empty office in the basement under the jurisdiction of the English department; he requested it for me. Later I was moved into the most spacious corner office in a new wing because no agreement could be reached as to who should be housed there. But it was only toward the end of my seven years in Manchester that the department acquired a telephone. Until then the janitor of the Arts Building would carry messages by hand up three flights of stairs and along two corridors, and I could then return the call from a pay phone in the corridor. Luxury was not the name of the game in British universities.

I was perplexed how to expand this department beyond the one course I myself could teach. I organized a second course on "Experimentation in the Twentieth-Century Novel" by inviting members of other departments each to speak about their favorite writer, while I acted as anchor. Every Friday I would tremble lest the Joyce or Svevo expert not turn up and leave me to conduct the class. It worked well, and was a stimulating course. With some help from the English department and with the addition of a junior faculty person, an M.A. curriculum was also offered, and several Ph.D. candidates began to appear, including some from France and the United States. The biggest challenge and my highest ambition was to evolve an undergraduate major. The English department initially voted against cooperation in this venture because the senior faculty supported it and the junior faculty therefore opposed it. Eventually a committee was appointed, which deliberated for a whole year to devise a major with our slender resources. The plan had to be presented to the Faculty Board, but I was not eligible to do this as I was not a Full Professor. The Professor of German was delegated to make the formal presentation; however, when he was faced with questions, he turned them over to me. Even after the major had been approved, the dean suggested that I should visit all the language and literature departments to deal with any further questions. The recurrent one was: "Why would you want or need to read in more than one national literature?" I was made to feel as if I were greedy, and Comparative Literature a superfluous discipline.

This experience undoubtedly played a central role in my ultimate decision to leave England. In 1970 already the economic prospects for developing a new department didn't look rosy. The universities operated on a quinquennial grant from the government, and I was promised another faculty position not in 1971, nor in 1976, nor in 1981, but in 1986. Was I guilty of impatience? It seemed like a never-never land, in which I was likely to grow stale and frustrated.

My disillusionment with British attitudes to Comparative Literature coincided with my increasing awareness of its liveliness in the United States. In 1967 I had invited Harry Levin, who was visiting Churchill College, Cambridge, to inaugurate the department (I had to look up where Harvard was in order to write to him); he very kindly agreed to give a lecture despite the paltry honorarium of $25 that was all we could offer. I met more American comparatists later that year when I attended the ICLA meeting in Belgrade, where I gave my first paper ever. It met with an onslaught of questions about my methodology, which was dismissed as merely "explication de texte comparée." I saw nothing wrong with that. The attack was abruptly halted when an authoritative gentleman on the front row commented that I did know what I was talking about. My defender was René Wellek! In 1968 I submitted an article to *Comparative Literature Studies* and met its editor, A. Owen Aldridge, at the FILLM meeting in Strasbourg. Aldridge asked me whether I would like to join his department, but I felt an obligation to Manchester, and turned him down.

I had further contacts with the United States after the publication of *Romanticism in Perspective*, which was reviewed in the *New York Times*. I received several appreciative letters, some of which invited me to give a lecture if I was in the United States. At first I laughed because it seemed so unlikely, but with four such invitations it began to be feasible. My mother died in October 1969, and my father's only brother lived in New York, so we decided to make a three-week trip in April 1970. I gave lectures at the Graduate Center in New York, Stonybrook, Dartmouth, Urbana, and Madison, where Eugène Vinaver was teaching in his retirement, and where I stayed ten days and visited some classes so as to get an idea of how an American university worked. While I was there, Stephen Nichols called me from Dartmouth and asked me to come back to talk about a position there. We agreed I should be a visiting professor 1971–72. This fitted in well with Harry Levin's invitation to teach Harvard Summer School in 1971. Already I was considering the possibility of a permanent move, although I hesitated out of loyalty to England, which had sheltered us during the war, and especially to Manchester, which had given me such a fine education. I discussed it in Madison with Eugène Vinaver, who told me firmly that allegiance to one's discipline took precedence over loyalty to a country.

From the hindsight of what has happened since, Vinaver's advice has proven to be the best I was ever given. Comparative Literature has never really prospered in Great Britain, partly, for sure, because of economic stringencies such as no American academic can conceive, even long before Mrs. Thatcher's notorious starvation diet for the universities, and particularly for the humanities. My struggle to get a telephone, let alone some secretarial assistance, was by no means exceptional. But in addition to the financial barrier, a matter of attitude was also involved. My experience in Manchester was pretty typical of the resistance of well-established English and Foreign Language departments to innovations of any kind. By contrast, in the United States there is an openness to experimentation, which has been conducive to the evolution of the discipline. Whereas in England anything new means "creating a precedent," which is perceived as a possible threat, a rocking of the venerable, stable boat, in the United States "new" tends to be equated with "better." Both stances have their perils; the American mania for the new and recent, as I learned to my cost in Texas, can lead to a jettisoning of an entire literary tradition in favor of the modern and postmodern on the grounds that choices must be made when resources are limited, and the latest is clearly the most desirable. However, the American willingness to try things out is certainly more propitious for the development of Comparative Literature. University organization plays its part too: it is easier here to get a new course approved, to amend or even scrap it after a year than in England, where curricula tended to be engraved in stone.

The record of Comparative Literature in Great Britain is in many respects one of missed or thwarted opportunities. There has been no lack of potential scholars in the field, yet they have been constrained by the prevailing climate of opinion and by the hegemony of restrictive departments. René Wellek, for instance, was at the School of Slavonic Studies of London University 1935–39, but decided to emigrate to the United States to a position at the University of Iowa because he objected "to the anti-theoretical bias of much English criticism."[3] Eugène Vinaver frankly regretted not having moved across the Atlantic until after his retirement because he wanted to remain close to France, and in the days before jet planes the distance seemed too enormous, psychologically as well as physically. This greatest Mallory scholar, who had discovered the manuscripts in Winchester cathedral and edited them, could never teach a seminar on him in England because his chair was in the French department. He told me an ironic incident about an American graduate student, who had written to the English department at Manchester University asking to come there (at his own expense) to work on Mallory; the reply he received was that there was no one in Manchester with any interest or qualifications in Mallory! It was evidently a source of frustration to Vinaver that he was not admitted to teach the author on whom he was the world authority simply because of departmental compartmentalization. Leo Spitzer, Vinaver told me with genuine annoyance, was denied a position in England on the grounds that his command of spoken English was inadequate.

By and large, the new universities, founded after the war, were far more hospitable to Comparative Literature than either Oxbridge or the so-called "Red Brick universities," for example, Manchester, Liverpool, Leeds, Durham, Bristol, Exeter, Hull, Southampton. The youngest generation of British universities, such as Essex, Sussex, East Anglia, and Warwick, were less bound by the burden of conventions, and opted for more adventurous approaches. At Sussex, for example, a School of European Studies was instituted, which comprised a Comparative Literature segment under the leadership of Anthony Thorlby, who had been a student of Wellek's at Yale. At Essex Donald Davie directed work in Comparative Literature before he took off for the United States. At Warwick translation studies became a specialty at the instigation of Susan Bassnett. East Anglia also had a School of European Studies, which benefitted from American immigrants, notably Elinor Shaffer, a student of Lionel Trilling and Harold Bloom, who remained in England on her marriage, and who is the founding editor and moving spirit of the *Yearbook of Comparative Criticism*, published by Cambridge University Press. Other immigrants, however, have fared less well. George Steiner was never fully accepted in Cambridge, where he held a fellowship at Churchill College, but no university position (as against his wife, a historian, who was accorded a university position in addition to her fellowship at New Hall). Rebuffed by Cambridge, Steiner was welcomed at the University of Geneva, to which he commuted from his home in England. At a more modest level, one of my American students, who did his Ph.D. in Manchester, Thomas West, taught at the University of East Anglia for several years, but finally settled in Paris. Nevertheless, Great Britain does now have a Society for Comparative Literature, which holds an annual meeting, and keeps the flag flying despite the difficulties of the past few years. Its first president, Frank Kermode, is another at least semiexpatriate; after resigning from his chair of English at Cambridge because of the refusal of tenure to the structuralist, Colin McCabe, he spent a number of years at Columbia. The brain drain from the United Kingdom in Comparative Literature has been quite pronounced, and no wonder. My department of Comparative Literary Studies at Manchester was taken off its life-support system and left to die a couple of years ago. This had not been done earlier because the saving entailed in this closure was too small to have been worth making sooner. Its sole tenured faculty member, Simon Curtis, who had been active in the British Society for Comparative Literature, headed for Australia. My predecessor in Manchester, Glyn T. Hughes, became an administrator at the University of Wales. On the whole, the picture of Comparative Literature in Great Britain is a sad one. I have sometimes recalled the words of the friend, who warned me, when I accepted the position in Manchester and was full of enthusiasm, that it was "a dead-end job"; at the time I regarded him as a cynic, now I see that he was a realist.

This does not mean that British comparatists have not made significant contributions to the field. But they have been made as individual initiatives rather than as part of a collective commitment, which always seems to have been lacking in England. Among those individuals, none perhaps is more outstanding than Siegbert Prawer, who held the Taylorian Chair of German at Oxford. Himself of European, cosmopolitan origin, he did his utmost to foster Comparative Literature both institutionally and in his own work. He requested copies of all my Manchester records of courses when I left. Oxford did indeed offer a B.Phil. (equivalent to an M.A.) in General and Comparative

Literature, while Prawer wrote a fine introductory book, *Comparative Literary Studies* (London: Duckworth, 1973), not to mention his monumental works, *Heine's Shakespeare* (Oxford: Clarendon Press, 1970), *Karl Marx and World Literature* (Oxford: Clarendon Press, 1976), *Caligari's Children: The Film as Tale of Horror* (Oxford and New York: Oxford University Press, 1980), and *Frankenstein's Island: England and the English in the Writings of Heinrich Heine* (Cambridge and New York: Cambridge University Press, 1986).[4]

When I was in England in 1989 to deliver the keynote address to the Association of University Teachers of German in Great Britain and Ireland, many younger scholars furtively asked me how to initiate the trans-Atlantic transition. Curiously, I had been invited to speak on a comparative topic because the then-president of the association felt weary of "the straight Germanistic line." I cannot conclude from this single experience that a trend is afoot in Great Britain toward Comparative Literature, but interest in the approach (if not material support for the discipline as a discipline) is still alive. Yet ironically, when I was urged to submit the paper for publication in a British journal, it was accepted on condition that the theoretical preamble be deleted. *Plus ça change, plus c'est la même chose*? I had to warn the young aspirant immigrants that getting a permanent visa was a complex undertaking.

In this, too, I was much helped by Eugène Vinaver's sound counsel as to what kind of visa to aim for, and what to avoid at all costs. Obtaining a visa was an almost full-time occupation for a year. There were endless forms to fill up and hoops to jump through; for instance, the original of my Ph.D. diploma had to be submitted as well as police affidavits from every place where I had lived since age sixteen to confirm that I had no criminal record. The consulate in London advised me to put myself in the category "Laborer, skilled or unskilled" as the best chance for a visa. A three-month postal strike in England caused such delay that I didn't think I would make it to Harvard Summer School. I had to go to London to be tested for tuberculosis, veneral diseases, and illiteracy. On 29 June 1971, clutching our chest x-rays, we landed at Logan Airport in Boston, were issued "green cards," and started a new life.

This new life proved full of unknowns and mysteries. Such common terms as "credit hours," "pass/fail," "drop/add," and "auditor" were new to me. When I read the "Instructor's Manual" issued by Harvard Summer School, I myself wanted to drop out immediately. I wouldn't have got through that first summer spell of teaching without the wise and patient guidance of Bette-Anne Farmer, the administrative assistant in the department of Comparative Literature. One of my two courses, "The Rise of the Romantic Movement in Europe," had only six students. When I was asked to teach Harvard Summer School again the following year, I said I probably shouldn't offer that again because of its small enrollment. The answer was: "No, it was a good course, but change the title." I did, to "The Romantic Revolution," and had twelve students! So I learned a basic American lesson: the importance of packaging. I could have learnt it too from the shirts we bought for my father at Filene's bargain basement; it was no simple job to extract the shirt from the welter of cardboard, pins, and bags, all designed to make it look good, and sell.

At the end of summer we went on to Dartmouth, which was just going coeducational. My first paycheck was made out to William Furst—it never occurred to anyone that a woman might be teaching there. We had to explain throughout that year that it was not my father, the elderly gentleman with a European accent, who was the visiting professor, but I. Generally this met with incredulous looks. I was also repeatedly asked what were the problems of a woman teaching at Dartmouth, and since I had always taught mixed classes, the question irked me. One day I replied: "The lack of a good ladies' haircutter in Hanover, New Hampshire," and promptly received a note from the President's wife recommending her Canadian haircutter in neighboring Lebanon. The resources and support services at Dartmouth were superb, and the students intelligent, but self-indulgent. They would ask me when we could discuss a book, and I would tell them, when they had read it. They were averse to reading and sought shortcuts. By the second quarter I was showing movies as an inducement to reading the text. The extensive Comparative Literature Program was quite an eye-opener to someone used to the relative narrowness of the British curriculum. I remember in particular a course in the winter quarter on "Tongan Music, Dance, and Literature," to be taught on the Pacific island of Tonga as an escape from the Northern New England winter. I welcomed the willingness to experiment, but wondered where the line ought to be drawn.

That winter I went to my first MLA in Chicago, a most confusing experience to a person unaccustomed to a meeting with multiple concurrent sessions in scattered locations. I knew no one, and stood by the elevators unsure in which direction to head. I found a haven in the book exhibits, but I recall waking at 3 A.M. and seriously considering a return to the quieter, if duller, pastures of England. Later I learned strategies for coping with the MLA: limit attendance to forty-eight hours, arrange to meet a friend within an hour of arrival, and map out in advance a route through the program. The best recipe for a tolerable MLA is to meet lots of friends, visit the book exhibits, and largely ignore the papers. Alternatively, of course, not to go at all.

While still in England, I had been approached by the University of Oregon about the Directorship of the Graduate Program in Comparative Literature, for which I had been nominated by Harry Levin. I knew of Oregon only as the home of *Comparative Literature*, in which I had published an article. So I looked it up in the *Encyclopedia Britannica* in the library, and read about its rain and logging industry. Later, in the United States I discovered a better way to research universities by reading up about them in *Barron's Guide* in bookstores. I flew out to the West Coast from Dartmouth via San Francisco because I was to give a lecture at Berkeley. The first glimpse of the Pacific at sunset as the plane landed was one of the great thrills of my life. It was late November, the sky was blue, the sun shining, flowers in bloom: very strange to someone used to the short grey days of Northern England. Oregon, wet and dark, was more familiar. I was unprepared for the American mode of interview, where the candidate is under constant scrutiny for two or three days, whereas in England it is a one-hour interrogation by a large committee seated round a table. After what seemed a long time, Oregon made me an offer of a visiting position at rather a low salary with the assurance that tenure would be a mere formality. I was naive, but not that naive. I insisted on tenure as a condition of giving up my tenured position in Manchester, and even held out for a little more salary.

Oregon was in some ways, *mutatis mutandis*, a repetition of Manchester. There, too, I went with the intention of settling, and there, too, I was disappointed by the lack of support and of funding. In contrast to Manchester, the Graduate Program at Oregon was well established; it had been founded, like the journal, by Chandler Beall, and probably because of the journal Oregon enjoyed a high reputation in Comparative Literature. On Beall's retirement, the journal and the directorship of the program were split. Tom Hart took on the journal, and with it took the typewriter, the secretary, and the budget. The NDEA funds, which had nurtured the program, were exhausted. So I found myself with a filing cabinet, a telephone (that, at least, was there!), forty-five students, and no help or funds whatsoever. The dean provided a half-time teaching assistantship to do the secretarial work, found a typewriter, and agreed to pay for paper and postage. The Department of Classics, which had all the trappings but few students, refused to merge with Comparative Literature: they didn't want to go sit in a grass-hut with a cannibal! The image of Comparative Literature as a cannibal was new to me. I decided to fight for the program, and went to plead with the graduate dean, the provost, and the president. Meanwhile my colleagues told me to stop complaining about the library, to relax, I had "made it" as a tenured full professor, and should cultivate my garden, play bridge, fish, bake bread, etc. The trouble was that I have neither inclination nor talent for any of those activities, whereas I do like to read books. I came to see that I was hitting my head against a brick wall, and that my head was likely to suffer before the wall yielded. I needed to move on.

Easier said than done, especially by the mid-1970s when the job market was drying up. I was handicapped by my ignorance of the United States, not to mention the absence of a network such as is usually started in graduate school. Playing for time on an ACLS Fellowship, I went back to the Boston area. There I ran into Regina Kyle, formerly an assistant professor of Comparative Literature at Harvard, and then Executive Dean of a new branch of the University of Texas just opening outside Dallas. It seemed an exciting prospect. The Southwest Institute for the Advanced Study in Science was to be turned into an upper level and graduate university through the addition of Schools of Arts & Humanities, and Social Sciences. Best of all, there were to be no separate language and literature departments; all literature faculty were to be comparatists, teaching a communal core curriculum with later specialization in individual fields. At the graduate level there were to be three tracks: Comparative Literature, History of Ideas, and Aesthetic Studies. To a comparatist it sounded most tempting. When I went to Dallas for an interview, I was impressed by the calibre of the scientists, who included a Nobel Prize winner, and I liked the idea of living in a city again. The move to Dallas was in some respects the greatest mistake in my career, and it was motivated by the lure of a central role for Comparative Literature.

I recognized my mistake in the first week. The campus was a building site, and for the opening semester the entire faculty huddled in the library. There was plenty of space there since the library was virtually empty. While I went to orientation sessions, totally disorienting to me, my father set up the furniture. I didn't like to tell him not to bother since it was clear to me that we would have to move again. We stayed, at least on paper, for eleven years, although five of those years we were away, "visiting," so much so that I was teased about being a visiting professor at my own university when I came back. There were good things about the University of Texas at Dallas, notably the solidarity among the forty-five struggling founding faculty, who supported and helped each other with real collegiality. It is no coincidence that when I needed major surgery, I chose to go back to Dallas, partly for its outstanding medical facilities, but also for the friends I had there. The bad things were the shortage of funding, which grew worse as the Texas economy slumped, the absence of library holdings (without the courtesy of Southern Methodist University we couldn't have operated), and the uneven preparation of the students, many of whom transferred from community colleges, while others returned to complete an education interrupted by marriage and child rearing. For a teacher it was a challenging and at times rewarding situation because the students were eager to learn. I developed not only new courses but also a different, more flexible style of teaching. The overriding disappointment for me was the collapse of the plan for a comparative approach; it foundered on the practical requirements for teacher certification in English or other fields, which mandated a certain number of courses categorically in one area.

The years in Dallas were the "journeyman" years of my American career. We went literally North, West, East, and South, to Case Western Reserve University in Cleveland, to Stanford, to Harvard, and to William and Mary, respectively, between 1978 and 1985. It was a demanding and disruptive way of life, rife with anxieties. On the other hand, I am convinced that it was the best way to learn about the profession in this country. My teaching obligations varied: at Stanford, for instance, I was in the German department, which was, however, under the chairmanship of Gerald Gillespie, very open to comparative approaches; at Harvard I was wholly in Comparative Literature, and charged with teaching the two introductory proseminars in Literary Theory, and Comparative Methodologies; at Case Western Reserve and at William and Mary

I was dealing primarily with undergraduates, for whom I evolved some broadly based Humanities courses centered on European literature. My travels around the United States were certainly the antidote to the staleness I had feared in Manchester. I gained valuable insight into the workings of different kinds of departmental structures and institutions, and I got to know a great many people.

After my hasty move to Dallas, I became extremely cautious about future permanent commitments. My cumulative experiences as a visitor, as well as in Oregon and Texas, raised my consciousness of the pitfalls to look out for. Comparative Literature programs are often in a precarious dependence on the goodwill of other departments, and that goodwill cannot always be counted upon, especially in times of financial stringency. I considered a number of positions and for various reasons decided against them. I continued to go to MLA to maintain visibility, which, I had been told, was vital, and I gathered some of the "scalps" prized in the American academic world: an ACLS fellowship, a Guggenheim, fellowships at the Stanford Humanities Center and at the National Humanities Center, directorships of NEH Summer seminars, publication by esteemed presses. To be sure, it takes persistent hard work for an outsider, particularly a woman, to break into the magic circle.

It also takes a certain amount of good luck, and this came my way when, as so often happens, two very attractive openings came along together. William and Mary asked me to stay on in the Kenan Chair, and the University of North Carolina offered me the Marcel Bataillon Chair in Comparative Literature. I accepted the latter because North Carolina has Ph.D. students and the best library in the South, and the propinquity of Duke and of the National Humanities Center creates a lively scholarly community. Comparative Literature at North Carolina has the status of a Curriculum with its own budget, secretary, and three faculty lines, which are supplemented by joint appointments from cognate departments, including Anthropology and Philosophy. This is a sound way to organize Comparative Literature institutionally. High language requirements are maintained along with an openness to diverse theoretical approaches. The recent revisions of our teaching curriculum and examination process have given me a sense of optimism about the future, clouded only by the current severe financial constraints. My Odyssey in pursuit of Comparative Literature has been long and arduous, but it has ended well: I can teach and write in accordance with my heart's desire.

NOTES

1. In *Concepts of Criticism*, ed. Stephen G. Nichols, Jr. (New Haven and London: Yale University Press, 1963), 128–98.

2. The French term, "littérature comparée" (compared literature) and the German "vergleichende Literaturwissenschaft" (comparative study of literature) are grammatically more logical than comparative literature.

3. René Wellek, "Prospect and Retrospect," in *The Attack on Literature and Other Essays* (Chapel Hill: University of North Carolina Press, 1982), 153–54.

4. Is it, I wonder, wholly a coincidence that Prawer's scholarly books were published by Oxford or Cambridge University Presses, while his introduction to Comparative Literature was put out by Duckworth in London, and is now, sadly, out of print?

11

On Wanting to Be a Comparatist

Marjorie Perloff

In the 1990s, when "Comparative Literature" has become an umbrella term for any number of "studies" such as critical theory, multiculturalism, nationalism, and Third World literature, we often forget that, although founded in the late nineteenth century, Comparative Literature came to prominence in the United States as the post–World War II invention of a group of fiercely intellectual, highly educated, multilingual, male refugees from fascist Europe: Erich Auerbach and Leo Spitzer, René Wellek and Roman Jakobson, Renato Poggioli and Claudio Guillén, Geoffrey Hartman, Michael Riffaterre, and so on. Like their counterparts in the newer discipline of art history—Erwin Panofsky, Walter Friedlander, Ernst Gombrich, Leo Steinberg—they took as a given the proposition that the object of their study should not—indeed, could not—be confined to a single nationality. "The great argument for 'comparative' or 'general' literature or just 'literature,' " Wellek declared in *Theory of Literature*, "is the obvious falsity of the ideal of a self-enclosed national literature."[1] And a few years later: "Comparative literature has the immense merit of combatting the false isolation of national literary histories: it is obviously right... in its conception of a coherent Western tradition of literature woven together in a network of innumerable interrelations."[2]

This last statement comes from the keynote address to the Second Congress of the International Comparative Literature Association (1958), an address that betrays a certain anxiety that has haunted our discipline from its inception. "The most serious sign of the precarious state of our study," complains Wellek, "is the fact that it has not been able to establish a distinct subject matter and a specific methodology."[3] And he proceeds to berate the positivism of the earlier French comparatists Paul Van Tieghem and Fernand Baldensperger, with their narrow source-and-influence studies and their penchant toward *Stoffgeschichte.*

All this is well known, but what we often ignore is that the European critics' powerful drive to "combat the false isolation of national literary histories" was motivated, whether consciously or not, by a certain condescension toward and impatience with English, not to mention American literature. In this sense, I was a "comparatist" by the time I was nine or ten. My Jewish family had fled Austria at the time of the Anschluss in March 1938; we landed in Hoboken that August when I was six years old and ready to enter first grade at P.S. 7 in the Bronx. My maternal grandfather Richard Schüller had been a prominent Austrian diplomat and became a professor of economics at the New School: he spoke French, Italian, and English more or less interchangeably, although not, of course, nearly as well as he spoke German. His wife, Erna Rosenthal Schüller, read these modern languages as well as Spanish better than did her husband and devoured the *Times Literary Supplement* every week, looking for "important" new foreign novels or nonfiction works. My lawyer father Maximilian (named for the emperor) Mintz had studied Greek and Latin for eight years at the Gymnasium and had belonged, in Vienna, to a group called the *Geistkreis* that met to read critical papers on writers such as Proust and Hofmannsthal, Nietzsche and Dostoevsky. Among the members of the *Geistkreis* were the phenomenologist Alfred Schütz, the philosopher Felix Kaufmann, the historian Erich Voegelin, and the musicologist Emmanuel Winternitz. My mother, Ilse Mintz, herself to become a professor of economics at Columbia, was one of the few wives invited to attend these meetings but evidently did so only rarely.

In my elementary school days in New York, my mother and grandmother would often read to me: Schiller's *Wilhelm Tell, Maria Stuart,* and *Götz von Berlichingen* (when I was eight, I regaled my father by dismissing him from my room with the words, "Wahnsinniger Jüngling, geh!"), Körner's *Zimri*, Gottfried Keller and Friedrich Raimund. A little later, I began to read French novels (*Madame Bovary, Le Rouge et le Noir*) without fully understanding them, and by the time I was sixteen or so, *War and Peace* and *Anna Karenina, Crime and Punishment* and *The Brothers Karamazov*. Shakespeare, my grandmother insisted, was really at his best in the Schlegel-Tieck translation. As for Milton and Wordsworth, these, my family opined, were "too English," which is to say, too solemn, colorless, Puritanical. In England and the United States these authors (along with Dryden and Pope, Arnold and Tennyson) were obviously considered important but only because readers confined to the English language didn't have the advantages of having grown up on the beauties of Goethe and Schiller, Heine and Fontane, Dante and Leopardi.

At the same time, my parents and grandparents began to "discover" English and American authors. Novelists like Dickens, Thackeray, and George Eliot had always been beloved; now Henry James was added to the list, my father devouring novel after novel with delight and pronouncing James almost as good as Proust, who was his great love. Edith Wharton was read as a lesser but adequate version of James. Such nineteenth-century authors as Emerson and Hawthorne were generally dismissed as provincials or bores, whereas Melville was considered too bizarre, as was, not surprisingly, Faulkner. As for poetry, it was the family consensus that nothing Blake or Coleridge, Yeats or Eliot had written could measure up to the poetry of Goethe or Heine, Baudelaire or Verlaine, the point evidently being that "English is not a musical language" and hence not really suited to poetry. Nor could the English philosophers—Locke, Hume, Bentham—compare to Descartes and Kant, Hegel and Schopenhauer. The British, after all, were mere empiricists. England, so the intellectual refugee scenario went, was blessed with a great political system, a system inherited and improved upon by the United States. One was deeply grateful to live under this system in such an open, democratic country. But for profound thought, one turned to the European continent even as one turned to the continent for great music and art.

The comparatists I cited at the beginning of this essay were obviously much more sophisticated than my amateur relatives, but it is curious how deep-seated their condescension to English and especially to American literature was. True, Geoffrey Hartman became known as a great Wordsworthian and Spitzer wrote on Yeats and Whitman. But continental Europe took pride of place so that when, in the early seventies, Paul de Man (this time not a refugee from fascism but himself a bona fide fascist) emerged as the most celebrated comparatist in the United States, he carried on, ironically enough, the emigré tradition in that, to the best of my knowledge, he never wrote an extended piece on any American literary text even though he lived in this country for some thirty years. De Man's canon—Rousseau, Nietzsche, Baudelaire, Mallarmé, Proust, Kafka, Blanchot, Heidegger—remained wholly what is now called Eurocentric.[4] Indeed, the only American hero, or better, antihero, cited in de Man's work was Archie Bunker.

It is customary today to scorn this Eurocentric canon and to castigate critics like René Wellek as guilty of "cultural imperialism."[5] But for me, as an undergraduate at Oberlin College in the early fifties, the Wellek model seemed, on the contrary, the very model of breadth and depth. I majored in English (Oberlin had no Comp Lit major at the time) but it quickly became apparent to those of us who considered ourselves at all advanced that the exciting courses were not Restoration Literature or Victorian Prose but such Comparative Literature offerings as the seminar called "The Four Theatres," taught by a Spanish exile professor named Centeno, whose first name I don't remember and of whom I have never heard since leaving Oberlin. The Four Theatres were defined according to their different sense of "scale," the relationship of the "characters" to their respective worlds. The "first theatre" was that of Sophocles and Shakespeare, where character was conceived as a "total human soul" and that soul was pitted against, not some paltry human environment, but against nature, the cosmos itself. Lear crying "Hear, Nature, hear!" was its epitome.

The "second theatre" was that of Molière, the theatre of types—the miser, the hypocrite, the impostor—in conflict, not with nature (which would have been out of scale) but with society. The third or "realistic" theatre was that of Euripides and Chekhov: it placed particular individuals in a particular environment and dealt, not with large questions of triumph or failure but with integration and adaptation. And the fourth—to which Centeno himself seems to have been partial—was the theatre of "life forces," of symbolic emanations of being, as in Aeschylus or, more recently, in Pirandello and Lorca. In the latter's *Blood Wedding*, the conflict was not between realistically portrayed individuals but, quite simply, between life and death. Hence Lorca's sparse stage directions: no clocks on mantelpieces, no period furniture, no distinguishing *objets d'art* on side tables. Although many dramatists, Centeno explained, fell between two categories (Ibsen, for instance, was somewhere between #2 and #3), the greatest fault, both for the dramatist and the audience, was to ignore scale and to assume that, say, a Chekhov character like Masha in *The Cherry Orchard*, could be silhouetted against the cosmic order or that Hamlet could dwell in a Chekhovian or Shavian drawing room.

I wrote a term paper for this course comparing two plays that had superficially similar subject matter, Lorca's *House of Bernarda Alba* (fourth theatre) and Chekhov's *Three Sisters* (third). I still remember how thrilled I was that the categories seemed to fit so nicely and that I could compare the plays point by point and come to terms with their structures. In retrospect, what seemed so exciting about Centeno's seminar was that we were working out larger theoretical problems, whereas English Lit courses like Chester Shaver's English Romanticism were more factual and practical. "Why," ran a quiz question in the latter, "did Michael [in Wordsworth's poem by that title] never lift up a single stone?"

The difference between Comp Lit and English Lit, in other words, was that Comp Lit was, from its inception, closely allied with the magic word *theory*. Not theory as we now know it, a discourse often wholly removed from individual literary texts, but Russian Formalist and Prague Linguistic Circle theory, the phenomenology of Roman Ingarden, the philosophy of symbolic forms of Ernst Cassirer and Susanne Langer. Whereas English Lit in these years was still confined to the study of specific periods and authors, Comp Lit was the discipline that asked the big questions: what is literature and literariness? what is the difference between specific genres and forms? how is "image" to be differentiated from "metaphor" and "symbol"? what is a "character"? how do we distinguish "free verse" from prose?

Not surprisingly, then, I wanted to be a Comparatist. But not right away. At Barnard, to which I transferred in my senior year, my transcript was held wanting since I hadn't taken all the English Lit requirements. I found myself taking the second half of eighteenth-century literature with James Clifford at Columbia, Milton with Rosalie Colie, and Chaucer with W. Cabell Greet. All three professors were fine scholars (and Colie, as I later learned, theoretically very sophisticated) but I disliked the courses, perhaps because they were requirements, perhaps because they were designed as vehicles to convey information rather than to raise speculation of any kind. The eighteenth-century survey, for that matter, was little more than a list of names, dates, and titles: the topographical poem one week, "bluestocking" writers the next, and so on.

The upshot of this training was that I decided never to go to graduate school. I managed to stay away for three years, during which time I worked as a movie subtitle writer for Metro-Goldwyn-Mayer and then accompanied my husband to London where he had a Fulbright at the Institute of Cardiology. In London, I had neither employment nor many friends and hence read more than I ever have before or since: all of *A la recherche du temps perdu, Die Wahlverwandschaften*, Roman poetry. By the end of the Fulbright year, we were to move to Washington and graduate school began to seem, after all, an attractive possibility. Comp Lit was what I wanted to study. I had seen, in the Harvard catalogue, a listing for a course called "Proust, Joyce, and Mann" taught by Harry Levin. That, I decided, was my kind of course.

As it turned out, however, I again took a degree in English rather than in Comp Lit. In Washington, the only university that offered a Ph.D. was the Catholic University of America. Georgetown, George Washington, and American University offered only the M,A.; Maryland had temporarily lost its accreditation; and from the perspective of a married woman student of the late fifties, Johns Hopkins was much too far away. An Oberlin professor recommended me to two friends at Catholic University: Craig LaDrière, later in Comparative Literature at Harvard, and Giovanni Giovannini, who was, among other things, a close friend of Ezra Pound's. Both LaDrière and Giovannini regularly called on Pound, then incarcerated at St. Elizabeth's. No doubt, my interest in Pound began here, although it would be many years before I studied the *Cantos* and wrote about them.

During my first semester at Catholic University, I tried to take as many "comparative" courses as possible. The director of the tiny program was Helmut Hatzfeld, known for his work in stylistics, and in the then-fledgling field of literature/art comparison. A one-time disciple of Spitzer's, Hatzfeld was a recent convert to Catholicism, and therein lay my undoing. In Hatzfeld's seminar on French Romanticism, I chose to analyze Alfred de Musset's *La confession d'un enfant du siècle*. I gave what I thought was quite a spirited report on this Romantic autobiography only to be greeted by consternation. "Ja, that is verry interr-esting, Mrs. Pehrloff," said Professor Hatzfeld, "but your tone is problematic. You don't seem to realize that Musset's adultery with George Sand was a sin."

There it was, sin. In Hatzfeld's class, everything was related to sin and redemption. Dostoevsky, we were repeatedly told, was a minor writer because his form of Christianity was nothing but "religiosity," whereas Chateaubriand was a true Christian. Deathbed conversions, for example, Paul Valéry's, were discussed with great relish. As the course went on, I realized I could never work with Professor Hatzfeld.

My other foreign literature class was a Goethe seminar with a priest-professor whose name I can't remember. There were only two students, myself and a young man from Gallaudet, the college for the deaf in Washington. The young man relied completely on my lecture notes and by the second lecture it was obvious that the priest wasn't saying anything so that I would doodle or write, "He isn't saying anything," and the Gallaudet student would look puzzled and shrug his shoulders. By the third week, I had dropped the course.

So began my career as an English doctoral student—on the whole, a happy experience. Catholic University had the advantage of requiring its Ph.D. candidates to have four courses in theory, mostly taught by LaDrière or his disciple, Father William Rooney. In the early sixties when I was in the program (I had taken time off after my M.A. in 1956 and had two children), the New Criticism was still dominant in American universities. But not at Catholic, where critics like Cleanth Brooks and W. K. Wimsatt (the latter said to be a renegade Catholic, having chosen to teach at Yale rather than a Catholic university!) were LaDrière's favorite whipping boys, their fault being that they paid too much attention to meaning at the expense of form. I am still amused today when I hear my colleagues and students dismiss the New Criticism as "mere formalism," because, by the lights of my professors, New Criticism was first and foremost thematically oriented: toward the paradox that lovers can be saints (Donne's "Canonization"), toward Blake's highly complex treatment of the "harlot's cry" in "London," and so on. The Russian Formalists, on the other hand, dealt, not with the isolated poem, but with *poeticity*, with *literariness*, with *sdvig* and *faktura*, with "orientation toward the neighboring word" and "making it strange." We also studied semiotics, linguistics, and rhetoric, this time American: Charles Peirce and Charles Morris (*Signs, Language, and Behavior*), Thomas Sebeok and Kenneth Burke. And behind these names stood the great edifice on which graduate students had to spend a full year: classical critical theory from Plato and Aristotle to Horace and Longinus and Cicero.

Ironically, therefore, it was during my doctoral years (1962–65) at the seemingly restrictive Catholic University that I had my first taste of formalist and structuralist theory, which would take another decade to become prominent in the Ivy League and major state universities. While my friends at Columbia were studying Pope's influence on Johnson, we were debating the merits of generative grammar. Of the five four-hour qualifiying exams, one was on language and linguistics, one on theory, one on English literature in general, one on a special period (mine was the twentieth century) and one on an author outside that period (mine was Jane Austen). I also had two minors: structural linguistics (taught by an anthropologist from the Smithsonian named Wallace Chafe), and American literature, where I had the good fortune to study with

James Hafley, who had written one of the first (and still best) books on Virginia Woolf and was now working on Southern women writers: Eudora Welty, Carson McCullers, and Flannery O'Connor.

My M.A. thesis, directed by Hafley, was on "Privileged Moments in Proust and Virginia Woolf" (a Comp Lit title), but the Ph.D. thesis, directed by Giovannini and LaDrière, dutifully concentrated on an English (or rather Irish) poet, Yeats. Still, its thrust was partly theoretical: namely, a study of the relationship of rhyme to meaning in Yeats's poetry that relied heavily on the prosodic theories of German and English nineteenth and twentieth century critics. So I was launched into the academic world, being asked to teach at Catholic even before I had completed the thesis. I began as an instructor in 1965, teaching, as one did in those days, four courses a semester, one of which was English composition. Within the year, I was substituting for my mentor, Professor Giovannini, teaching the graduate course in modern poetry. At the same time, I was boning up on all the English literature I had never quite learned so that I could teach the "Sophomore Survey" of English literature (Beowulf to the present), using the Norton Anthology.

In retrospect, it strikes me that my relative ignorance of certain "major" English authors was not untypically Comparatist. One of the great strengths of the Eng Lit curriculum was that students came to see the "great" writers as part of a dense literary and historical network that included many lesser lights. Not "Proust, Joyce, and Mann," as in Harry Levin's course, but Joyce in relation to the Irish Jesuit culture in which he grew up and to his reading of Aristotle and Thomas Aquinas, Joyce in relation to the English nineteenth-century novel, Joyce in relation to the photojournalism of his time. Comp Lit, on the other hand, had a way of hitting the high spots only, especially in the days when "AND-" studies dominated the field: Joyce AND Mann, Yeats AND Mallarmé, Wordsworth AND Hölderlin, and so on.

In my early professorial days, I was acutely conscious of the "gaps" in my English Lit training. British academic friends were often dismayed to learn that my knowledge of Dryden was very sketchy and that I had never read the novels of Walter Scott or Elizabeth Gaskell. I often told myself that in my spare time I would fill in these lacunae, but the fact is I didn't. For by the late sixties, I had become very much absorbed in the American poetry of my own time and place. I wrote a book on a contemporary American poet, Robert Lowell, and then four years later on another contemporary American poet of a very different stamp, Frank O'Hara. But even the Lowell book contained a whole chapter on the issue of translation, Lowell having chosen to "imitate" rather than translate literally such poets as Heine and Baudelaire, Montale, and Pasternak. And the O'Hara book was "comparatist" in its focus on the relationship of poetry to the visual arts, so central to this poet's work, as was the influence of Apollinaire and Blaise Cendrars. I had also, by the early seventies, written essays on Yeats and Goethe, on Goethe's *Dichtung und*

Wahrheit and on Pound's debt to Rimbaud, which became the heart of *The Poetics of Indeterminacy: Rimbaud to Cage* (Princeton, 1981).

By this time I had become especially interested in problems of framing and contextualization. Pound's *Cantos*, for example, looked very different when one read them against Rimbaud and Marinetti, from the way they appeared when one read them in the tradition of the Romantics, Browning, and Ruskin. John Ashbery, who had spent a decade of his life in France, made a new kind of sense when one read him as an heir of Reverdy and Roussel rather than as the ephebe of Emerson and Whitman. And so on. At the same time, I found postwar French theory, first the phenomenologists like Jean-Pierre Richard and Jean Starobinski, later Barthes, Todorov, and Derrida, more useful to my purposes than, say, American reader-response theory (Stanley Fish, Norman Holland). For however many arguments Fish could mount that there was no inherent difference between "literary" and "ordinary" language, my own instinct was that such controversies could never be half as interesting as the analysis of what made texts that did purport to be "literary" work as they did.

At the same time, my interest shifted somewhat from individual modernist authors to the Modernist period itself, especially to the years preceding what Guy Davenport has called, in *The Geography of the Imagination*, "the war which extinguished European culture."[6] Like Davenport, I felt and continue to feel that the great experimental period in twentieth-century art and literature was the *avant guerre*, the period suddenly and unexpectedly cut off by World War I. Perhaps I am haunted by this particular period because it marked the decisive end of the *fin de siècle* Vienna which was the seemingly glamorous world of my grandparents. Accordingly, in *The Futurist Moment: Avant-Garde, Avant-Guerre, and the Language of Rupture* (1986), I studied the poetic and aesthetic of one particular "moment," 1913, with respect to its hybrid art forms—collage, artist's book, manifesto, prose-verse mix. But there was no way to understand the aesthetic of the avant-guerre without including Russian works and so I spent a happy summer in an intensive Russian program, trying to master the Byzantine verb forms and cases and then trying to see (in bilingual editions) how Malevich's manifesto style compared to the manifestos of Futurism and Dada.

At the University of Southern California, where I taught between 1977 and 1986, I was given a dual appointment in English and Comparative Literature. Comp Lit at USC was small but I did get to teach courses like "Proust and Joyce" and to include French poets in my Symbolism seminar. Imperceptibly, of course, Comp Lit was undergoing a sea change. More than thirty years had elapsed since the generation of European refugees had come to the United States. The new young American Comparatists could hardly be expected to have the command of languages that characterized their predecessors. Even those educated at the top universities, where the language requirements continued to be rigorous, were more at home in two languages than in three or four. Increasingly, foreign literature was taught in translation, and increasingly, given the theory explosion, Comp Lit became associated with theory. What this meant in practice is that a given university would have an English department that continued to teach the historical periods and genres, whereas Comp Lit tended to become a kind of super-department where the "interesting" and "sophisticated' theory types congregated. The name "Comparative Literature" thus became a complete misnomer, there being little literature studied and even less comparative study.

At the same time, Comp Lit came under attack for its Eurocentricity. In the 1986 report of the Committee on Undergraduate Affairs of the American Comparative Literature Association, the chair, Claus Clüver, announced that "the supranational perspective" Comparative Literature claimed as its own had by and large failed to "challenge the assumptions on which the prevailing institutional model [of the individual national literature] has been based." Indeed, the "Euro-centricity" of the profession had become little more than a cover for the "cultural imperialism" that dogged the field. And since "canons are always ideological constructs perpetuating a system of values that supports the existing power structure,"[7] we must develop ways "to see the other as truly Other. Taking our "clues from Feminist theory," we might, for example, "consider the literary system [Third World Writers] have inherited from the colonizers as an embodiment of patriarchal values. These values are seen to manifest themselves not only in themes of dominance and submission, but also in the whole concept of hierarchical structures and in the Euro-centric view itself."[8] And Clüver concluded: "Ideological criticism...appears altogether one of the most fruitful approaches of the contemporary critical enterprise."[9]

That this "emerging new paradigm" effectively spelled the end of Comp Lit as René Wellek and his colleagues had conceived of it was not immediately clear to those who taught the subject. The proposed revision of the curriculum seemed at first like a simple and much needed opening of the canon, the broadening of the base to include Asian, African, and Latin American literatures. Why, after all, foreground French literature when there was an appreciable "boom" in the Latin American countries? Why Italian literature rather than Japanese or Indian? In the abstract, the demand for the "opening of the field" made perfect sense. As Japan gained prominence in the Western Hemisphere, it seemed odd to make so much more fuss about the literature of small European countries than that of large East Asian ones. Then, too, the new multiculturalism and increasing diversity of the student body could no longer justify the emphasis on the European Continent characteristic of Comp Lit.

How vexed the problem was became clear to me when, in 1986, I accepted an appointment to a professorship at Stanford. I told the Chair of the English department that if I came, I would want a subsidiary appointment in Comp Lit and since, at that time, Comp Lit was a program rather than a department, I was granted a "courtesy" appointment. It meant little since Comp Lit at Stanford had almost no separate courses or separate faculty, relying primarily on cross-listings. A courtesy appointment thus meant that one's courses were sure to be cross-listed in the catalogue. I was satisfied with this arrangement, my chief contact in Comp Lit being the program's former chair, Herbert Lindenberger, whose work on Georg Trakl and Rimbaud had been very important to me when I worked on *Poetics of Indeterminacy*, and whose book on Wordsworth's *Prelude* provided me with a model for the way different critical approaches could be combined. Lindenberger had been one of the people most instrumental in bringing me to Stanford and he had also been my daughter Carey's mentor when she majored in Classics and Comp Lit between 1976 and 1980. I thought, then, that I was in good hands and looked forward to my exchanges with Lindenberger and with another one of my idols now at Stanford, namely Joseph Frank, whose famous essay "Spatial Form in Modern Literature" gave me the idea for my first published essay.

Ironically, all went smoothly until 1988, the year Comp Lit at Stanford finally achieved departmental status. In response to a number of personnel disputes, the then Associate Dean in charge of the Humanities decided to appoint, as co-chairs of the new department, one professor of English and one of German literature, the rationale being that the two professors in question had been active in trying to formulate a possible Comp Lit curriculum and that both wanted greater scope than their respective departments could provide. Once again, then, Comp Lit was to be defined as a "more than" discipline, with the proviso that "more than" was now given a new spin. Membership in the new Comp Lit department was reconceived as a kind of reward for those who felt, understandably enough, that the foreign language departments had lost the prestige they once held in the university. How much of an impact, after all, could a professor of German have in the new multicultural (but no longer multinational, at least so far as the nations of Europe were concerned) American university of the eighties? Solution: put the dissatisfied professor of German (or French or Italian or Slavic) in Comp Lit; never mind that the professor in question might not know another language (or literature). The conduit—and this became the Solution of the Eighties—therefore had to be "theory," but this time around, theory always already in translation. Theory had of course always been central to Comp Lit, but whereas the earlier paradigm foregrounded the relationship between theory and literature, the new theory model was conceived of as an independent field of study, quite aside from its relationship to any literature to which it might be applicable. More important: theory now meant social (primarily Marxist) rather than literary theory: Bourdieu rather than Barthes, Raymond Williams and Stuart Hall rather than Frank Kermode. Thus, while the drones of the English department continued to "do" literature—so the scenario went—those who were *au courant* were debating theoretical issues and arguing as to what Foucault *really* said in *The Archaeology of Knowledge* or what Deleuze and Guattari *really* meant by the "rhizome."

If I found it difficult to participate in this discourse, it was not because I took myself to be in the "literature" rather than the "theory" camp but because the issues that especially interested me (e.g., How did a High Modernist poetic transform itself in the 1930s and again in the 1950s into something rather different? Why is so much "poetry" now written in "prose"? What is the relationship of poetic imagery to video imagery?) could not be tackled by submitting to yet one more analysis of Paul de Man's essay "The Rhetoric of Temporality" or Derrida's "White Mythology." I wanted to explore, not the hermeneutic question ("How do texts mean?") but what Gregory Ulmer called, in his book by that title, *applied grammatology*, with its opening of the field to include the films of Eisenstein and sound texts of John Cage. Again, for me, the general question, "What is painting vis-à-vis writing?" could never be as interesting as the more concrete one, "Why did Malevich turn to 'abstract' painting in 1915 and what does it mean to 'do' abstraction?

Meanwhile, I was getting many more invitations than I could handle to write for "Comparatist" journals and speak at international conferences. Because I had, in *The Futurist Moment*, written on the Italian, Russian, and French avant-garde, I found myself invited to an increasing number of symposia in these individual fields: a conference on Italian Futurism in Rome, one on the Russian avant-garde in Los Angeles, and so on. *The Futurist Moment* was taken up by the *Noigandres* poets in Brazil and has recently been translated into Portuguese. It was reviewed in East German as well as Scandinavian journals and sold especially well in museum bookshops. At the same time, a number of my essays on contemporary poetry were translated and reprinted in French, Italian, and German journals. In one sense, then, I felt I had, so to speak, realized my childhood "comparatist" dream.

What I didn't realize, however, is that the actual practice of comparative literature in which I was now engaged did not accord with the academic institution that had now appropriated the familiar title "Comparative Literature." On the contrary, I was to learn that the historical and formal study of contemporary poetry, and to a lesser extent fiction and drama, was judged to be not quite "serious" enough to be studied in "advanced" courses. When one meant business, one turned, not to Proust or Perec or to Ingeborg Bachmann (old-fashioned comparatists, after all, were known to teach these writers!), but to Foucault and Habermas, Dick Hebdige and Anthony Giddens, Eve Kossofsky Sedgwick and Judith Butler. Thus, just as I had been reprimanded by Helmut Hatzfeld at the Catholic University for treating Musset's adulterous union with George Sand too lightly, I now found myself considered too literary for the Comparative Literature department.

The English department, however, was very supportive, and, in 1990, I received an endowed chair, the Sadie Dernham Patek Professorship of Humanities. When the deans, who were being very solicitous because I had received a prestigious offer from another university, asked me what they could do to keep me at Stanford, I told them that I felt it was time to regularize my Comp Lit status. I was already serving on numerous Comp Lit doctoral committees and dissertations and giving courses like Theory of the Avant Garde or Theory of Lyric, courses which included French, German, Italian, and Russian texts alongside English and American ones and which were taken by students from such varying disciplines as Drama, East Asian Studies, and Art History, not to speak of Comp Lit.

By this time a new Chair had been brought in to run Comp Lit, a professor formerly of the University of Siegen in Germany, who had begun his career as a student of Hans Robert Jauss at Konstanz. As a native German speaker, expert in French, Italian, and Spanish literature and the relevant continental theory, this German professor seemed to the then co-chairs of Comp Lit to be the perfect choice. That a Comp Lit department chair in an American university might have an easier time of it if he or she had at least some acquaintance with the literature and culture of the adopted country was evidently not considered an issue, the Comp Lit emphasis on a German-dominated Continental theory having remained remarkably stable since the days of Spitzer and Auerbach, despite the new call for Third World Studies and multiculturalism. Under the new regime, in any case, the Germanification (or, more properly, the German-theorification) of the Stanford Comp Lit department now proceeded quickly. A faculty seminar was held on Niklas Luhmann's model of Systems Theory. A Comp Lit conference called *Ecriture / Schrift / Writing*, featured, aside from the French Roger Chartier, a contingent of critics almost exclusively German, including Friedrich Kittler and Luhmann himself. It was not long before Comp Lit students were much more familiar with Habermas than with Heine or Hölderlin.

My own relationship to this new version of "the German problem" was equivocal. On the one hand, writing as I now happened to be on the role of World War I in Wittgenstein's *Tractatus*, I was certainly interested in Austrian and German culture and philosophy. On the other, I found a good deal of the New German Theory turgid and pretentious. On the whole, however, I did not connect the choice of Comp Lit guests or symposia to my own role at Stanford. I wanted to be in Comp Lit because I was myself working on what most literary scholars would consider comparative topics, no more nor less. It was not a case of honor or status; I simply took it as a given that *descriptively* I belonged in the Comp Lit department as well as in English. Moreover, the new chairman, evidently at the urging of the deans, assured me that his plan was to bring me into the department, together with another newcomer, the great Russian semiotician/theorist Viacheslav Ivanov, recently arrived at Stanford from the former Soviet Union. Ivanov's "comparatism" belonged to the tradition of the European refugees I spoke of earlier; indeed, together with such other recent arrivals from the Soviet Union as Alexander Zholkovsky and such somewhat earlier Romanian exiles as Matei Calinescu, Virgil Nemoianu, and Mihai

Spariosu, he promised to provide a new and exciting influx into the Comp Lit curriculum. I was honored to be paired with Ivanov and supplied the chairman with the vita he requested.

A few months went by, during which I more or less forgot about the matter, and then one day the chairman of Comp Lit phoned to tell me that my "case" was coming up and he would need samples of my course evaluations and syllabuses. I found this request somewhat puzzling at this stage of my career, but since I had just received absolutely beautiful course evaluations for the "Introduction to Theory" course and the Postmodern Poetics seminar, I sent those over to his office with a set of syllabuses from a variety of courses. It did not occur to me that these syllabuses would be scanned for their ideological content or that the whole procedure was somewhat bogus, my candidacy never having included a faculty lecture or so much as a meeting with interested graduate students and faculty.

At any rate, one morning, a few weeks after the syllabus request, the chairman called in great embarrassment with the news that I had been turned down for membership in the Comp Lit department. I found out later that Ivanov (who has since moved to UCLA) was also turned down. At first, I was simply incredulous: if Ivanov and I were not Comparatists, whom might the label fit? No reasons were ever given me, but, as I was to learn in due course, it seems that we simply didn't "fit the agenda." And what was that agenda? Evidently a projected move toward cultural studies, third world, and minority studies, as well as media studies. That last item should have been right up my alley since my forthcoming book *Radical Artifice* was subtitled *Writing Poetry in the Age of Media*. But it seems, so I later heard via the grapevine, that mine was evidently not the "right" kind of media theory. Moreover—and here was the real caveat—it seems that I was judged neither sufficiently "feminist" nor sufficiently "multicultural."

Absurd as this objection seemed at the time, it now strikes me as not entirely unreasonable, given the earlier anomalies and aporias of the Comp Lit paradigm. The drive toward cultural studies, which has since accelerated in Comp Lit circles around the country, represents what I take to be a kind of logical Endgame for what was never really a separate discipline. Indeed, if no premium was to be put on the knowledge of the so-called "great" literatures and cultures, beginning with those of Greece and Rome and the Hebrew Near East, then Comp Lit could only survive as *an institution* by transforming itself yet again. "Comparative," in this scheme of things, would now refer to the comparison of "high" and "low" cultures, wherever they were to be found. And "literature" would now function in the paradigm "literature-as-only-one-discourse-among-many."

Of course the situation at Stanford was rife with ironies and hypocrisies. That the anti-white hegemonic, anti-imperialist, anti-essentialist, new Comp Lit department was chaired by a white male German, trained in medieval

Romance languages and literatures, who expressed little interest in the literature (as opposed to the theoretical fashions) of his adopted country or, for that matter, in the literature of England in which U.S. literature has its roots, that the members of the Stanford Comp Lit department were almost exclusively middle-aged white men—these factors were tactfully ignored. For of course the real game in town had become not equity or justice but, as Foucault had so well understood, power. Given a large and powerful English department, the issue for Stanford Comp Lit became: who should control the new gender studies: English or Comp Lit? Who would receive a budget line in Native American studies, English or Comp Lit? Which department could claim the agency to teach a course in Agency? English or Comp Lit? And so on.

In my own case, at any rate, the precedent established at Oberlin, Barnard, and Catholic University, the precedent of *wanting* to be "in" Comp Lit but actually being "in" English, has remained operative. And perhaps this has been a good thing, English departments surprisingly being more open to diversity than their more rigid Comp Lit counterparts. Or perhaps not so surprisingly, given the democratic force of the Anglo-American tradition, a tradition that has always been suspicious of the sort of institutional constraints of Continental (especially German) educational theory and practice. Indeed, being "in English" is perhaps not the worst place a Comparatist (even the President of the American Comparative Literature Association, an office I hold at this writing) can be, the margins being quite a good place to observe the function of Comp Lit at the present time. And ironically, as in the postwar period when Comp Lit first became prominent in the United States, it may well be "English" that is hospitably opening its doors to comparative study. Or so it occurred to me just the other day when a prospective graduate student admitted to our English department said that her decision whether to attend Stanford or a rival university would depend on which program had a stronger "comparative component," her desire being to continue the study of French poetics she had begun as an undergraduate at Columbia.

"English with a Comparative Component" may well become a code term for the renewal of literary (as opposed to gender-race-culture) study. And as such, the field seems to be far from dead. Judging from publishers's lists and journals, the "comparison" of different literatures is once again flourishing, the irony being that those who are doing the "comparing" tend to be, as they were long before Comp Lit was institutionalized, the writers themselves. Just as Joyce studied Norwegian so that he could read Ibsen, so the American poet Lyn Hejinian has studied Russian so that she could read and translate the poetry of Arkadii Dragomoschenko and, conversely, the Russian poet Alexei Parschchikov, now at Stanford, is working on his English so that he can translate Lyn Hejinian and Michael Palmer. Michael Palmer, in turn, has tapped into his native Italian (the family name was Palmieri), which he never learned properly until he was grown-up, so that he could translate the great contemporary poet Andrea Zanzotto. Again, the best single anthology of experimental American poetry now in print may well be the French *49 + 1*, edited by Emmanuel Hocquard and Claude Royet-Journoud at Royaumont. And, in what is perhaps the most important development in comparative studies, the break-up of the Soviet bloc has produced, for the first time in half a century, the possibility of real exchange with East European literatures. The program initiated by Jonathan Brent at Northwestern University Press is a case in point: from the reissuing of the *Diaries* of Witold Gombrowicz to the novels of Danilo Kis, a whole new body of literature is now entering our world. At the moment, it is being read largely in translation, but this may change as contacts are expanded. One of our finest graduate students is writing a thesis on the problems of closure in postmodernism, using as her examples both American models and those of her native Yugoslavia. But—and here is another irony—this student belongs, not to Comp Lit, but to the MTL (Modern Thought and Literature) program.

The literary curriculum, we know, is never innocent; it always has a political dimension, a certain ideological charge. But we don't often stop to think that the "political unconscious" takes many forms. One of the spin-offs of Japanese global power today is that in cities like New York, performances of Noh theatre, of Kabuki, and Bunraku now take place side by side with performances of Shakespeare and Shaw. The study of such forms and of related works in dance, painting, architecture, and literature is bound to become part of our curriculum, and I would venture the guess that such study will have greater staying power than the current preoccupation with "Asian-American" (at best, a patronizing category, lumping together as it does such disparate cultures as Chinese-American, Korean-American, and Vietnamese-American) studies. Indeed, as I was watching a performance of the amazing Bunraku puppets recently, it occurred to me that this theater's extreme stylization of gesture might shed interesting light on Roland Barthes's aesthetic (see the chapter on Bunraku in *L'Empire des signes*) or, closer to home, on a recent performance piece by John Cage called *One6*, in which a sculptural installation by Mineko Grimmer becomes the locus for the complex sound play produced by ice melting and pebbles falling into a water tank, to the accompaniment of a single note, played with long intervals of silence, on the violin. But as I was mentally working out the relationship among Bunraku, Barthes, and Cage, I had a sudden shock of recognition. Wasn't Bunraku the perfect exemplar of Centeno's "fourth theatre" as we had studied it at Oberlin? And, if so, where did Kabuki fit in? Was that perhaps the second theatre? To ask such questions is perhaps the heart of the comparatist enterprise, an enterprise that will happily outlive its current institutional formations.

NOTES

1. René Wellek and Austin Warren, *Theory of Literature*, 3d ed. (New York: Harcourt, Brace and World, 1956), p. 49.

2. René Wellek, "The Crisis of Comparative Literature" (1958), in Wellek, *Concepts of Criticism*, ed. Stephen G. Nichols, Jr. (New Haven and London: Yale University Press, 1963), p. 283.

3. Ibid., p. 282.

4. De Man's writings on Wordsworth, Shelley, and Yeats, much cited as they are, don't really contradict this pattern, since they are used primarily to support theoretical arguments (e.g., the famous discussion of the last stanza of Yeats's "Among School Children") that foreground continental philosophy.

5. See for example, Claus Clüver, "Third-World Literatures in the Canon of Undergraduate Curricula," *ACLA Newsletters: American Comparative Literature Association*, 17, no. 2 (Winter 1986): 9–17, p. 10. Subsequently cited as CC.

6. Guy Davenport, *The Geography of the Imagination* (San Francisco: North Point Press, 1981), p. 314.

7. Clüver, p. 13.

8. Ibid., p. 15.

9. Ibid., p. 16.

12

Self-Portrait in the Unembellished Mode

Herbert Lindenberger

INTERLOCUTOR: Was it all that different when you began?

AUTHOR: Like the difference between urban America right after the Second World War and the way it is today. Less dangerous, more predictable, less interesting.

INTERLOCUTOR: And you feel no nostalgia for the time you started in this field?

AUTHOR: Nostalgia's not in my character.

INTERLOCUTOR: What made it different from now?

AUTHOR: There were only two models available, in English studies at least—the old positivistic method, which is where the old farts hung out, and the New Criticism, which was what one identified with, and of course that's become the place for the old farts today. Like with any style—whether in art, or clothes, or food.

INTERLOCUTOR: How did you decide what you were going to identify with if it was always going out of date?

AUTHOR: I suspect one chooses by people more than ideas. When you think you're embracing ideas you are actually embracing people you happen to find appealing—teachers, fellow students, writers who seduce you with their style. But things didn't date nearly as fast in the old days as they do now. In the over forty years since I started graduate work we've moved from a written to an oral academic culture.

INTERLOCUTOR: Explain what you mean.

AUTHOR: There was much less communication then. Long-distance phoning was once prohibitively expensive—and so was air travel. In fact, when I began, it was still common to cross the country by train, which, since I was on the West Coast, meant four nights to New York. You pretty much sat at home and read and meditated, and hopefully there were a few colleagues to talk to. Today there's an incessant movement from one conference to another at each of which, by the last day, you've managed to bond with a whole new set of characters with whom you can now mutually arrange letters for promotion, job offers, book acceptances, and, for that matter, more conferences. The intellectual world in which I began would look pretty provincial, perhaps even unbelievable, to anybody today.

INTERLOCUTOR: You liked it better before?

AUTHOR: I'm not making value judgments, just describing historical differences that, as I see it, also amount to cultural differences. Today knowledge in the so-called humane sciences is no longer produced according to some ancient model of prolonged, silent meditation but by means of interpersonal contact, whether electronic, face-to-face, or even (dare I say?) sexual.

INTERLOCUTOR: You're making more value judgments than you claimed to, and you also seem to be confounding academic novels with the real world.

AUTHOR: I wouldn't know since I don't read those things.

INTERLOCUTOR: But you wrote one yourself—*Saul's Fall*, I mean.

AUTHOR: If that's how you care to classify it. You could as well call it a piece of critical theory—or as I myself suggested dubbing it in the text itself, an "anatomy" of genres and rhetorical situations. But I certainly never saw myself writing an academic novel, much though I like to observe and comment on what I've seen go on around me, just as I've been commenting to you. In any case I intended that book to resist any easy classification.

INTERLOCUTOR: That's fine with me if that's what you wanted. But as we speak I sense you're wanting to resist anything that others—or at least I—suggest.

AUTHOR: I confess I've always found it easier to resist rather than embrace ideas, as well as the people identified with them. I feel most comfortable being against the grain.

INTERLOCUTOR: You mean you see yourself as oppositional, revisional?

AUTHOR: I don't use those terms—they're the most establishment of establishment terms today. These are the slogans of people who want the satisfaction of feeling rebellious yet are only too content to follow the pack, like certain dog breeds. Sorry, chumminess is no more my style than nostalgia.

INTERLOCUTOR: Then how did you ever manage to shape a career in *this* profession? Surely you must have recognized long ago that being a literary scholar meant being part of an ongoing, collective enterprise in which you submit yourself to mutual giving and taking.

AUTHOR: You're feeding me the traditional justification that covers up the power relationships and machinations guiding what we call intellectual work. But let me approach this from a different angle. In recent years I've tried to investigate this very thing, figuring out precisely how institutions work—and not just academic institutions. I've even been giving a seminar called "Literature and Institutions," and this was, in fact, one of the issues that my last book, *The History in Literature*, was centered around—how institutional pressures of all sorts are implicated in the writing of literature and the writing of criticism.

INTERLOCUTOR: Did you ever imagine thinking about this when you started your career?

AUTHOR: Not in the least, but then I've always conceived of myself as wanting to deal with problems, or with what I saw as problematic, though at the beginning it was the problems I thought I saw *in* literature rather than, as now, what is problematic about the whole process by which literature is created, demarcated, defined, disseminated. But as I said before, the world of forty years ago seems grossly naive in retrospect. Naive in the Schiller sense, which meant you weren't selfconscious enough to figure out why you were doing the things you did.

INTERLOCUTOR: How was it you chose to go into literature?

AUTHOR: You make those decisions in late adolescence when you have a lot of psychological tensions you want to explain to yourself. Literature, especially the literature of the last century or two, seemed to offer explanations, or at least certain consolations.

INTERLOCUTOR: Then how was it you first thought of doing Comparative Literature? Did that provide better consolations than, say, English or some other national literature?

AUTHOR: The idea for Comparative Literature came to me well before I had any notions of what studying literature might do for me. I was somewhere between twelve and fourteen and walking along the top of

Capitol Hill in Seattle, where I'd grown up. I'd vaguely heard the term Comparative Literature, which was supposed to mean reading several literatures in the original language. So I said to myself—maybe that's what I want to do when I grow up since I happened to have some languages on me.

INTERLOCUTOR: How extraordinary! And you knew that early where you intended to go?

AUTHOR: Not in the least. I promptly forgot about that just as I forgot about all the other possible careers that flitted through my mind in subsequent years—newspaperman, book reviewer, magazine editor, actor, movie director.

INTERLOCUTOR: Such verbal professions! Did you never consider law or medicine or business?

AUTHOR: Law yes, but that came later—after I'd been settled in academia. During my undergraduate days I associated all of these careers with people whom I took to be, shall we say, not particularly cultivated? None of these standard vocations seemed to me to be particularly noble.

INTERLOCUTOR: Noble! Acting, editing! Surely you've got your priorities a bit confused.

AUTHOR: These all had to do with art, or some form of artfulness. I've since learned better.

INTERLOCUTOR: Then how did you come to reject those other verbal trades?

AUTHOR: I went to Antioch College, where you worked part of each year, so I tried out a number of things. My senior year I had a great newspaper job, but the people there drank too much, and the writing, though I found it great fun, was too quick and unreflective. Earlier, I had tried out the media by being a page-boy for NBC in New York, which meant I could stand in uniform for a season of Toscanini's concerts carrying smelling salts in case some lady in the audience fainted. Later I was a copy boy at United Press in Washington—something designed for Antioch students as a sort of internship—and this got me into things like Harry Truman's press conferences, but the Washington world seemed too glitzy for me to want to make a career of it. I also needed to satisfy what one called one's social conscience in those days, so I did unskilled factory work and tried (unsuccessfully) to organize a union. But social causes in those early years of the Cold War seemed hopeless. By my junior year I opted for literary study, which seemed the only noble thing you could do, except to write the literature itself.

INTERLOCUTOR: And then you decided to apply to graduate school?

AUTHOR: Well, to Harvard and Yale, which seemed the only respectable places in Comp Lit at the time, but I didn't get in, so I decided to try for publishing or the media after all. And probably that's where I would have landed, or I might have continued the fiction- and play-writing I'd been fooling around with until I could make some success of them, except the month I finished college the Korean War broke out and I desperately needed a draft deferment. I promptly enrolled—on a month's notice—in a brand-new Comp Lit program at the University of Washington, where I could go free of charge and live with my parents till the war was over.

INTERLOCUTOR: You owe your career, I see, to an accident of history.

AUTHOR: But aren't all decisions made like that? In fact, as I look back, I'd say my whole career has been a series of improvisations with nothing leading inexorably anywhere else. If I'd written this in the form of an ordinary essay, I suspect I'd have felt the need to concoct a narrative—something to show, say, how the seeds of later ideas were planted in some incident or other during graduate school or earlier, or how one day some vision opened up that set the path for everything I've thought or written since.

INTERLOCUTOR: And what was it like doing Comp Lit in those days?

AUTHOR: Remember I went to a rather backward place, especially in the foreign languages. English at the University of Washington had a certain vitality because it was one of the first departments to institute the New Criticism. But that too was provincial. Comp Lit had little identity of its own. Later on when I developed my own Comp Lit programs, I decided their real justification was to provide theoretical underpinnings for literary study as a whole. But in my graduate days Comp Lit justified itself simply as a clearinghouse between literary traditions that otherwise had no contact with one another. In those days if you were one of the few identified with Comp Lit, you immediately excited the suspicion of everybody in the various individual national literatures. These people seemed all-powerful, and I quietly declared myself their enemy. One was always under suspicion. Could you possibly be "expert," they believed, in any author or period (let alone a whole national literature) in the way that a "real" scholar was? In the early 1950s Comp Lit had none of the glamour it enjoys today. But somewhere about twenty years ago, when the Stanford Comp Lit secretary handed me a *New Yorker* sketch by Woody

Allen about a pretentious young woman doing Comparative Literature—
that day I knew the field had arrived.

INTERLOCUTOR: How did you manage dealing with all the traditional literary scholars around you?

AUTHOR: You practiced the double-voicedness that minority groups
supposedly cultivate to survive. Except for us it was more a triple- or
quadruple-voicedness. The people in English wanted to hear you mouth
the moral meanings emanating from a text, the Germanisten expected
to hear you link their texts to some anomalous German spirit, the French
simply wanted to hear your accent, which for me at least got worse the
harder I tried. Every dog, after all, has its lair to guard.

INTERLOCUTOR: You aren't showing a lot of charity, whether to
persons long since dead or, for that matter, to dogs.

AUTHOR: Let me assure you of my affection for my own, late beagle
Mickey, who sniffed a large proportion of the people studying literature
at Stanford during his all-too-brief ten years.

INTERLOCUTOR: I understand the need you must have felt to develop
disguises, and that's precisely what you're doing with me right now. Just
tell me directly, were there no redeeming qualities to your studies?

AUTHOR: One or two courses, though I don't complain, since people
of my generation who went to even the best graduate schools expressed
the same disappointment. Is it possible that disappointment is simply built
into the framework of formal study?

INTERLOCUTOR: Maybe you should tell me about your good
experiences.

AUTHOR: There was first of all the reading I did on my own—most
importantly the German romance scholars—Curtius, Spitzer, Auerbach—
since they had a breadth missing in the provincial world in which I was
studying. Today of course we complain of their Eurocentrism or of their
bias in favor of "high" art, but that's beside the point since they
commanded a range you rarely find even among those today who've moved
beyond Europe or broken down the barrier between "high" and "low."

INTERLOCUTOR: If you heard yourself talking, you might recognize
yourself chanting the characteristic litany of the aging as they look back
nostalgically to their good old days.

AUTHOR: I never said they were good. They weren't good at all. I
merely named exceptions—but these exceptions were good enough that
I've tried to keep these Romance scholars alive for my students—to the
point even of co-editing a volume of Spitzer's essays just a few years ago.

INTERLOCUTOR: To get back to your student years: was there nothing in your coursework that you can remember with any shall-we-say charity?

AUTHOR: Two courses maybe. Certainly a fine seminar my first year from Arnold Stein on *Paradise Lost*—essentially an attempt to look at the poem from the point of view of the New Criticism, which of course had been resisting Milton.

INTERLOCUTOR: And did Milton fit?

AUTHOR: That hardly mattered. At least I learned something about how intellectual frameworks operate—how some things fit and others don't and how you tinker with them to make things fit the way you want them to fit. It helped break down the illusion you have when you're young that all knowledge is there already and all you can do is learn it and apply it obediently to other things.

INTERLOCUTOR: You said there was another course.

AUTHOR: Oh yes, and that was the most important of all. It was when Northrop Frye visited the University of Washington the summer of 1951. That was the end of my first year of graduate work. He was thinking out *Anatomy of Criticism*, though he didn't seem aware of that at the time. I know he later considered that summer an intellectual breakthrough since he asked his biographer to have me describe the seminar.

INTERLOCUTOR: It's refreshing to hear something from you so positive.

AUTHOR: Actually I was very negative during the first half of Frye's seminar—in fact fought the teacher with every exception I could muster up to the examples he was giving. You see, I'd been indoctrinated into a New Critical world while still an undergraduate and all of this was reinforced by the New Critical department I was in—I never really took seriously the positivistic approach that reigned in my French courses or the *Geistesgeschichte* in the German.

INTERLOCUTOR: But didn't you recognize Frye for what many people see him as today—as just an extension of the New Criticism?

AUTHOR: That's only if you look back in time, and I'm none too sure if I go along with that. Retrospectively, all sorts of things that seemed different at the time they happened later come to exhibit underlying similarities. What mattered to me was the difference, since Frye was working out a theory—and with vast numbers of charts on the blackboard. Every seminar session he started with his fourfold chart of Blake's geography:

Eden

Beulah

———

Generation

Ulro

Note the line between Beulah and Generation, since that separates Blake's higher from his lower worlds. In the course of any seminar session he moved through the whole of literature—the Bible, Virgil, Dante, Spenser, Shakespeare, Coleridge, Eliot, and vast numbers of other writers—to fit their characteristic imagery (and this was the word he always used for what he saw as the central verbal unit in literature) to a single, larger scheme that Blake typified for him. You see, Frye was extending his earlier study of Blake to a general theory of literature, and I was acting skeptical—to the point of making myself thoroughly obnoxious in class— mouthing the various New Critical clichés about the uniqueness of the individual work of art, its organic wholeness, its refusal to allow itself to be co-opted by some large, capacious theory. By concentrating on the differences I saw between works (we said "works" in those days, not "texts"), I was always able to find some exception to the theories he was voicing. The seminar pretty much turned into a dialogue between us.

INTERLOCUTOR: He must have felt tempted to throw you out of class.

AUTHOR: I wouldn't know since he was unendingly patient with me. But something happened in the middle of that summer. It suddenly dawned on me that the thinking that Frye engaged in was wholly different from anything I'd ever been trained to do, that no matter how sure I was of my own notions, these notions belonged to only a single, limited category, that this mode of thought was not nearly as "natural" as I took it to be. And so the seminar turned into an important lesson—doubtless the most important lesson I learned from any course I took. It was from Frye that learned to think theoretically.

INTERLOCUTOR: And you became a Frye disciple?

AUTHOR: God no! At the end of the summer I went into Frye's office and told him what had happened to me—that smack in the middle of the course he'd convinced me he was really on to something—to something important, in fact. But I added I had no intention of becoming a disciple. His ideas, I said, would be badly served that way—and he fully assented, adding, "I certainly don't want disciples." Which made me feel pretty good, and let me say I've always disapproved of teachers imposing their egos on their students.

INTERLOCUTOR: Still, you must have seemed insufferable to Northrop Frye. How old were you at the time?

AUTHOR: Twenty-two, but he obviously took me for younger the way I acted. When I made tenure many years later, a senior colleague broke confidentiality to the point of telling me that Frye began his letter as referee by citing his memory of me as a "precocious eighteen-year-old."

INTERLOCUTOR: Whether you were eighteen or twenty-two, we're half way through this interview and have never even got you started on your career proper. You are dawdling à la Shandy.

AUTHOR: Listen, I came close to never having a career at all, or at least an academic career. That's where my flirtation with law came in. I raced through graduate work writing the quickest thesis I could possibly think up, and of course they passed it, though I shall always respect one of my readers for signing his name only on condition I never try to publish it.

INTERLOCUTOR: Do I dare ask what you wrote about?

AUTHOR: It was on Georg Trakl, who was not yet so well known in those days. I'd come across his poetry during a Fulbright year I spent in Vienna. The thesis was an undigested mishmash of Heidegger (who'd recently picked Trakl as one of his pets), of Frye (who'd taught me to think intertextually, though we never used that term then), and the New Criticism (where I'd learned how to read poems, or at least to read poems with a certain set of biases).

INTERLOCUTOR: But you *did* publish that thesis after all, despite your teacher's prohibition.

AUTHOR: That was twelve years later, and anyhow my teacher was dead. Let me assure you the book had little to do with the thesis, from which I was able to retain only one sentence—a metrical analysis of a few Trakl lines—so I speculated that the only part of your mind that's mature by age twenty-five is your ear for language. Otherwise it was a totally new, though relatively unambitious project.

INTERLOCUTOR: And how do you justify doing what you call a quickie thesis, especially since you're known to boast about how slow you write?

AUTHOR: You see, I was not convinced at that point I could stand being committed to an academic career, particularly if I had to teach in the sort of place people from my graduate school were likely to end up at in those days—Oregon State, Idaho State, or some other ex-normal school. I knew I'd appear intellectually arrogant in that context, with the likelihood of being fired early my first year. I'd finished graduate work in four years, and if I didn't get to a respectable place right away I decided I'd go to law school since by that time my notions about the inherent nobility of humanistic study were fast wearing off.

INTERLOCUTOR: How early to feel disillusioned! But surely your students over the years weren't aware of this.

AUTHOR: I'm a bit like Unamuno's priest San Manuel Bueno, who hid his atheism from his parishioners.

INTERLOCUTOR: What happened to law school then?

AUTHOR: A decent job—or what I thought would be a decent job—fell into my lap without any effort on my part. I was hired to a not-yet-opened campus of the University of California, the one at Riverside.

INTERLOCUTOR: And everything worked out after all?

AUTHOR: Yes and no. The first two years I got to teach a single, one-semester literature course per year out of six courses, the rest being beginning German and freshman English. The literature course was a kind of introduction to theory, though we called it simply criticism in those days. I still teach this course to undergraduates—though of course I've let it evolve. But I keep a section on the history of *Hamlet* interpretation that was there from the first time I taught the course in 1954; it was meant to problematize the whole problem of interpretation, and the idea seems more current than ever now.

INTERLOCUTOR: You must have been glad you stayed in the profession.

AUTHOR: One interesting course out of six wasn't nearly enough to sustain a career. I started an undergraduate Comp Lit program, but the students with the necessary language background were too few. Frankly I felt useless and bored to death and wondering what to do with my life. During my first two years I kept intending to apply to law school (I'd picked Boalt at Berkeley), but somehow it was too painful having to become a student again. So I knew the only way out, despite a back-breaking teaching schedule, was to find a project that could engage me. A colleague who worked primarily on Dr. Johnson was teaching Wordsworth's *Prelude* in an introductory literature course, and he asked me to discuss some passages with him. He said he'd been unable to find any useful critical commentary on the poem. When we'd finished the conversation, he told me I must write a book on *The Prelude*. Since I had nothing better to do, I went at it. Luckily I'd never had a formal course in English romanticism, which meant I had no antiquated knowledge to cast off.

INTERLOCUTOR: Had you been attracted to Wordsworth before?

AUTHOR: No more than to a lot of other writers. But I loved mountains. So I spent the following summer in an idyllic retreat north of Seattle doing nothing except repeated readings of two books, *The Prelude* and the *Philosophical Investigations* of Wittgenstein, which curiously fed on each other.

INTERLOCUTOR: I never had the impression that Wittgenstein played any role in your book.

AUTHOR: I never mentioned him, since I didn't use him directly. But I now realize that this tandem reading of Wittgenstein / Wordsworth was precisely what I needed to loosen up the thinking process. Mulling over the Investigations reinforced and confirmed the skepticism I'd always been tempted by—a skepticism toward any enterprise that pushed for big truths and essences, which meant that everything I'd learned, including Frye's big truths, could be put to the test. And Wittgenstein also sharpened my sensitivity to language in a way that the by-now-quite-rigid New Criticism had been unable to do.

INTERLOCUTOR: But didn't you also have to do some homework on Wordsworth and romanticism besides reading a contemporary philosopher?

AUTHOR: I left that for later—if I'd done the homework first I'd probably have written a thoroughly conventional book. The next summer I scrounged through many shelves of the Berkeley library reading up what had been "done" on Wordsworth and the other English Romantics, and along the way I also tried to recapture Wordsworth's own reading in many long-forgotten eighteenth-century poets. People in those days wondered why I'd ever choose a poet like Wordsworth to work on since Romanticism was very out of fashion. My friends in English (except for the colleague who told me I must write the book) thought I was wasting my talent when it'd be so much more interesting to work on, say, a Metaphysical poet or on Faulkner or Joyce. Still, the body of scholarship I had to work my way through was so dull—or at least so out of date—that I felt the latitude to do something new. My original intent was to do what we then called a close critical reading of *The Prelude*, but after a chapter and a half I'd exhausted that vein—

INTERLOCUTOR: You mean you covered a fourteen-book poem in such short shrift?

AUTHOR: No, I simply gave the poem some suggestive—and highly evaluative—jabs à la Leavis. But since I'd come to see a critical method as just a framework that you think your way through and nothing you "believe" in as such (maybe this was the Wittgenstein legacy), I decided to try placing the poem within some other frameworks that interested me at the time—for example, Curtius's *topoi*, Poulet's time-consciousness, Lukács's version of the political unconscious.

INTERLOCUTOR: What heterogeneous components!

AUTHOR: That hardly mattered! Or you might say the more heterogeneous the better for my purposes. To me the whole thing was above all an exercise in the possibilities of critical thinking. I wasn't even too much concerned as to whether I'd "illuminated" the text I was supposedly writing about. And I managed quite to forget about law school.

INTERLOCUTOR: How did you redirect your career?

AUTHOR: I improvised as usual without planning out my moves very far. Of course I was now, from an institutional point of view, a specialist in English Romanticism, and various universities called me to solicit my interest in positions they had to offer in that area. The idea of spending the rest of my life twiddling around with the six poets deemed canonical in those days was more than I cared to contemplate, and I reminded all inquirers that my training and my interests took me in other directions.

INTERLOCUTOR: Where did you go from Wordsworth?

AUTHOR: To Georg Büchner. I'd put six years into Wordsworth, and now I wanted a less demanding project that I could finish in a year or two.

INTERLOCUTOR: What attracted you to Büchner?

AUTHOR: First, he'd written very little when he died at twenty-three so I felt I could quickly master a handful of texts (they turned out to be harder than I thought). Second, I liked his politics, which is something you can't say about many canonical writers (his politics also turned out to be more complicated than I thought). Third, I felt haunted by the French Revolution, which of course brought Wordsworth and Büchner together for me (the relation of the Revolution to subsequent writers turned out to be trickier than I thought).

INTERLOCUTOR: By then, surely, you must have seen yourself headed for some larger book on Romanticism—I don't just mean the English variety, but European Romanticism as a whole.

AUTHOR: Yes, after the Büchner I knew I should be writing that sort of book—something that would bring together Wordsworth, Shelley, Scott, Kleist, Hölderlin, Büchner, and a whole slew of others. But studies in the Romantics—this was the mid-1960s—had moved in a direction I didn't feel any too comfortable with: too introspective, Heideggerian, consciousness-ridden. That wasn't where I belonged, so I bided my time for a while writing plays. Then I got a Guggenheim to write the book on Romanticism that I was supposedly destined to write.

INTERLOCUTOR: Why didn't you write it?

AUTHOR: I balked. I sat in the library going about it according to the schedule I'd submitted for the grant, but this was the summer of 1968, and there were other things on people's minds, and certainly on my own. I found myself zeroing in on the new theories of history, as well as the new forms of historical writing, that had developed during the Romantic period, and above all I noted the pressure of actual historical events on those who were rethinking history at the time. The pressure of real events on the streets of Paris, Prague, Chicago that spring and summer made this just the thing to be reading.

INTERLOCUTOR: Obviously you chose not to observe the traditional model of scholarship as cool and detached contemplation.

AUTHOR: That model had its own historical roots in a far more quiet time. Just the same I felt detached enough to note the events of that year as performances little different in kind from the sort of history one saw performed on actual stages. Next thing I knew I was writing not the period study of Romanticism for which I'd been given a grant but rather a genre study of historical drama—but I shouldn't call it a genre study since that sounds much more traditionally literary than I meant it to be, since I was really using history plays to explore borderlines—between drama and narrative, between public and private, between what we call literature and what we call reality.

INTERLOCUTOR: It's proving hard to pin down any continuities in your work. How do you justify doing a project like *Saul's Fall* right after that book?

AUTHOR: I've never had sufficient patience to establish continuities. To keep from feeling automatized, I've had to keep developing new seminars, new undergraduate courses as well, all these years. One's personal evolution is like literary evolution the way the Russian formalists described it. And that's why both in my writing and in my teaching I've moved back and forth among various languages, periods, genres, media. And I suppose that's why I'm so uncomfortable with the way ideas get developed within groups: you're too busy having to defend a single idea, a single perspective, as well as the people in the group, even after they've all ceased to be interesting.

INTERLOCUTOR: Fine, I'll stop badgering you and I'll settle for the fragmented image with which you seek to represent yourself.

AUTHOR: But in the case that you just brought up there actually *were* continuities, though not quite what you might think. For one thing, after working six years on history plays I found myself thinking about the more extravagant, histrionic side of historical drama, and before I knew it I'd moved—quite naturally, wouldn't you say?—into opera, which was supposed to be the subject of my next book.

INTERLOCUTOR: But that *wasn't* your next book.

AUTHOR: No, but I got an NEH to write what I thought would be a poetics of opera, though almost as soon as I started work, I was asking myself about the relations between historical drama and opera and before I knew it I was writing a history play of my own that was meant to be as operatic in nature as possible. That was *Saul's Fall*.

INTERLOCUTOR: You've lost me. I never thought of it as a play, though I know that there was a play embedded in there.

AUTHOR: The play came first, but I didn't quite know what to do with it—it was too bizarre to perform. So I created a context for it, invented an author, created a larger bunch of writings he'd written, gave him an editor, critical commentaries, and made a huge Norton sort of edition out of all this. Without quite thinking it out beforehand, I'd found a way of trying out a whole bunch of genres, literary or critical or both at once. In fact, the book was intended—or at least it ended up seeming intended— to be read at once as a novel or as a piece of literary theory. Again, you see, I was playing with borderlines, this time the borders between what we call literature and what we call criticism.

INTERLOCUTOR: Obviously you *do* have your continuities, namely an obsession with borderlines.

AUTHOR: Or maybe just questioning other people's ideas of what constitutes a border. But don't think I'm always going against the grain. I actually finished the opera book that I got the grant for, though not until a number of years later. In retrospect, each of these three books seemed to lead naturally into the next, but that's of course only if one glances backward. That's what I was trying to say earlier: everything can be made to seem inevitable in retrospect. So now when I look back from *The History in Literature*, I tell myself that it too had its roots in the preceding book. What had started out as a poetics of opera (and certainly also remained that) had opened into an inquiry into how an exotic and irrational entertainment, to cite Johnson's famous terms of abuse, was actually embedded in history and could also speak out as history.

INTERLOCUTOR: And now you yourself decided to let history speak out for itself?

AUTHOR: That's a bit overblown, but there's no question that the word *history* was the key term of the 1980s for most of us. The NEH grant I had for that book was for a project originally entitled "Social and Historical Factors in Criticism," and for once I think I actually wrote the book to which I had committed myself and at the appropriate time. But not quite in the way I'd first intended. As I started, I found it hard to sustain a single argument, so I went about writing a series of independent essays, things I could try out as lectures or as contributions to collections. After several years of this, it occurred to me that these essays, if set in the right order and made to relate explicitly to one another, together constituted the argument I'd been looking for in the first place. And then it also occurred to me that that's what my earlier books really were like even when they pretended to be sustained arguments.

INTERLOCUTOR: What were you arguing in the essays?

AUTHOR: Not so much arguing, I suspect, as exploring—matters such as the processes by which literary values have been shaped, or by which canons have been perpetuated, or by which literary institutions have created the conditions both for the writing and the mediation of texts.

INTERLOCUTOR: Sounds like pretty fashionable late 1980s stuff.

AUTHOR: I admit I felt more at home intellectually in the '80s than I ever did before.

INTERLOCUTOR: I see you're not so down on fashion as you pretend.

AUTHOR: Fashions are fine as long as you know they're fashions. Which means you can create them, wear them, dump them.

INTERLOCUTOR: And now you finally found yourself identified with a group, namely the New Historicism.

AUTHOR: Not in the least. In fact, I never used that term. I said "new history" for what I was advocating though of course I shared certain key assumptions with those who called themselves New Historicists. The dangers of group action were brought home to me a few years ago while I was on the *PMLA* editorial board and we were faced with a polemical piece attacking feminist Shakespeare criticism. Though I disagreed with much in that piece, I thought it needed to be printed in order to stimulate discussion. After it had appeared, twenty-four people, some of whom I greatly admire and one of whom was my former student, signed a letter not simply taking issue with the article but slapping the editorial board for its bad political judgment in even allowing it to be printed. They were acting like packhounds.

INTERLOCUTOR: You're being uncharitable to dogs again.

AUTHOR: Though I actually felt some sympathy with the group's own politics, I also recognized what must be a generational gap between them and me. Let me assure you, I took myself to be politically correct long before anybody ever thought up a concept by that name, but I'll be damned if I join any bandwagon now that the concept exists.

INTERLOCUTOR: Finally you're willing to act your age.

AUTHOR: It may well be that people have to act in groups the way they do to survive in academia—or at least the way it's been the past twenty years or more.

INTERLOCUTOR: So what do you do when the young ask you to sponsor them in this profession?

AUTHOR: I hate to undeceive them if they can't imagine themselves doing anything different (they're often too rigid to imagine other satisfactions in life), but as I've watched this spectacle over the years I've kept wondering how anybody is fool enough to undertake graduate study in the humanities—an undefined number of years being a student and putting off any sort of grown-up life; floating from one temporary job to another; struggling to get into some journal or a conference that will allow you to meet somebody who can get you into some other journal or to some later conference; and maybe, once your hair is white and your spirit thoroughly broken, finding a tenure-track job in some God-forsaken place like South Dakota.

INTERLOCUTOR: Your cynicism sounds strange coming from somebody who's had your luck.

AUTHOR: My generation got off easy. These others did not.

INTERLOCUTOR: I assume you are content now that you didn't do law.

AUTHOR: Not really.

INTERLOCUTOR: What is it that's still bugging you?

AUTHOR: A feeling that there's always quicksand underneath everything we write and teach. One day not too long ago it occurred to me that we are all rhetoricians and that that's all we amount to, though we manage superbly to put on airs that we are something considerably more than that. Yes, we' re nothing but rhetoricians defending whatever grand cause or idea we think to identify with. We all come to see ourselves as oppressed minorities of one sort or another, and it's no wonder we expend our best energies lashing out preemptively against any group we think might threaten our space.

INTERLOCUTOR: How are lawyers any less rhetoricians than you people are?

AUTHOR: Lawyers make no pretense to be otherwise. Still, as I've thought about it over the years, I realize that if I'd made the change into law, it's possible, maybe even likely, I would have ended up teaching in a law school.

INTERLOCUTOR: So what's the difference, I ask you once again. You would have ended up interpreting texts just as you've been doing all your life.

AUTHOR: They would have been real texts about real things, even when I chose to destroy their verbal underpinnings. I'd have had a chance to change the world.

INTERLOCUTOR: Fat chance.

WORKS MENTIONED, FOLLOWED BY RETROSPECTS

Lindenberger, Herbert. "The Poetic World of Georg Trakl." Ph.D. diss., University of Washington, 1955.

———. *On Wordsworth's 'Prelude'.* Princeton: Princeton University Press, 1963.

———. *Georg Büchner.* Carbondale: Southern Illinois University Press, 1964.

———. *Georg Trakl.* New York: Twayne, 1971.

———. *Historical Drama: The Relation of Literature and Reality.* Chicago: University of Chicago Press, 1975.

———. *Saul's Fall: A Critical Fiction.* Baltimore: Johns Hopkins University Press, 1979.

———. "Re-viewing the Reviews of *Historical Drama*." In *The Horizon of Literature,* ed. Paul Hernadi, 283–98. Lincoln: University of Nebraska Press, 1982.

———. "aFTER *sAUL'S fALL*: An Interview with the Author." *New Literary History* 21 (Autumn 1989): 37–57.

———. "Wordsworth by Accident." *Studies in Romanticism* 21 (1982): 566–69.

———. *Opera: The Extravagant Art.* Ithaca: Cornell University Press, 1984.

———. "Teaching Wordsworth from the 1950s to the 1980s." In *Approaches to Teaching Wordsworth's Poetry.* Ed. Spencer Hall with Jonathan Ramsey, 32–38. New York: MLA, 1986.

———. *The History in Literature: On Value, Genre, Institutions.* New York: Columbia University Press, 1990.

Spitzer, Leo. *Representative Essays,* eds. Alban Forcione, Herbert Lindenberger and Madeline Sutherland. Stanford: Stanford University Press, 1988.

13

Home Truths and Institutional Falsehoods

Gerald Gillespie

An invitation to write about professing what loosely we call Comparative Literature is one of those attractive propositions in life designed to teach humiliating lessons. I feel unready to select from among the dozens of mentors and companions who have been significant living guides; to single out just a few lights seems a premature arrogation of wisdom by someone not yet an emeritus! A sketch of my own career stretching from the waning days of the New Criticism to the waning days of the New Historicism may, nevertheless, at least have some practical value as one outline of what it was like for a native-born American of my generation to follow in the ample wake spreading behind the giants of the "restart" of Comparative Literature in the United States, most notably Harry Levin and René Wellek, and to feel the wash of further waves in an increasingly turbulent sea of critical discourse and practice. A cross-section of such individual accounts can help clarify where the profession stands at century's end in a large part of North America.

My parents, who migrated to the United States from Ireland by way of Great Britain, were avid readers. Perhaps an inherited susceptibility predisposed me to soak up the heady lessons about cosmopolitan openness and cultural depth imparted by such early teachers as the translator-poet Dudley Fitts at Phillips Academy, Andover. Secondary education in Cleveland and Andover introduced me to the typical fare of good American schools in the forties: among other things, in my case, to several practical trades, Latin and Spanish, ancient, medieval, and modern history, including that of the United States, English and American writing, advanced math, chemistry, and biology. Rounding out secondary school and my teen age years at Felsted in East Anglia allowed me opportunity to wander through Great Britain, France, and Spain and to fit in as more than a cultural tourist on some occasions. Not just to read Jean-Paul Sartre's novels (in translation still) but to glimpse the existentialist master leaving his hotel nextdoor to mine in Paris; to report my own impressions of battlefields to a Glaswegian uncle who (using Esperanto initially!) had fought on them in Spain; to meet filmable characters in the shabby postwar German citiscapes that bristled with refugees—this kind of immediacy whetted a lifelong appetite for sharing and witnessing on the home grounds of other cultures as well as exploring the American past and present, both in the cultural record and at memorable sites.

I entered the History and Literature program at Harvard for the advantage of studying modern Europe from several angles—for example, of hearing William Langer's lectures on the age of imperialism, while reading French Romantic writings with René Jasinski, Victorian with Howard Mumford Jones, German from the Goethezeit onward with Stuart Atkins, Henry Hatfield, and Wolfgang Kayser, and sharing in the excitement of Harry Levin's course "Proust, Joyce, and Mann" as a lowly auditor. I owe a lot to fellow students (who may read in their own names!) for countless conversations winning me to Beethoven's quartets, Hazlitt's criticism, Mallarmé's lyrics, or Barlach's sculptures, reviving my interest in Eliot or Picasso, critiquing Existentialism, Skinner's behaviorism, Tillich's theology, commenting their own films (e.g., of the Bushmen of the Kalihari), their short stories, poems, and paintings, and so much more that my head spins recollecting the sheer wealth of life at Harvard in the early 1950s. As an exchange student in Tübingen after graduation, I was still addicted to combining Western literatures and history and enjoyed Kurt Wais' seminar on Romantic poetry in the one-man Comparative Literature institute of those days. During the holidays I roamed through more corners of Europe north and south.

Opposing the hysteria of the McCarthy period during the Cold War had been one of the rites of passage marking the start of college. Now the tragic drama of the Hungarian insurrection so close at hand during my Tübingen sojourn served to reinoculate me with a reminder of the power the totalitarian virus still packed. The Republican Irish, who celebrated the collapse of the British empire, could readily sympathize with the Hungarian aspiration for national independence. I remember, from thirty-five years ago, trying to sort out for kin in Donegal the longer-term indebtedness of the world to Britain and the newer complexities flowing from the settlement of World War II. Uncle Connell, a shaughraun for whom the Grand Armada still counted among notable news, restored my perspective as a student of literature by regaling me in turn with lore that seemed straight out of a course in Indo-germanic philology—for instance, one night reciting what sounded like a local version of the *Völuspá*.

I turned down a fellowship in Comparative Literature at Yale extended by René Wellek in order, first, to indulge my growing interest in German culture with Ohio State's great department of the mid-fifties to mid-sixties. It boasted such notable critics as Oskar Seidlin, Sigurd Burckhardt, and Walter Naumann. Seidlin and Burckhardt ranked among the finest interpretive and theoretical talents in the New Critical direction, the German expression of which had largely been overridden by World War II. Naumann, a student of Husserl and Curtius, was a Germanist as well as Pan-Romanist and represented the great tradition of Comparative Literature shunted aside in Germany under the Nazis. These teachers encouraged my pursuit of graduate work in Italian and Spanish classics, while I was feasting on a main diet of courses from the Middles Ages to Modern period in German. Naumann had completed a path-breaking dissertation on *Der Sprachgebrauch Mallarmés* (1935) under Curtius; he had recently published a major book on the Romantic playwright Grillparzer; and he was pursuing his interests in twentieth-century German poetry and the European Middle Ages and Baroque at the end of the 1950s when I asked him to guide my doctoral thesis on the seventeenth-century tragedian Lohenstein. Willy-nilly my Germanistic byway was reconnecting with the comparatist highway. For instance, my awareness of Wellek's role in stirring fresh attention to the Baroque was, a few years later, the initial basis for a lasting friendship with his student Frank Warnke.

I met my wife as a fellow graduate student in French at Ohio State. Beginning a saga of family trips, we went on the most improbable honeymoon to Castro Cuba before the start of the next school year, out of sheer curiosity over how things might look and feel. In 1961, I returned stateside from a second fellowship year in Europe, split between research libraries and theaters in Munich and Paris, to join the University of Southern California as an Assistant Professor; and in 1962 Naumann returned to Europe permanently, to found the Institute for Comparative Literature at Darmstadt. David Malone, a product of Werner Paul Friederich's outfit in Chapel Hill, arrived about the same time to create a Comparative Literature program under the aegis of USC's English Department, and I was involved for the Germanic linkage. That meant for me, as a newly minted Ph.D., teaching mainly standard topics such as German Romantic and Baroque literature, and a few general courses, while doing a share of the serious committee work, advisement, and examination of the few pioneering graduate students at that time in the interdisciplinary field, and of course, doing even more of the same program support work for the German department. There was not yet a core faculty dedicated to CL (henceforth my abbreviation for Comparative Literature), only some cooperative colleagues located in a few relevant humanities groups. What I experienced at USC in the early 1960s was and still is—with exceptions as usual proving the rule— typical of the first steps toward establishing CL as a discipline outside of the old self-confident citadels such as Harvard. Most American universities never get past that point, nor can many, even if willing, really muster the required team of experts out of small literature groups whose members' teaching time is already fully committed. I never shared in second steps at USC, because, despite my forthcoming promotion, toward the end of my fourth year in Los Angeles (and many delightful adventures all around the western states and Mexico) I decided to return to the East Coast. One motive was to be closer to Europe. I accepted a position at SUNY-Binghamton, effective autumn 1965.

No reader of Proust will presume to step back imaginatively into yesteryear's flowing stream in less than seven volumes. I can offer only a wildly foreshortened assessment of the "feel" of CL from the mid-fifties to mid-sixties for a tyro, in my case prior to working in Binghamton. Even the youngest beginners seemed aware that the sound pre-college education for native-born Americans, still widely available in the years immediately after World War II, was a significant asset. I remember hearing fellow students of literature reflect that the vast migration of writers and scholars in the World War II period had led to a shared North American-West European monopoly in literary theory and to a floration of critical practice. Successive editions of Wellek and Warren's *Theory of Literature* (1942 ff.) were sweeping the nation and world. Remobilizing insights from East European Formalism and Western history of criticism and history of literature, they proposed a general system of analysis that could better serve to situate literary works and processes within actual cultures, and to grasp similitudes and divergences among cultures, not just in formal or synchronous cross-sections but over time. Claudio Guillén's *Literature as System* (1971) is exemplary for finer American efforts in the Levin-Wellek vein to expound a Structuralism that takes proper account of historical dynamics. The American scene meanwhile was rife with local and exile Formalists, Marxians, Freudians, intentionalists, poetic anthropologists, and intellectual historians. The master historians of culture, Ernst Robert Curtius (*Europäische Literatur und Lateinisches Mittelalter*, 1948) and Erich Auerbach (*Mimesis*, 1946), were enormously influential in translation.

Before the breakthrough of the French varieties, Wolfgang Kayser's looser brand of Structuralism in *Das sprachliche Kunstwerk* (1954) skirted the pitfalls of extremist positions. But by far the favorite rival Structuralism around 1960 in North America was that set forth in Northrop Frye's *Anatomy of Criticism* (1957). It was successful in no small measure because Jungians, New Critics, and others could co-opt its atemporal system of genres and modes, while its functional approach to features of works offered very inviting points of contact to the various heirs of Formalism. As Geoffrey Hartman commented in *Beyond Formalism* (1970), the highly literary Frye was truly radical, because his abstract approach to specific patterns as actualized possibilities arising from an extant repertory demystified literature without having recourse to one of the contending ideologies of the moment. Some time was to pass before intellectual history paid closer attention to Frye's relationship to the anthropological-psychohistorical tradition from Vico over Nietzsche—just as in the soon-to-unfold case of Jacques Derrida a whole generation intervened before scholars undertook more careful historical assessments of his relationship to older Idealism and Romanticism.

From the 1960s onward, the young American entrant in literary studies could count on being helped and confused by a rising tide of advice for our restarted field that included handbooks such as Newton Stallknecht and Horst Frenz's *Comparative Literature: Method and Perspective (1961)*, visions of the next great challenges such as René Étiemble's exhortation to move beyond Europe in *The Crisis in Comparative Literature* (1966), excellent histories of critical theory since antquity, and conspectuses of current trends. When I look at old syllabuses and book lists for theory courses that I gave at SUNY and as a guest at New York University at the end of the sixties and start of the seventies, what stands in relief is the juxtaposition of psychological and "worldview" approaches and the new range of Structuralism. For example, one of my seminars for doctoral candidates, recycled in 1972 at Binghamton, featured as topics the Geneva School, Gestalt and Jungian psychology, hermeneutics, phenomenology, philosophy and language (Cassirer, Wittgenstein, Heidegger), Existentialism, and the onrolling newer "French" wave (Lévi-Strauss, Barthes, De Man). I recall giving a paper on "Postmodern Mannerism" in a panel with Paul de Man and Ezio Raimondi at a *Diacritics* conference at Cornell in 1973 and noticing the amazement of many in attendance over my qualified indifference to Derrida, whose *De la Grammatologie* (1967) I indeed thought witty, but not a new evangel.

Although I sensed an odd fervor among Deconstructionist groupies in the assemblage, it never occurred to me that, a mere decade later, when they saw an opportunity, some scholars of this and other contemporary persuasions, newly arriving in the academy, and some older colleagues latching onto the *nouvelle vague*, would literally attempt to persecute persons who disagreed with them. Especially mean treatment was to be accorded many a comparatist who well understood, and might in fact borrow devices from Deconstruction, Foucaultian "archaeology of consciousness," neo-Marxian analysis, and so forth, but who explicitly rejected specific "Poststructuralist" doctrines. They knowingly donned the mantle of latter-day heresy. But I am getting ahead of my story and ought to sketch the institutional setting in which CL came together at Binghamton contemporaneously with the breakthrough of Postmodernism.

The sixties boom in the New York state university system occurred before the drastic drop in educational standards nationwide began to dampen the effective scope, but not the appetite, for cross-cultural and interdisciplinary literary studies in American institutions of "higher learning." Luckily for people like me, Frederick Garber, another Wellek student (as well as one of America's top-flight Romanticists), chose to chair not English but the young CL program at Binghamton. He guided it to desired departmental status by 1969 with the cooperation of the chairs of several key humanities departments, just before the state economy—and SUNY's prospects for creative experiment—began sliding. It was one of the bold ventures that has lasted: At Binghamton, a diverse group of practicing comparatists with solid European and Western Hemisphere credentials gained *actual* disciplinary independence. They enjoyed not merely a nominal status through split appointments—today still the norm across the United States—but complete intellectual sovereignty by virtue of disposing of undivided billets and wielding the same power to negotiate occasional collaboration and crosslisting that any established department enjoyed. The internal migration of a few comparatists from split to full appointments cemented the arrangement.

Nonetheless, fairly predictable turf problems threatened to muddy the picture. The English Department fumed for a long while because it claimed charter rights over anything that constituted "General Literature," liberally interpreted to be anything taught or conveyed in English, whether or not deriving from other cultural streams and/or represented by specialists in other humanities fields. In that climate, foreign literature groups were concerned to apply their expertise to teach the non-English literatures in translation. At the same time, some individual scholars in these departments were convinced that CL was perverse in not elevating a favorite direction in theory from their enclave to dominant status for any generalist approach. In yet another inherent conflict of interest, certain irreparably monoglot members of the Philosophy Department who claimed expertise in specific areas on the basis of translations were angry both at some of their own colleagues and at comparatists who read theory and intellectual history in the original languages. My experiences outside the United States were already deeply influencing the way I thought about these routine cultural tensions at work within the American institution.

More than a battle between opponents and proponents of CL was occurring at a number of universities. The circumstances of comparatists in other cultures—so I had become aware—could explain a lot also about the unfortunate cleavage at home between scholars who were more generous proponents of CL and others who indeed wanted to crowd into the new disciplinary space being created but who were, in fact, "single-issue" or "single-enclave" advocates with a culturally narrow vision. To my delight, when I first ventured overseas to one of the congresses sponsored by the International Comparative Literature Association (Belgrade, 1967), I encountered a good number of native-born and immigrant Americans in various age brackets who were already actively engaged in direct dialogue with their counterparts from a wide range of nations and who exemplified international openness. A few names must serve to represent all—colleagues such as Haskell Block, Burton Pike, Claudio Guillén, Anna Balakian, Henry Remak, and Ulrich Weisstein.

Some old lessons were confirmed, and new ones learned. Just from random conversation at this sort of congress one soon realized that at many important universities in most Western European nations, as in the United States, the "national" literature departments more often than not presented a big obstacle to a richer development of CL because they sought to maintain hegemony in criticism and theory by co-opting the newer field. In contrast, "foreign" literature departments frequently produced the seed from which CL could grow in an exponential spurt. However, there was no guarantee that the role of the "foreign" literature exponents would be constructive. It turned out that in other nations too, just as one might expect, there were colleagues who specialized in being "professional foreigners"—representatives of another culture, whether as a result of their migration or intellectual choice—and passed this off as credentials in CL. It was fine, of course, to enjoy the collaboration of specialists, and there were many who contributed important topics in a sensible way. But anywhere one worked or visited, there were troublesome ones, too, especially those who, rather than acknowledging the limits imposed on what a single person could encompass in cross-cultural studies and theory, insisted that their fellow countrymen should humbly receive through them profound messages from some preferred extraterritorial oracle.

Another lesson to be gained in the 1960s by visiting other peoples' home territories was one which all of us might have garnered (and often did) in our easy chair from reading accounts by the finest imaginative writers and historians, but which impressed itself with greater immediacy on the itinerant scholar's mind. Discourse with many counterparts from a variety of nations in person at ever shifting venues sharpened awareness of differences within and between large sectors of the world—for example, differences inside the Soviet block of the Stalin era, and between the Soviet block and the "West." It also made linkages and sharing across boundaries more vivid. In addition to discreet *tête-à-tête* exchanges, there were those telltale public moments at earlier ICLA congresses, such as when all the East Germans disappeared daily at exactly the same hour to report to their control, or when a Russian colleague stormed toward the podium during a plenary paper to protest Harry Levin's aberrant definition of "realism" in the novel since Cervantes. There in the drama being staged before my eyes was somatic evidence of the enormous importance which a formidable state system attributed to our testing of literary definitions of "realism." It is to the credit of the ICLA members from older democratic nations that for four decades they have managed to keep the lines of communication open with scholars in countries until recently or still under repressive regimes. In upholding individual participation as inviolable, ICLA may well be unique among international organizations. Starting in 1955 and continuing in a triennial pattern, the major world congresses of ICLA have been held at Venice, Chapel Hill, Utrecht, Fribourg, Belgrade, Bordeaux, Ottawa-Montreal, Budapest, Innsbruck, New York, Paris, Munich, and Tokyo. Other meetings between members of ICLA's scholarly committees and learned academies or regional societies of CL have been held at least annually at venues around the world for some four decades now.

I became more involved in this international flow at the end of the seventies, when at Innsbruck I was elected to my first term as Secretary General of ICLA. This sort of CL was a movable feast, but serving in person as a transactional channel imposed a formidable burden. Many traditional specialists remain dismissive of efforts to be in touch with scholars across a broader front on several continents. I recall one British colleague, in the discussion after a lecture in Bristol, expressing his horror over the idea of collaborating on a project with scholars from incompatible worlds, rather than conveniently operating within one's own frame of reference. I was not then and am not now insensible to the creative and social logic of working in splendid isolation as an individual in the great libertarian tradition of Western Europe. It costs a real price to practice CL because sometimes the historical demands of the field compel scholars to engage in unwieldy, collective efforts. (As if to illustrate my point, I have just closed off such a project requiring collaboration by a team of experts in European and Western Hemisphere cultures, the manuscript of the volume *Romantic Drama*, in the series *A Comparative History of Literatures in European Languages*.)

During the 1970s and 1980s, the evidence coming my way has suggested that the authorities at very few American universities have seriously appreciated the nature or value of a full range of comparatist activity. Deeply ingrained institutional habits of mind trammel our field. American administrators tend to "see" the supposed specialization of a faculty member as his or her "main" field, and CL as a secondary embellishment or level. They also tend to identify people in CL as pushing contemporary fashions that will enhance their university's reputation for being "up-to-date." Recognizing this foible, self-appointed trendsetters eagerly strike their institution's innovation gong; its chime is keyed to the cultural sensitivities of the campus rulers. Thus the by-far easier messages of "single-enclave" and "single-issue" simplifiers have gained a powerful hold in many institutions. The inertial effect of compromising with them has been to deprive CL of a distinct disciplinary identity and authority. Rendered marginal by being made "useful" to established fields, CL is all too easily co-opted by special interest groups.

I sensed in the cross-currents of the 1970s what outcome aggressive co-optation might bring about, but my mind was turned in those years to the large job at hand. In the immediate offing our CL group at Binghamton began to thrive as a nexus for European studies and literary theory. We also had some special expertise in Western Hemisphere subjects, such as contemporary drama in Latin America and the Caribbean, and took modest initial steps to add competence in Far Eastern literature (Japanese). I founded a center for translation studies that my colleague Marilyn G. Rose subsequently expanded as a lasting component of the department. Most American scholars were not yet aware of the growing importance of translation studies at the core of one of the most promising developments in general theory of the past two decades, the "polysystem" approach. The coherence and legitimacy of CL at Binghamton early on resided in its competence as a Eurocentric program. I use the term Eurocentric as purely descriptive and in no wise pejorative. Very important for the development of CL in the United States was the way in which American institutions approached the task of widening competence beyond the European core. I shall return to this subject.

The CL group at Binghamton were privileged to be direct observers of William Spanos' success in founding the journal *Boundary 2* under the roof of the neighboring English department. He quickly opened its pages to important currents of Postmodernism and general theory in Europe as well as the United States and devoted special issues to contemporary American poets and other writers. On a couple of occasions Spanos, an existentialist committed to some key Postmodern attitudes, generously welcomed me to comment as a devil's advocate in *Boundary 2*. Through its many stimulating overlaps with our interests and those of foreign literature departments (e.g., relevance for Nietzsche and Heidegger enthusiasts in German, Structuralism and Deconstruction buffs in French and Philosophy, etc.) *Boundary 2* played a significant part in fostering one layer of an intellectual identity for our combined fields. Paul Bové, successor editor upon the journal's recent twentieth anniversary and its shift to Duke University Press as publisher, has reoriented it more heavily to sociological and anthromarxist approaches—and no doubt his decision reflects the drift in a large part of its readership. Since, for example, *New Literary History*, a natural rival of the 1970s, has long shared a good deal of the same conceptual space, it remains to be seen how many prominent journals can survive by specializing in sociological levels of "poststructuralist" debate.

In 1966–67 I was fortunate to be a Mellon fellow at the University of Pittsburgh and to follow that research spate in Baroque and Romantic topics with a year as a Guggenheim fellow in Munich where I completed a book on German Baroque poetry and prepared commented bilingual editions of Tieck's *Der gestiefelte Kater* and the then still- anonymous *Nachtwachen* of "Bonaventura." I happened to be directly on the scene to witness the 1968 manifestations in Paris and Munich; I had observed their earlier phase in summer of 1965 at Berkeley. Increasingly after 1968, spontaneous antinomian eruptions posed a problem in Western cultures. The rancor at the end of the Vietnam War and the bitter flavor of social crisis in the cities (drugs, failed schools, broken families, etc.) were admixed in the collective hysteria washing about in American universities by the early 1970s. Critics who issued abundant apocalyptic and millenarian statements tended, more and more, to feel comfortable grouped under the Postmodern banner. Published at what is likely to prove out as approximate midpoint in the PM trajectory, Jean-François Lyotard's *La Condition postmoderne: Rapport sur le savoir* (1979) is characteristic of treatises that sought to straddle the moment in polysemous safety. Through concepts like "instability," it flirted with the antinomian foible for transformational drama, while preserving the appearance of connection with scientific speculation (e.g., catastrophe theory) and sound academic enterprise. Lyotard merged social criticism (with a bow toward a repristinated Marxism), discourse theory, epistemology (flavored to be acceptable to Foucaultians), and language-gamesical thought (accessible to Derrida-trained deconstructors) into a "performative" model that accommodated almost anything likely to constitute a trend during the author's remaining years.

In 1973–74, I moved to Paris as a Senior Fellow of NEH to extend my research in the European Baroque, and by springtime I decided to accept a split appointment in German and Comparative Literature at Stanford. The experiences of my first years in the Bay Area seemed to justify a return to the old-fashioned, awkward yoking of fields which, of course, is the common curse imposed on comparatists. For example, in Binghamton, I had found it exhilarating to mount a graduate course in Renaissance and Baroque poetry and poetics because a sufficiently large contingent of students could work seriously in one, two, or even three languages besides English. At the start in Stanford, I was able to replicate that sort of bridging in a graduate course on Romantic lyricism. But, "progressively," the dire fact of the shrinkage of the pool of students already preliminarily trained or trainable with timeliness made itself felt. Comparativistic classes in topics, genres, and periods devolved inexorably into being mixed affairs, even though they frequently attracted excellent students. It was not atypical to bring together a few majors in this or that "national" literature who had a strong interest in a particular author, work, or topic, a few students from allied fields who associated some elements of the course with a particular theoretical stance, and a minority of CL aspirants proper. It soon became habit to devise a core syllabus that used original texts and translations in tandem; and to conduct discussions with an eye on problems of communicability across language systems, lest those students using a translation in this or that connection be left in the dark. This inhibiting factor for work in depth began to intrude even into seminars.

To avoid misunderstandings, I want to caution that my comments about the preceding decade should not be read as applying to the recently reenlivened program at Stanford. As of the 1980s, no adminstrator "in charge" of the humanities at Stanford seemed acutely concerned any longer over the fact that, after its implementation in the late 1970s, the university's own policy of reducing the number of students in the allied fields was perforce transforming both CL and, to a lesser extent, the study of continental European literatures into a species of General Literature. This was a predictable result of jumbling together the levels of amateurs and specialists, as well as younger and older students. Some colleagues who averred dedication to CL were actually resistant to a higher standard of reading capacity and happy to fall in line with administrative pressures to level requirements in order to accommodate the squeeze-down of a severe *numerus clausus*. I finally had to admit there was a significant correlation between the privileging of theory by some colleagues and their own dependence on translations in many key connections affecting theory as well as literature.

It was hardly surprising that several single-enclave and single-issue types at Stanford as at other major universities militated to make theory in general the touchstone of academic virtue in the 1980s. Their advocacy of what comparatists were already zealously pursuing as a major sector of their multifaceted enterprise confused institutions about the nature of the total field; of course, some institutions had a proclivity toward being confused or saw oversimplification as an opportunity. This trend appeared to be happening at Yale on a higher, elegant level up to the death of Paul de Man, and the examples of Yale, Johns Hopkins, and Cornell were often invoked elsewhere in rationales for "switching" to theory. But just as smaller sheep were managing to reach a cancer theory-ward, the literary sector (literary history, interpretation of imaginative writing, contemporary criticism applied to a variety of actual literatures) at Yale, Princeton, and other citadels of learning demonstrated a will to maintain its prestige and it reemerged with vigor. The erection of a distinct, explicitly so-named Theory program alongside the extant CL program at the University of California at Irvine in the 1980s was an honest as well as bolder move, because this arrangement acknowledged the importance of both orientations in scholarly work. One kind of essential work was not arbitrarily and wastefully damaged to gratify proponents of the other.

I was very pleased when Thomas R. Hart invited me in 1977 to join Paul de Man, Harry Levin, René Wellek, Phillip Damon, and Victor Lange on the editorial board of *Comparative Literature*. The program of this journal, the discipline's American flagship, was and has remained open to all areas of theory and critical practice in the United States and internationally; and the board has been steadily enlarged in the past decade to cope with new interests. The natural kaleidoscopic variety of studies in organs like *Comparative Literature* which resolutely resist promoting specific themes, but as resolutely welcome airing them, contrasts with the pseudo-universalizing under the label of CL prevalent in much of the American academy.

What I feared when I wrote down the title of my remarks now bulks larger as my thoughts gravitate toward 1990 and the aftermath in the American academy. It is incumbent to distinguish between two poles in the generalized addiction to theory in the 1980s. On the one hand, some colleagues spoke of Theory (with a capital T) as if it promised some kind of bypass around the contingency of actual cultural life. On the other hand, the energy and acumen which certain thinkers (e.g., Derrida) exhibited in the passionate pursuit of specific theoretical questions were impressive. The jury is still out, but thus far it appears we do not have any preponderant evidence (e.g., a wealth of first-rate critical applications) of the efficacy of much of recent theorizing. For whatever reason, the theories still wait to be tested out with rigor through impressive uses. Disquieting, so far as the prospects for that are concerned, is that a very large part of the interest in currents loosely labeled as "theory" over the past twenty years has been neither intellectual nor aesthetic but instrumental. Extensively, the variegated lobby for "using" theory is made up of persons who are willing to engage in an ideological accommodation based on the common denominator of a desire to displace and replace (actual or supposed) cultural authority as a servant of political power. Older ideological crusades in refurbished dress (e.g., Marxism spruced up with Derridian and Foucaultian vocabulary), worldviews based on psychosexual specializations (e.g., a range of gay and lesbian proposals to alter society), and various transformational doctrines (e.g., Heideggerian ontological oracularity) cast their crossover threads to weave a colorful tapestry. What a considerable number of theory promoters share, in the final analysis, is a mood of resentment against a baffling "reality": the complexity of the actual world—a complexity not amenable to single-issue approaches. Thus a literal horde of "critics" in the academy function today, with their "outsider" consciousness, much the way religious dissidents have in earlier centuries.

In a traditional reflex, universities first encouraged academic fields to accept some of the most anti-intellectual dissidents. Eventually, advocates of an outright destabilization of higher education compacted with sympathetic, reform-minded moderates to form blocks that could decisively influence curricular policy making.

Some were taken up into the administrations to placate the lobbies; and when the moment arrived when the balance could be tipped, it was tipped at a number of American institutions, so that in many places an antinomian alliance gained control of important aspects of the curriculum, of the shaping of core departments, and of funding for the encouragement of new initiatives—principally in the humanities.

There have been parallels in other parts of the total educational establishment of the United States. Real and supposed reformist innovations and antinomian preachments have become so entangled as to be effectively indistinguishable to many academics. This confusion has been permeating public school systems, colleges, seminaries, and other institutions for a long while now. Lobbyists of antinomian persuasion seemed useful allies to specific single-issue political factions when they began pushing for radical changes through the state and federal legislatures. The consequences of the altered cultural climate have often been devastating for CL as a field whose mission was inherently elitist. At certain universities, the antinomian alliance set out with deliberation (I now use a term coined by one of their own) to "colonize" the discipline and use its lingering prestige for their own purposes. They found ideal conditions in the 1980s in a number of instances, because various administrators (whose sensibility sometimes had not advanced much beyond Flower Power) were eager to proclaim a self-congratulatory vision of a transformed America as a model for the whole world. The idea of assembling a high-level theory combine that could crank out dazzling justifications for a chaotic smorgasbord of courses and explain away the lowering of cultural consciousness as the dawn of a thrilling transformation was just too tempting to be resisted. The academic triumphalism of the 1960s resurged in new channels.

CL in general across the country was too compliant in letting itself be used by administrators as a device to meet demands for "inclusion" of attention to groups within the diverse American population, while the same arbiters were withholding adequate support for in-depth study of other cultures around the world. The disciplinary integrity of CL was compromised one small step after another as hard-pressed practitioners learned to tolerate the most banal assaults on one of the most complex civilizations imaginable (Europe and its extensions). They suffered the presence under their roof of colleagues who read crude versions of other cultures back onto the American scene or carelessly projected American situations and values onto the misconstrued variety of patterns around the globe. The field of CL was particularly vulnerable to the vulgarizers because it was and is dedicated to the serious study of "otherness" and because it paid and pays attention to the internal systems of cultures, including the role of other media of communication and other arts. It was in the cards that CL should have powerful ties with "culture studies" and "les sciences humaines"; that also opened the field to being absorbed into the social sciences. By 1950, coping with the phenomena of the related huge European and North and South American civilizations already exceeded the capacity of any individual scholar. By 1970, it was abundantly evident that coping with the phenomena of sets of entire civilizations and of smaller-scale cultures required the coordinated effort of *teams of elitists*. Yet at too many American universities in the 1980s, comparatists were being dragged down into the vortex of clichés about "innovation" and "multiculturalism" while a collapse of capacities actually gripped the humanities.

How profoundly the failure of vision affected CL in the past decade can be illustrated by the story of one major university. Out of hope for its eventual recovery, let it be called X in these pages. As early as 1980 some in the broad configuration of comparatists at X began building an alliance with persons in various fields across the humanities and social sciences and professional schools with interests in "les sciences humaines." These wider ties were based on two main attractions that did not necessarily overlap: One was a fascination for theory in general, reinforced by curiosity, on the part of some, about the newer French waves. A second area of mutuality for a significant minority was adhering to one or another brand of the persuasion that Western culture per se, or major aspects of it, had to be coopted or demolished. A yet smaller set of people within these two larger sets gradually promoted the idea that their own much-touted devotion to Theory constituted the only valid credentials for CL. Eventually, by secret agreement, a tiny nucleus moved to separate from other already tenured comparatists who were well-established in theoretical debate or were versed in older and contemporary theory but more interested in literary studies. The aim of the cabal, which succeeded within a few years, was to co-opt the name of the richer discipline, rather than form their own institute under an appropriate rubric (such as Theory, or Culture Studies).

When new administrators who needed something "innovative" to put on their résumés came into office, the moment was ripe. With decanal connivance, the tiny nucleus of ringleaders arranged an academic putsch. The "innovating" administration, as rulers of a virtually sovereign city-state, assisted in the birth of a reconstituted CL by using legalistic dirty tricks. They worked behind the scenes to redefine the entire enterprise of CL. They annointed the key putschists high priests of the new dispensation and allowed them to banish any comparatists they wanted to push out. There followed a remarkable period of symbiosis in which lead figures in the redefined CL directorate acted as consultants on administration plans to engineer sweeping changes in undergraduate and graduate education in the humanities! One of the public pieties since the mid-1980s at X was to pretend that an ever increasing share of the university's funds and psychic energies would be devoted to purging such grave cultural deficiencies as Euro-, logo-, and phallo-centrism.

Many will credit the case at X to the column of occasional "aberrations" that crop up in American universities. But my own awareness of practices under totalitarian regimes (accrued in twenty-five years of contacts worldwide) make me less sanguine about the implications of the story at X. I regard this sort of gross manipulation as entailing more than the destruction of collegiality and proper procedure. The flagrant disregard for the rights of seasoned colleagues practicing over a much richer range in CL amounts to a massive assault on the academic freedom of proven scholars. It is an authoritarian attempt to redefine a discipline without the agreement of the experts involved in it. Characteristic was the unwillingness to engage in open, thorough debate of positions. The behavior of the dean at X, assisting in the hijacking of a whole field, is reminiscent of Pope Urban VIII's quashing of Galilean astronomy, Stalin's interference in biology, and similar intrusions based on a political agenda. The intolerance, anti-intellectualism, and arrogance of the infamous CL coup d'état at X betokens the endangerment of the discipline in the kinds of societies which originally nourished it.

As of the 1990s, the contradictory patterns in the huge realm loosely labeled Comparative Literature prohibit any simple prediction. The historical picture in the older homelands of the field is as mixed. States in Western Europe take important steps toward union and even states in Eastern Europe hope eventually to enter such a club. Significant numbers within smaller cultural entities (e.g., Welsh, Basque, etc.) and intermingled population subgroups, whether characterized by ethnic identity (e.g., Turks in Germany), religious heritage (Protestants in Northern Ireland), or by sociolect (e.g., lesbian activists), insist on a greater degree of recognition, while the old Soviet empire devolves into constituent nations many of which contain unhappy minorities. Internal faultlines indicate a cracking apart of the older Atlantic enterprise in which Western Europe and the United States-Canada have dominated.

In the special case of the United States as an immigrant nation, this process of fragmentation appears under such guises in the academy as the theme of overcoming "Eurocentrism" and the demands by a plethora of subgroups to participate in discourse and/or replace all older dominant theory-makers who are construed as belonging to a hypothetical oppressive majoritarian consensus. (It is uncertain whether the numerical majority of ethnically mixed persons, who by assimilation share a common heritage of Anglo-American law, may yet be galvanized into an effective "mongrel" backlash against particularist demands.) While neo-nationalist quarrels flare up in Europe and Canada, and ethnic internal separatism is a major theme in the United States, very large blocks of literary scholars in alternate civilizations with deep cultural histories have been enjoying increasing success in putting the relevant materials about their cultures and politics before a world audience. Japanese, Chinese, and Indian savants have been leading, and they enjoy notable support from Western experts dedicated to the study of non-European literatures. On balance, the definitely enlarged, and definitely international *respublica litteraria* now on the horizon because of such sharing is still dominated by the Northern Hemisphere. Latin American and African studies are gravitating at a slower pace into a stronger intercontinental bonding with a global system in which Europe is "decentered" but still provides vital leadership.

Comparatists who aspire to analytical praxis or theorizing that is "extraterritorial," in the positive sense of their work being liberated from local cultural norms, now face a puzzling question. Should African, American, European, Indian, and other competent investigators, regardless of their nominal social allegiances (e.g., "politics," "religion," "nationality," etc.) be exploiting newer knowledge based on kinds of literary awareness found in the various "native" traditions under scrutiny, or should they continue to adapt European tools to do the job of dealing with home cultures and communicate their findings in European critical terminology as a global *lingua franca*? We can turn this same question around. Let us stipulate outright one of the worst-kept secrets of the ending twentieth century: that applying Marxian concepts to African literatures, Foucaultian to Japanese, etc., amounts to a "Eurocentric" game, a game that has widely been transposed onto "colonialized" minds. (Of course, paradoxically, these latter terms, too, are a European invention!) If we follow the logic of genuine reciprocity, we should then conclude that applying Japanese poetics to Swedish literature, Hindu dramaturgical categories to Italian opera, etc., would likewise be an arbitrary act in a potentially distorting game. But the idea that "Japanocentric" discourse is relevant only to Japanese people, Indocentric only to Indians, and so forth, is obviously a shallow racist approach analogous to the stultifying notion that "Eurocentric" paradigms can bring no profound human benefits to non-Europeans.

The fact that there have been so many failed or misguided attempts to transfer categories across resistant cultural boundaries does not rule out the possibility that some theoretical and critical traffic crossings can be helpful. Earl Miner's book *Comparative Poetics* (1991) has contributed valuable insights into the reasons for fostering what ultimately would constitute a multidirectional awarenness of poetic systems. He has pointed out how the natural processes of longer-term reinforcement in great literary cultures produce conceptual gaps and lopsidedness, so that a whole web of sensibility underpinning creativity and responsiveness in one poetic world simply is absent or marginal in another. Thus to understand some important aspects of non-European works will, finally, require our understanding that many supposed "universals"—even rival universals proposed to displace older ones—actually all are virtual automatisms in our Western repertory; and that sheer blanks in our repertory prevent our noticing certain phenomena.

Older Western Formalism suggested a starting point toward an awareness that tries to achieve an operational "value-neutrality" and therefore, in principle, is open to admitting the variety of values in a plurality of systems. Older Formalism made that advance by the strategy, and at the price, of reducing literary phenomena to their smallest constituent units. The newer Polysystem approach—pioneered by scholars such as Itamar Even-Zohar—aspires to discriminate units and processes of all magnitudes of complexity within indentifiable cultures, and to chart the internal dynamics of a culture in time and in its interaction with other cultures. What people like Miner and Even-Zohar propose, from two independent perspectives, cannot be built on the inherently self-blinded emptiness of that sector of Western theorizing that wraps itself in the assumption that comparatists can generalize about the cultural behavior of the entire human race out of the limited resources of various pseudo-universalisms now in vogue in the academy. I have already cited as a particularly banal case the contemporary "multiculturalism" wave in the United States. There are more subtle, Janus-headed instances such as Hayden White's treatment of components within cultural belief systems or "mentalities" as rhetorical subgenres. Careful scrutiny of writings in terms of a rhetorical typology certainly can and does yield valuable insights. Even when the critic may overinterpret in lining up the indicative features, the whole business depends on our general knowledge of cultural repertories. Not to mirror something authentic about Western texts would require a perverse special effort on the part of a reasonably well educated Western critic (which does not exclude this happening). The latent dangers of a "mentalities" approach become more apparent as soon as a Western critic, poorly informed in relative terms and too comfortable with Western paradigms, turns to non-Western literatures. The consequences of the widespread bad habit of slighting the substance of Western works, in the name of privileging "theory" (methodology), are magnified when the analyst has no reliable sense of the alternate poetics behind a non-European work, let alone of its substance.

Persons who want to profess CL at the end of the twentieth century in North America appear to me to be facing a set of choices that more or less are the same on other continents. But many institutions of higher education inhibit the pursuit of the fuller range and certain combinations. I do not intend the following set as a hierarchy, but merely as a schematic indication of several legitimate modes of involvement that in fact are knotted together at multiple intersections: (1) CL can take the decision to avoid losing a firm grasp on literature and literariness as its primary object of inquiry and eschew the dilation and distraction of a quest to describe total semiotic networking. Without serious literary history and constant renewal of critical interpretation, we shall lack safe moorings for this endeavor. (2) CL can be centered around an informed interpretation of literary texts and textual repertories, but pay considerable attention to other artistic media and to associated cultural patterns and events within a large sector of a civilization. For example, one can strive to be an expert in the European Renaissance at large, or in the interrelationship of filmmaking and older and newer literature in modern India, etc. (3) CL can promote not only individual efforts (such as Miner's *Comparative Poetics*) but also team efforts (such as the ICLA projects in literary history, theory, translation studies) to achieve understandings that are attainable only when, reaching across cultural boundaries, we contextualize actual differences. We must also test our views in mutually illuminating conversation with comparatists based on other continents and rooted in different traditions. (4) CL can attempt to elaborate general theoretical models for the analysis of literature and culture applicable anywhere in the world (for example, Polysystem analysis).

There is no reason why the United States should remain in the forefront of CL if it abandons sound principles. I would prefer to see vibrant activity at home, but excellence anywhere else is preferable to acceding to regional subsidence. Of course, there is no special mandate for CL to continue if it is emptied of a vital inner purpose, and it may well fade away into the archives to be remembered in one or more generations as a rather long-lasting series of loosely related ventures in literary and cultural studies. The CL that we inherited from Modernism had its deepest taproots in two major strands of nineteenth-century development. CL as the passion to know more about art in relation to "the" (one's own) psyche and social circumstances flowed out of egotistical Romanticism. CL as a passion to know the world and participate more widely and deeply in the great adventure of mankind was nurtured by a generous, cosmopolitan Romanticism. But for me personally there is nothing salvational about CL except perhaps in its specific case-by-case lessons about human variety that put us on our guard against those cultural particularists who attempt to co-opt CL as a cover for tyrannical designs in the American academy.

What have I omitted about CL from these fugitive notes that have rapidly grown too long? I have not spoken of the pleasures of all the texts, works of art, and performances which become part of one's life, and all the sharing that connects lives. The urgent need to express concern over the possible loss of CL as a coherent enterprise by the time I retire has postponed exploring the important biographical matters: which authors, which works are the true loadstars that appeared in my sky? Thank you, irritating institutional falsehoods, for helping me to preserve this precious topic for another day, when I may be more ready for it.

14

Remembering Paul de Man: An Epoch in the History of Comparative Literature

Stanley Corngold

I met Paul de Man for the first time in September 1966, soon after he had begun to teach Comparative Literature at Cornell. I had just returned from Europe in order to begin graduate study. I remember his very bright, slightly bulging eyes, wide, gap-toothed smile, and the collar of his white shirt buttoned, even though it was very warm and he did not wear a tie. He smiled a lot, but one detail of our conversation, the only one that bore on literary matters, greatly interests me today.

I happened to be carrying a copy of the book I was reading—Kafka's novel *Amerika*—and I alluded to the hero Karl Rossmann's first disaster. Even before disembarking he had already lost his small steamer trunk; and I, too, absorbed in *Amerika* on shipboard, had managed to lose my typewriter. De Man *might* have said something about the dangers of reading, but he surely did say something remarkable—remarkably pejorative—about Kafka. He said he was "a second-rate writer." I heard this remark with amazement and absorbed it in silence.[1]

In the memoir to follow, I am tempted to spell "America" with a "k" throughout, if only to point up the ironical connection, not now between the life of *Amerika* and my own, but rather with the vastly more novelistic life of Paul de Man.[2] For like the Prague youth Karl Rossmann, the Antwerp youth Paul de Man, as we now know, fled a shameful past in Europe to begin again in New York under a protective identity—nephew of a powerful politician. The uncle who assists Karl in *Amerika* is Senator Jakob; the uncle who helped Paul de Man begin again in America in the early 1950s is the former Belgian Socialist Minister Hendrik de Man. The continuing cogency of Kafka's first novel—

above all, for its frame of dislocation, technology, arbitrary authority, and apocalyptic rumor—will I hope, emerge, as I proceed.

My concern is with the work and person of Paul de Man, whom I am remembering for a purpose. I want to recollect something overlooked in the remarkable impact his criticism has had on his American colleagues and students—namely, a specifically American factor in his writing and in the character of his most receptive audience.

Between 1949 and 1983—except for a couple of intervals in Zurich—Paul de Man taught Comparative Literature in America. The period covers his first appointment as a lecturer at Bard College up the Hudson in New York State, the same venue as Chapter 2 of Kafka's *Amerika*. It includes his three years of independent study in the 1950s as a member of the Harvard Society of Fellows, followed by his lectureship in Comparative Literature at Harvard. It includes his tenure at Cornell during the 1960s, whence he moved to Johns Hopkins University after 1967,[3] and, finally, his arrival at Yale, as Sterling Professor of the Humanities, where he taught until his death in 1983.

Each of these axial years—circa 1950, 1955, 1962, and 1966—is one of which I am able to give a personal account, because each also marks a stage of my initiation into American university life. And so, as a way of getting to the conditions of de Man's employment in the system—especially conditions economic and ideological—the better to grasp the fit between his teaching and these conditions and hence his impact on American students, I shall now begin to remember my own experience, in the hope that it will lead to factors more pertinent and more general.

The fifties and the sixties were Cold War years; to be in the university then was to be, willy-nilly, a scholar-warrior (short form: "scholwar"). When in 1953 de Man, an over-age graduate student of 34, was studying Yeats with J. (Corny) Kelleher the Gaelicist at Harvard and I, a sophomore, had begun to study Yeats with Lionel Trilling at Columbia, the president of my university was, not untypically, an Army general, no less than General Dwight D. Eisenhower, at the time on leave as military head of NATO. I happened also to be supported to some extent by the United States Navy Department. Like a dozen or so others at Columbia, I had decided at sixteen to join the Regular Naval Reserve Officers Training Corps, whose plain purpose was to graduate scholwars—in this instance, officers who would spend four years, the equivalent in duration of their college education, manning outposts on the defense perimeter. And if I mention now that I was not commissioned because I failed my exam on Bofors guns and boilers, having pored too long the night before over the lines of poetry that in those days had all Columbia English students gaga, namely: "...Hamlet and Lear are gay;/ Gaiety transfiguring all that dread"[4] ("gaiety" in the modern and not the post-modern sense, as in Nietzsche's *Gay Science*)—if I mention this fact, it is only to emphasize the presence of the "military-industrial complex" in American universities in the 1950s. For, on failing to pass my examination, I was to discover the disciplinary practice in place at Columbia College for students who for one reason or another had been provisionally denied degrees (as I was denied a degree, on the grounds of having *purposely* failed Bofors guns and boilers with the *intention* of escaping perimeter defense watches for the next four years—a theory afterwards confirmed by an Instructor of Fine Arts, who was able to recall that I had once *deliberately* failed a quiz on the Parthenon). In fact, I had deliberately failed neither.

It was the practice at Columbia to warn deferred baccalaureates like myself—whose dread of having so much purpose imputed to them, gaiety did not succeed in transfiguring—that Columbia was an independent degree-granting institution, hence not bound by rules in the matter of whom it granted degrees to, even in the case of students like myself who had already satisfied all ordinary published requirements for a degree. In truth Columbia's independence amounted to a show of autonomy masking an unacknowledged dependency on the military budget for its science program and much more. An "autonomous" but "dependent" power? Yes—to say this again simply: you could pass all the required courses, fall afoul of the Naval Reserve Officers Training Corps, and be told by Columbia College to peddle your papers—the corporation of the university reserving the right to decide who got his B.A. at the normal time and who might qualify for it later—"later," meaning, in my case, as in a number of others, after you had taken the opportunity offered you by Columbia to spend the next two years as an *Army* draftee and erase, in this way, your indebtedness to "the government." "Columbia," I was told—in the person of the no doubt impartial Dean of the College who heard my case, a Commander in the Naval Reserve—"Columbia is not dictating to you." Only, if I still wanted a degree, I should know that Columbia might look favorably on my case in two years' time, in 1957, assuming I had used the interval productively—namely, as a soldier—to "discharge my debt," a putatively pan-U.S. nationally-owed debt.[5]

(Readers unfamiliar with the draft should be apprised that the debt of military service was one universally owed to the government by all U.S. citizens, with a few exceptions—such as women, pacifists, students, children, elderly people, and anyone else to the proper degree lame, retarded, illiterate, crazy, indispensable to the civilian sector, or otherwise figuring outside of local draft board quotas—which may explain why the rule of universal conscription was administered by the *Selective* Service.)

Memory jogged by the peddle-your-papers image, I shall mention one other aspect of life at Columbia in the 1950s, and that was the Administration's anti-Semitism, though of what has nowadays been called, in reference to the de Man case, the blessedly "non-virulent" kind. After the professor for Shakespeare had sounded me out on my interest in spending two years after graduation studying English at Cambridge (it interested me enormously), I was asked whether—as a mere formality—I was indeed the son of "native-born

Americans." In the 1950s that didn't mean American Indians. Indeed, for such a one as myself in 1955, who looked and spoke in the manner I did on the way out of Brooklyn, the likelihood of my having Algonquin parents—however delicious, as Kafka's story "The Desire to Become an Indian" bears witness— was probably even greater than that of my having been born of non-immigrant Americans. Actually, I had come fairly close to acquiring that token of civility, my father having been born in Harlem, Manhattan, and my mother (as I boasted to the professor for Shakespeare) having taken the trouble to be born on the boat midway on her parents' journey from the Ukraine to New York harbor. But my story made an only unpleasant impression on this savant, who thereupon closed his books, having good grounds to perceive now that I was, after all, quite unsuited to read English at Cambridge.

What has it do with the critical power of Paul de Man that I, a future and typical de Man student, left Columbia with the impression that as a Jew I belonged somehow outside the life that for four years I had imagined burgeoning there (the "liberal imagination," that abundance of "variousness and complexity") at the same time that I had been identified, by the Dean's office, as a person conspicuously lacking in moral knowledge of the "debt" I owed "the American government"—a lack made abundantly plain by the excess of intention that had been attributed to me—I mean, the intention of deliberately putting down wrong answers to examination questions?

I must have perceived, first, that the life of the liberal imagination had nothing to do with the life of government—whether of universities, courts, or armed forces. And that that rich, imaginary life, though attractive as an object of study and desire, was helpless to assist me to its actual and local realization. Hence, whatever the meaning of my felt indebtedness to that wider life, it had nothing in common with the meaning of my inculcated indebtedness to the military-educational complex, which was a caricature of genuine obligation. So here I was at Columbia, all in all getting (1) early lessons in political demoralization, learning it was futile to attack the injustice of the institution that had taught me to hate injustice, and (2) lessons in moral apathy, having become skeptical of the value of interpersonal relations, since at any moment they were liable to turn into a whirl of maliciously attributed intentions. After all, I had been punished by the willful application of an idea of intention and had seen how readily it could be used by the military-educational complex as a disciplinary instrument—and, by extension, by anyone else. (I believe, incidentally, that young people—who play more than they work—are more readily subjected to judgment on the matter of their intentions than their elders, who are likely to be found toiling at institutions where they are assumed to be carriers of the ethos of the place. There, they are more likely to be judged by the profitability of their actions than by the bias of their intentions. So if they are "bad" [i.e., bad "brokers" or "actors" or "teachers" or other members of the entertainment industry], that is because they are unproductive and not because they are *deliberately* unproductive.)

Assuming, then, my experience at Columbia to have been mediated by objective and generally obtaining structures of university and governmental power (and I shall be giving some further examples)—structures of power necessarily constitutive, too, of Paul de Man's experience (with, of course, important differences to be provided for)—can it be that his—de Man's— exceptional immigrant's, chameleon's, adaptive intelligence found a way, even and especially through literary critical theory, to acknowledge such structures of coercion, denigration, and indebtedness and also to suggest a way to triumph over them? In other words, despite the very palpable differences between him and us—differences of age, experience, nationality, taste, dress, and grammar— could de Man appear to speak triumphantly for "us"?

So, here, rapidly, are the last empirical circumstances I shall mention to substantiate this view. Most of my classmates at Columbia—with our taste for "variousness and complexity" stimulated by the study of English and American literature (and also, importantly, German, French, and Russian works in translation)—determined, in 1955, to become novelists, meaning that almost no students of English went on to graduate school for the professional study of literature. This, at the time, would have been only to choose four more years of oppression in the shadow of the military-educational complex—professional school seeming even more than college an extension of military service. Secondly, the decision not to go on to graduate school also opened the way to crossing the Atlantic sooner, to getting to Europe and staying longer in Europe—and this is a very important point. For—an idea that cannot be over-emphasized—in the 1950s we were mad about Europe; we were not *Europa-müde* but *auf Europa verrückt*: nuts about it. "Europe"—a certain anachronistic, pre-NATO Europe—was the secular religious ideal of students of literature during the Eisenhower era, an era, I should like to stress, that I had been among the first to experience, since I began conscious life at the university where Eisenhower was already president.

And so, characteristically, I think, in July 1952, when my training battleship sailed to Europe and anchored, and I was released in the evening to rush into the port, I kneeled down and kissed the dark, rain-wet cobblestones—of yes, Antwerp (I do not lie)—crying out, "Here, at last!"— although ten years later, when I began the study of Comparative Literature at Cornell with Paul de Man of Antwerp, it did not occur to me to make this Antwerp connection explicit. The scene and the connection, however, have often been with me ever since the wartime behavior of my "doctor father" came to light. ("Doctor father" is the literal translation of the German word *Doktorvater*, the national catachresis for "thesis adviser.")[6] In 1941, it has since emerged, Paul de Man wrote for the collaborationist newspaper *Le Soir* of Brussels an article entitled, "The Jews in Contemporary Literature," in which he declared that "a solution to the Jewish question which envisages the creation of a Jewish colony isolated from Europe would not lead to deplorable consequences for the literary life of the West. It would lose, all told, a few personalities of mediocre value and would continue, as in the past, to develop according to its own great evolutionary principles."[7] Now I suffer from this morbid connection of Antwerps, additionally chastening my enthusiasm for Europe and bringing my view of the Old World closer to that of my father's, who remembered his father's stories of humiliation and pogrom.[8]

My remark about the two Antwerps is meant to make the following point: in 1955 I had assumed, like many students of my generation, that the great life of the mind was one that had been pre-lived in Europe, by activist European intellectuals like Malraux, Trotsky, Sartre, and Orwell. (We did not, by the way, make a clear distinction in such matters between England and the Continent, partly, perhaps, because our teacher, Lionel Trilling, regarded Wordsworth as a Hegelian poet of the Unhappy Consciousness). So in my case Antwerp in 1952 turned out to focus symbolically my generation's passion for Europe.[9]

The further irony of this post-1955 conjuncture—and here I shall definitely conclude the personal note—is that for those like myself, seeking, after two years in the Army near Heidelberg, to stay on in Europe, if only to go on breathing that *Geist*-filled atmosphere, the one plausible sort of work available was teaching American literature to airmen and soldiers at one of the many Army and Air Force bases throughout Europe. This opportunity had been created in the 1950s by legislation urged by the industrial-military complex requiring that all officers of the U.S. Army and Air Force hold Bachelor of Arts degrees—requiring, in a word, that all our warriors be scholwars. It had obviously become necessary in an age of increasingly complex warfare to raise the technical consciousness of the officer class; but another consideration was in play: legislators believed that a generally heightened literacy among officers and soldiers would be pleasing and impressive to the semi-occupied countries in postwar Europe, supposing that it is better to be ordered about by a scholwar than by some thug who cannot tell "Lapis Lazuli" from a Bofors gun. This legislation provided a new educational opportunity in Europe for enterprising American universities selling B.A.s cheaply to a freshly created, literally captive market—an opportunity exploited at first but soon afterwards abandoned by the University of California, which was evidently doing well enough selling B.A.s in California—and then afterwards taken up by the University of Maryland, which even now maintains in England and Germany remnants of its Overseas Division once as farflung as Reykjavik and Ankara. This final apprenticeship in Europe completed, in our perspective, the merger of the values of the university and "the military": American expatriates teaching at such camps could not fail to confuse the authentic content of their work (rhetoric and composition) with its inauthentic circumstances—the fact that their workplace, the classroom, was enclosed by barbed wire and guarded by bayonets.

There appeared to be no way out of this confusion, until the homeopathic route suddenly provided in 1957 by the success of Sputnik. The Russians' launching of a satellite into orbit provoked Congress to a new plan for winning the Cold War, which of course had always included winning Europe's mind.[10] It passed the National Defense Education Act, now explicitly merging the values of the Campus and the Pentagon, the plain purpose of which was to strengthen the American aerospace engineering plant, with Congress once again choosing to define this project as more generally humane than that of mobilizing hard-science technologies. The government undertook simultaneously to create new foreign and critical language programs, including the Department of Comparative Literature at Cornell University, little realizing what witch's brew it was preparing: for when it gave Cornell NDEA money, which Cornell matched, to hire Paul de Man—cast off from Harvard—as well as provide fellowships for new Ph.D. students of Comparative Literature, it was decreeing the career of deconstruction in America.[11] In 1962, de Man, now functioning as admissions officer to his newly fledged department, found impressive my years of exposure to the intellectual life of France and Germany—an atmosphere in truth much attenuated by the barracks-climate of Army classrooms at Captieux and Butzbach; and thus I once again began training in America, now under the former Nazi-sympathizer Paul de Man, and both of us under the paternity of the U.S. National Defense Education Act.

So I came riding in (as did de Man) on the support of the American military-educational establishment, an artificial family arrangement which we both accepted even as we shrank from it.

Now what had Paul de Man been learning in America while making his journey from Bard to Harvard to Ithaca, New York? Certainly, he had not been detained by the notion of a large, various, hierarchically ordered Life (to be found either in Europe or America). One of his earliest and most influential essays, called "The Dead-End of Formalist Criticism," repudiates the view of poetry as the representation of lived experience.[12] De Man had long before experienced the great collapse of the ideology of European *Lebensphilosophie*, with himself playing the role of traitor-intellectual. Thomas Mann had written (in his *Reflections of a Nonpolitical Man*)[13] of a certain good thing: Mind's self-betrayal in the name of Life, the name of the betrayal being a kind of invigorating, "Life"-furthering Irony. De Man was all set to betray (a large, hierarchical, variously ordered) Life in the name of Mind, so long as Mind was Irony yet not of a notably "Life"-furthering sort. When de Man arrived in America it was all in all as a thoroughly disillusioned European mandarin. In him a pride of negative Intellect (as a critique of Life) joined with his political cunning into an Irony that kept him going, although it must have robbed his going of the certainty of any particular direction. His irony was not inconsistent either with opportunism or with keeping a low profile. His life would be nourished by one inexhaustibly good thing—literature; as a new American

I think he was satisfied enough with the native tone of a relative freedom from persecution.

We know that after the war, it is true, when he could have feared retaliation in Belgium, he was cleared of the charge of significant collaborationist activity; on the other hand, just after he left *Le Soir*, another cultural reporter associated with *Le Soir* was assassinated by a member of the Resistance and de Man's own photograph reproduced in a Resistance pamphlet entitled "Galerie des Traîtres"—whereupon he fled Brussels for Antwerp. De Man spent the remainder of the war years in the provinces; and furthermore in the late 1940s or so, the years of de Man's emigration, he had been on the point of being prosecuted in Antwerp, it has been seriously alleged, for forgery and other sorts of business swindle.[14] So the young immigrant had a couple of things to fear being turned in for, during his early days in America, which indeed could have made it an Amerika for him: especially when you add to the entire constellation of collaborationist journalistic activities and ventures in fraudulent signatures the fact that in America de Man became a bigamist by marrying his student at Bard College—a matter of some vexation for his Romanian wife, whom with their three children, he had left behind in Argentina. She resurges here as the rumored author of a letter denouncing de Man after he had settled in Harvard with his new wife and child. Such a letter is mentioned in the draft of a reply de Man wrote to Renato Poggioli in 1955 while still a member of the Society of Fellows.[15] In it de Man claimed that his journalistic activities had been decent—though they had not been—and had been limited to the years 1940–41—though he had published collaborationist and anti-Semitic articles at least as late as summer 1942. So the timely award to him of his Ph.D. at Harvard would also have been in some jeopardy at the hands of an administration ready to impute intent of a damnable kind to him.

Now what was de Man thinking about in Harvard over and above "gaiety transfiguring all that dread"? He had been asked to leave Bard College, so he was available. Furthermore, he had averted deportation to the homeland thanks to the intervention, not this time by an uncle but by another American Senator— his new father-in-law. De Man moved to Boston, where, while considering an education at Harvard, he began teaching French at the Berlitz school, numbering among his pupils a future Secretary of State, with whom, de Man related, he had made a private arrangement by which both stood to profit—the professor would pay de Man less for lessons than the school charged, and de Man would also prosper, because the school's cut would not be skimmed off the top of these fees, but it did not help, since the future Secretary did not pay—another unsavory episode from the annals of the military-educational complex.[16] From his situation in Boston, however, de Man was able to gain entry to graduate seminars at Harvard, owing to the sympathy of Harry Levin, head of Comparative Literature. Levin, precisely because of his extraordinary learning, was inclined to be impressed by the Real Thing, namely, by an authentically polyglot European intellectual, one perhaps associable with the impressive group of émigres from Hitler who came to this country after the War ("Hitler shook the tree," J. Robert Oppenheimer reportedly said, while directing Princeton's Institute for Advanced Study, "and I picked up the apples").[17] Levin kept de Man on, but something went wrong—quite possibly de Man's insistence that the true subject of literature was, again and again, just this: literature itself and nothing less. Yet Levin and Renato Poggioli were protective, and given Paul de Man's boast that he was not the nephew of Hendrik de Man the Belgian collaborator but rather his son (a lie both self-accusing and likely to evoke an unearned commiseration), the authorities were reluctant to put any more pressure on a son who had presumably suffered enough from the sins visited on him by his "father."

Here I recall a passage from de Man's essay on Rousseau's *Confessions*— his wildest piece of writing, and now we know why—called "The Purloined Ribbon." De Man says, "With the threatening loss of control [of the meaning of a text], the possibility arises of the entirely gratuitous and irresponsible text, not just. . .as an intentional denial of paternity for the sake of self-protection, but as the radical annihilation of the metaphor of selfhood and of the will."[18] De Man's life-texts and assertions, this essay says, could, like Rousseau's, amount to something other than an intentional denial of paternity for the sake of self-protection; these texts are events bringing about the entire annihilation of the individual personality of the author and the assumption of a sort of allegorical existence. This is the end-state of de Man's—and quite possibly Karl Rossmann's—trajectory in America.

Let me try to extrapolate from de Man's American experience up to this point to those structures of power I claimed to have identified from my own experience. Like upcoming Jewish faculty members at American universities in the 1950s, especially in departments of English literature, where they were unwanted, de Man had practical reasons to play down his empirical identity, while at the same time teaching that the empirical identity was in principle vacuous—inauthentic and contingent—so it did not finally matter how you used it. If it turned out that you used your so-called empirical self to your so-called advantage, that mischief was no worse than the naivety of regarding your empirical self as an agent and repository of true experience, for thinking of it this way would inevitably magnify (if this were possible) personal inauthenticity and bad faith into a profitable inability to understand anything let alone literature. (That may be why, for one thing, de Man has left behind him such conflicting stories, which can be heard from his students, about what he'd done during the war: to Juliet Flower McCannell he said he'd gone to England; to David Quint, to Switzerland; to me, to Paris.) You might say there is deplorable mendacity in such a stance or a liberating relief from the ideology of "identity." De Man preferred, at any rate in the classroom, not to examine the motives of renunciation too particularly.

To enlarge this point: de Man would have been acquainted right from the beginning at Bard, and then at Harvard, with the harsh face of power—of administrative power—at universities, which did not much smile at him. These were realities with which, as I have been saying, I and many ethnic and political minority students of my generation were acquainted. What was new to us in the early 1960s was the rigor and severity with which de Man dismissed the value of "lived experience"; the real subject of our concern should not be a large, various, complex, and hierarchically ordered Life. The impossibility of pursuing such an ideal was based not just on individual human weakness but on an ontological reality. For the beginning condition of all human experience (even and especially in places and conditions where experience could seem to be most seductive—such as Europe, as American students in the 1950s were inclined to see it) was not wholeness and intensity but catastrophe, negation, and sacrifice. This was the most heavily charged part of de Man's teaching, the strangest and the hardest to believe. I remember when, after being puzzled by a lecture on Rousseau, I asked de Man what the practical upshot was of Rousseau's thoroughgoing insistence on negativity and difference—the difference not only of selves to other selves but of selves to themselves. De Man replied, with a mixture of weariness, incredulity, and what seems now a trace of hope of being proved wrong: "It means the impossibility of happiness!" As an American Euromane of the early sixties feeling cheated by Europe—by an Americanized, militarily-educationally resectioned and commodified Europe—I was getting ready to understand this. Still, it felt like a leaden cloud—de Man's attack on what he called "the empirical self." An example of how it sounded can be found in the first essay of *Blindness and Insight*: "Considerations of the actual and historical existence of writers are a waste of time from a critical viewpoint."[19] De Man was teaching a position that had been philosophically validated in Heidegger's *Being and Time*—which happened to be the one set book for our first seminar, our introduction to methodology seminar, in Comparative Literature. It was a position interesting to himself. In the French department de Man was teaching a seminar on Mallarmé—offering dialectically differentiated, Hegelian-phenomenological readings of *Igitur* and *Un Coup de dés*. At the end of the seminar, in a rare gesture of classroom curiosity, he asked us our opinion of Mallarmé's poetry, and I said, "I have the feeling in the case of Mallarmé's poetry you cannot do anything except explicate it." De Man looked very amused, grinned, and nodded, saying, "That is true," and meaning, "*You* would think that was a drawback." Encouraged, I continued: "I look to poetry to mobilize my experiences and my feelings" (I remember that I actually used the word "mobilize"—scholwar to the last). De Man grinned some more. "Yes," he said, "that is your very engaging aberration." I was to understand that my view was "naive."

But after a few months at Cornell, in Ithaca, upstate New York, where "experience" could mean very little more than having Chinese food on Saturday afternoons, I was ready to agree that it was naive to regard personal experience as the base of interpretation. It all became gradually very convincing, because it was so very convenient to believe that there in the rural academy, that zone of no experience, we were actually being initiated into the one authentic teaching of literature—namely, that literature is the zone of no experience, except for one distinguished one: the experience of the "nothingness of all human things" (Rousseau).[20] It was an additionally impressive teaching as coming from a genuine European (who carried about him a certain tattered aura of Europeanness even while he cultivated a reasonably friendly, assimilated—American—manner of speaking and behaving). For if de Man could repudiate experience, then experience was nowhere and no longer worth having. Abandon all experience, all ye that enter here: thus passed away the large, hierarchically ordered life of the mind, full of variousness and complexity.

In the classroom, I am saying, de Man produced a special sort of transcendentalism which worked well in the increasingly antidemocratic and professionalized atmosphere of American social life in the years before and after 1968–70. I find it tremendously suggestive that he spent these years out of America and in Switzerland (the years when university students struggled most to cast de Gaulle out of France and the "k" out of America); and it was only in 1969, on the publication of "The Rhetoric of Temporality,"[21] the text which allegedly completes de Man's turn to rhetorical analysis and inaugurates his kind of deconstruction proper and its corollary—professional formalism—that he resettled in this country. De Man's own remarks on this subject are pertinent.

> I have been teaching in the United States for the last thirty years, and it's an experience which I take so much for granted that I don't reflect on it very much anymore. I became aware of it because for a time I taught alternatively at the University of Zurich, at Cornell, and at Hopkins. I had then the possibility of comparing the situation of teaching in Europe and of teaching here: in Europe one is of course much closer to ideological and political questions, while, on the contrary, in the States, one is much closer to professional questions. So the ethics of the profession are very different. I found it difficult in Europe to be teaching material that was so separated from the actual professional use that students, who were mostly destined to teach in secondary school, would make of it. So there was a real discrepancy between what one talked about and what the use value of this could be for the students. So it had a very special feeling of alienation to me, very different from here, where since one teaches future colleagues, one has a very direct professional relationship to them—which, however, has its own ideologies and its own politics, which are more the politics of the profession, the relation of the academic profession to the American political world and society [I never heard de Man say a word about this relation—SC]. I ended up finding the function

of teaching in the United States—the function of an academic as distinct from the academic function—much more satisfactory than in Europe, precisely because of the contract one has with the people one teaches. Here you can actually carry out your contractual relation to them, whereas in Europe you can't.[22]

At this point it is obviously important to consider de Man's understanding of contractual relations.

In the chapter on autobiography in *The Rhetoric of Romanticism*, de Man writes: "Writers *of* autobiographies as well as writers *on* autobiography are obsessed by the need to move from cognition to resolution and to action, from speculative to political and legal authority." De Man cites the critic Philippe Lejeune, "who," de Man says, "stubbornly insists. . .that the identity of autobiography is not only representational and cognitive but contractual, grounded not in tropes but in speech acts. The name on the title page is not the proper name of a subject capable of self-knowledge and understanding, but the signature that gives the contract legal, though by no means epistemological, authority. The fact that Lejeune uses 'proper name' and 'signature' interchangeably signals both the confusion and the complexity of the problem."[23] We are to understand that the poverty of truth in autobiography is an affair of its desire for legal and political authority—an authority which is recognized for what it is whenever autobiography is theorized about in terms of contracts. Contracts, of course, are based on force, or, in the manner of speaking de Man came to prefer, on "potential violence. " At the outset of *Allegories of Reading*, de Man also wrote: "We speak as if, with the problems of literary form resolved once and forever, and with the techniques of structural analysis refined to near-perfection, we could now move 'beyond formalism' towards the questions that really interest us and reap, at last, the fruits of the ascetic concentration on techniques that prepared us for this decisive step. With the internal law and order of literature well policed, we can now confidently devote ourselves to the foreign affairs, the external politics of literature."[24] When this piece first appeared in *Diacritics* in 1973, it was regarded by many as a courageous thrust at the violence of the American intervention in Vietnam. But when, some ten years later, de Man reprinted the essay in *Allegories of Reading*, leaving the allegedly political reference unchanged, the question was raised (first, I think, by Jonathan Arac) about the authenticity of de Man's political intention. Was America—for all decades hence—always to be violent overseas because blinded by the only specious order provided by its "internal police"? At best, we have de Man repeating his disdain of the satisfactions provided by relations and models based on potential violence—such as, for example, the notorious so-called "aesthetic ideology."

It was, however, during his later years at Yale, the time of concerted deconstructive attack upon the most recalcitrant of Romantic and Idealist writers, that de Man most conspicuously upheld the ethos of professionalism. Which is, of course, an affair of contracts, enforced by agencies of law and order. That is the living gist of the ethics of deconstruction, and it makes vivid exactly what term of lesser worth is being subordinated and eclipsed. This term is "intention." It is precisely the aberrations of intention—especially, as intentions are imputed to persons by institutions and vice-versa—that the appeal to the police, to which de Man finally succumbs, might be supposed to regulate. In light of de Man's own past, a famous passage from *Blindness and Insight* reveals a different sense:

> In the act of anthropological intersubjective interpretation [he writes], a fundamental discrepancy always prevents the observer from coinciding fully with the consciousness he is observing. The same discrepancy exists in everyday language, in the impossibility of making the actual expression coincide with what has to be expressed, of making the actual sign coincide with what it signifies. It is the distinctive privilege of language to be able to hide meaning behind a misleading sign, as when we hide rage or hatred behind a smile. But it is the distinctive curse of all language, as soon as any kind of interpersonal language is involved, that it is *forced* to act this way. The simplest of wishes cannot express itself without hiding behind a screen of language that constitutes a world of intricate inter-subjective relationships, all of them potentially inauthentic. In the everyday language of communication, there is no a priori privileged position of sign over meaning or of meaning over sign; the act of interpretation will always again have to establish this relation for the particular case at hand. The interpretation of everyday language is a Sisyphean task, a task without end and without progress, *for the other is always free to make what he wants differ from what he says he wants* (emphasis added).[25]

I hardly need to point up the sheer oddity of these arguments when they are put forward as universal principles, and their vastly greater clarity when they are read as the temptations of a confidence man—one who, as Thomas Mann wrote in *Felix Krull*, lives forever only figuratively, *im Gleichnis*.

Consider, with respect to de Man's statement about the impossibility of truthful interpersonal recognition, the following question: What are the conditions of thought about the self, what are the assumptions about the self, that would allow one to claim that one was forever free to make what one has intended different from the intention attributed to one by another as the meaning of one's words?

Perhaps I admired the audacity of this position for all its superiority to my own. Whereas I, a Columbia senior under suspicion, could merely claim that an intention had been attributed to me *where I had had none*, de Man was raising a significantly more powerful defense: no intention attributed to me has to be recognized as right, because I am free to change at will the truth of my initial intention. I can always deny what I intended—and not be wrong!

It appears that when you give up the category of intention in order to destroy its efficacy as an instrument of political discipline—a renunciation that would greatly appeal to individuals harmed young—you wind up empowering the same principle of disciplinary law and order in order to control the aberrant behavior of persons no longer responsible for their words and actions. This is not a point you will actually find clearly stated in de Man. It is, however, a point that needs to be emphasized, especially in the present climate, where, as an undeniable part of his legacy, academic work has more and more come to mean naked opportunism in the pursuit of power, ostensibly for the sake of enforcing contracts but in reality for power's own unlovely sake. This crisis comes as no surprise when so little has been done—and so much undone—in the effort to clarify the spirit of the contract.

NOTES

1. Many years later I reminded de Man of his judgment, and he denied all recollection of it. Nor did he any longer agree with it: it was true, however, that he did not know Kafka, he said, although, of course, he added, he had read Maurice Blanchot's essays on Kafka. It was unlikely that de Man was thinking then of the notorious sentence he had written in March 1941, which appeared in an article judging the emigration of Jewish writers from Europe to be in no way deplorable. In that article he had singled out the following writers as "continuateurs" of an authentic novelistic tradition: Gide, Hemingway, D. H. Lawrence, and a novelist called "Kafha." "Les Juifs dans la Littérature actuelle," *Le Soir* [Brussels], 4 March 1941, 10, in *Wartime Journalism, 1939-1943 by Paul de Man*, ed. Werner Hamacher, Neil Hertz, and Thomas Keenan (Lincoln and London: University of Nebraska Press, 1988), p. 45.

2. A life that did in fact key a novel by one Henri Thomas, entitled *Le Parjure*. (Paris: Gallimard, 1961). The refrain throughout the novel is the hero Stéphane's passion for "Hölderlin in America"—de Man having early translated into American that German Romantic poet and schizophrenic in exile and been his explicator.

3. The year of the famous meeting with Derrida, when each divulged to the other his intense preoccupation with Rousseau's *Essay on the Origin of Language*.

4. W.B. Yeats, "Lapis Lazuli," *Collected Poems of W.B. Yeats* (London: Macmillan: 1958), p. 338.

5. This is not a footnote for historians of Comparative Literature, who can return immediately to the text without missing anything. Moral pathologists with time on their hands, however, might like to learn why I have not put this matter more directly and said "a debt I owed the Navy!" But I cannot say exactly what I owed the Navy. I was

paid to drill, and drill I did. But didn't the Navy also pay my tuition? Indeed, but so did the Regents of New York State and so did the Pulitzer scholarship. Columbia, it emerged, had collected payment for my tuition three times over, then withheld my degree not for any act I performed (failing gunnery) but for the intention of so doing—which it attributed to me. It is true I felt remiss for failing to meet my obligation to the Navy: in return for its paying my tuition at Columbia, I had implicitly promised to qualify for a commission. But aside from dismissing me, the Navy had no other penalty in place; it did not, for example, withhold B.A.'s. It did not have to, since dismissal from the program normally meant financial hardship for the culprit. And so I continued to grieve—until the scholwars at Columbia College entered the scene; then I felt not sorrow but indignation. If the Navy Department had paid my tuition, so had two other institutions. Columbia, I felt, could at any time give my tuition back to the government instead of keeping three times what it was entitled to. I chafed to think that the product of all my exertions was to help provide the Dean's office with the opportunity to misjudge my case.

6. In the early 1960s, in upper New York State, where I studied with de Man, I did not conceive of him as my "father" in any sense whatsoever. But as my career more and more took on the direction of German studies, I began by that Freudian logic of deferred action to regard him as a certain kind of academic father—a point that has since been emphasized for me by German and Dutch correspondents, who refer to my present position on de Man as constituting a *Vaterrmord*—a parricide.

7. Hamacher, Hertz, and Keenan, eds., *Wartime Journalism. 1939–1943 by Paul de Man*, p. 45.

8. In 1942, several months before de Man once again took up his anti-Semitic pen, Antwerp was itself the scene of pogrom, its own party-directed Night of Shattered Glass, when the Jewish community was assaulted and humiliated at the instigation of Flemish Nazis.

9. The flight to Europe ends in a darkest Amerika of the spirit. And whatever direction the quest for redemptive experience is conceived as taking, the point of the Antwerp joke seems to dawn most clearly in the American West. Thus the book entitled *Responses: On Paul de Man's Wartime Journalism*, in which Paul de Man's career comes to an end in a sort of apotheosis of denigration, has been published in Lincoln, Nebraska [Werner Hamacher, Neil Hertz, and Thomas Keenan, eds., *Responses: On Paul de Man's Wartime Journalism* (Lincoln and London: University of Nebraska Press, 1989). Karl Rossmann's end, in Kafka's *Amerika*, is also far-Western. Not trivially, wanting, like de Man, to be an engineer, Rossmann flees Europe for America, seeking the redemption that he singularly fails to find—witness his negative apotheosis and literal denigration at the Oklahoma Nature Theater (I say "literal," because he is given the name "Negro"). I am alluding here to another apotheosis of de Man produced in Norman, Oklahoma [the proceedings of a conference held at the University of Oklahoma, *Deconstruction at Yale*, edited by R.C. Davis and R. Schleifer]. De Man died before he could enter this Oklahoma Nature Theater.

10. It became important to assure the Germans that our up-through-the-ranks officers maintaining a defense perimeter across their country were capable of accurately

punctuating something more than the silence of provincial evenings with scattered bursts of M-2 fire.

11. De Man remarked at Cornell: "I thought the students at Harvard were primitive...!"

12. *Blindness and Insight: Essays in the Rhetoric of Contemporary Criticism*, 2d rev. ed. (Minneapolis: University of Minnesota Press, 1983), pp. 229–45.

13. Thomas Mann, *Reflections of a Nonpolitical Man*, trans. Walter D. Morris (New York: Unger, 1982).

14. According to the declarations of de Man's boyhood friend Georges Goriely—now an emeritus professor of sociology at the University of Brussels—made on the occasion of a conference held on Paul de Man at the University of Antwerp in June 1988.

15. *Responses*, pp. 475–77.

16. This anecdote comes from Professor William Flesch of Brandeis University, author of one of the most distinguished and nuanced discussions of de Man's wartime journalism ("Ancestral voices: De Man and his Defenders," Hamacher, Hertz, and Keenan, eds., *Responses*, pp. 173–84).

17. "What interested me the most [at Princeton] was the famous Institute for Advanced Studies. Since so many great German *exiles* work there, I thought that with the outbreak of Hitler it had been founded especially for them. But that is not true. The plan had been in existence for a long time...." Erika and Klaus Mann, *Escape to Life: Deutsche Kultur im Exil* (Ignoto: Edition Spangenberg, 1991), p. 269.

18. *Allegories of Reading: Figural Language in Rousseau, Nietzsche, Rilke, and Proust* (New Haven: Yale University Press, 1979), p. 296.

19. *Blindness and Insight*, p. 35.

20. In 1793, at the Festival of the Supreme Being, an effigy of le Néant was burnt. De Man restores this martyr of Reason to its rightful place.

21. *Blindness and Insight*, pp. 187–228.

22. *The Resistance to Theory* (Minneapolis: University of Minnesota Press, 1986), pp. 115–16.

23. *The Rhetoric of Romanticism* (New York: Columbia University Press, 1984), p. 71.

24. *Allegories of Reading*, p. 3.

25. *Blindness and Insight*, p. 11.

15

Out of a Gothic North

Lionel Gossman

Lionel Gossman was born in Glasgow, Scotland, at a time when it still styled itself the "second city of the Empire." He attended public schools in the city and, during the worst of the war years, in the surrounding countryside, where he had been evacuated. It was a solid Scottish education, strict, thorough, strong on the basics, except for science, since virtually all the science teachers (who were overwhelmingly male) had been conscripted into the armed forces and their replacements were less than competent. He was drawn to foreign languages early, for three reasons, or so it seems to him in retrospect. First, he was good at them and liked grammar in any language: English, Latin, French, or German. Second, they gave him the opportunity to assume momentarily different identities, and in those freely assumed, alien identities, the things that made him, as a Jew, feel uncomfortably different from the Scottish children who were his friends and playmates no longer counted. (This was a major advantage of the modern languages over Latin, which did not allow for role playing in the same way.) Finally, his teachers took a great interest in him and opened up an unsuspected world of beauty and elegance that contrasted with the raw energy and austerity of grimy, wartime Glasgow. One in particular, a pretty and graceful woman, whom Gossman considered the acme of Parisian stylishness, would gather her classes round an old piano in the school's draughty assembly hall and have them sing Reynaldo Hahn's settings of Verlaine and Hugo, or would pack a half dozen at a time into a tiny Morris Minor, for which she received a small petrol ration on account of her father's being an invalid, and drive them off to the Municipal Art Gallery to look at the Manets and Degas. In addition, reading novels and poems in French and German, which he had begun to do more and more, Gossman was discovering exotic conditions quite unlike those he was accustomed to. There were ideas, feelings, and ways of expressing them in the world beyond Glasgow, it seemed, that were different both from the blunt, matter-of-fact Scottish style to which he was accustomed and from the rarefied upperclass English manners that, like most Scottish adolescents, he found alien and threatening. (In his mature years, he feels it is only fair to add, Gossman has come not only to value that Scottish bluntness and plainness but to understand how deep a mark they left on him.)

When he went up to the University of Glasgow at the end of the war (not something that could be taken for granted, since most places were reserved for returning servicemen and servicewomen), Gossman thought briefly about Law and Classics, but the opening lecture of a course in conveyancing quickly dissuaded him from the former, and as he had only Latin and no Greek, he did not feel adequately prepared for the latter. He therefore felt justified in continuing to do what gave him most pleasure. A degree in French and German in Scotland at that time led almost inevitably to a career as a schoolteacher, and that is what he expected to be.

There was no question of Comparative Literature. Gossman had never heard of it, and there was no Comparative Literature program at Glasgow or probably anywhere else in Great Britain. (Only four representatives from Great Britain attended the 1958 Congress at Chapel Hill, compared with twelve from France and nine from Germany, and not one of those four held a university position in Comparative Literature). Students of foreign languages and literatures at Glasgow were required, however, to major in two. Gossman majored in French and German.

The dominant form of criticism in French, he recalls, to the degree that there was one at all, was a version of New Criticism applied to French Literature, mixed with Lansonism and traditional French explication de texte. Gossman recalls that in the first class on Nineteenth Century French Poetry, Sam Hackett distributed an unidentified poem (no title, no name of author, no date) and instructed the students to write what they thought of it. He has often wondered whether the results confirmed I.A. Richards' claim in *Practical Criticism*, by which the exercise was obviously inspired. In German, the old philological method predominated and the program was heavily weighted toward Old and Middle High German texts. Mostly the students translated them and commented on the linguistic forms. It was, however, in the German Department Library that Gossman discovered the critical writings of Georg Lukács (how they got there he still cannot fathom), and it was in a German class taught by Harold Betteridge, the only liberal in a department of arch-conservatives, that he was introduced to the correspondence of Goethe and Schiller on questions of esthetics. He considers that Lukács's writings on the historical novel, on the classical age in Germany, and on German expressionist poetry—which he appropriated uncritically and imitated shamelessly—together with the prolonged exchange of ideas between Goethe and Schiller on the relations among the different genres, the conditions of literary production in antiquity and in modern times, and the effect of these conditions on the genres, were the two formative influences on his studies and that they determined what turned out to be a lifelong interest in the ethical, political, and ideological conditions and implications of different esthetic practices.

It was not by accident, or because of an interest in literary theory (he would not have known what that was) that he was drawn to Lukács. He did recognize, obviously, that there was a coherent underpinning to Lukács's criticism, and he responded to that out of frustration with critical writing, especially in French, that seemed to him impressionistic, personal, capricious, and impenetrable. But in German there were several critics' who appeared to be systematic: the Hegelian literary historian August Korff, for instance. If Lukács, in particular, appealed to Gossman it was almost certainly because of the social philosophy and the social and cultural criticism that are an essential part of his work. For in the years after the war, there was an expectation in Britain of major social change, and Gossman shared it. While Herbert Lindenberger was trying to organize unions in the state of Washington, Gossman was campaigning for the Independent Labour Party in the slums of Glasgow. Lukács's appeal was that he made it possible to reconcile the love of art and literature with a social conscience and a strong interest in social and political issues.

All the writers in German that Gossman particularly liked were those admired or discussed by Lukács: besides Goethe and Schiller, Hölderlin, Büchner, Fontane, the expressionist poets. In addition, he discovered Franz Kafka, whom he thought of as a model, since he had turned his complex personal situation as a Jew writing in German in Czechoslovakia to brilliant account. Kafka's works were then (1945–51) available in German only from Schocken Books in New York. There were no credit cards in the 1940s, international communications were just beginning to pick up again and in the pre-jet age remained slow and expensive, and currency was not convertible. So it was a major undertaking for a seventeen year old, who for five years had lived in virtual confinement (during the war years travel was difficult, sometimes dangerous, even within the British Isles), to procure those books. As a result, they acquired an almost magical significance. They stood for all the knowledge and thought of which young people in those days felt they had been deprived by the war. They forecast the end of intellectual isolation and undernourishment, and released troubling questions and sensitivities that had been interned, so to speak, during the war years, for reasons of national security.

On reflection, Gossman considers that French represented for him a culture that seemed more intellectual and cosmopolitan than the native culture. To a naive, uncertain undergraduate from a modest background in a big working-class city at the outer rim of Europe, it also offered what the remote Amazon had offered the superbly gifted, sophisticated, and urbane Lévi-Strauss: a critical position from which to consider and evaluate his own culture—which in Gossman's case had come to seem almost unquestionable as a result of wartime propaganda and the remoteness and provincialism of early twentieth century Scotland. German too might have offered an outside position, though a very different and, to a Jew, certainly a far darker and more problematical one. Gossman was strongly attracted to it, but in the end, having been warned by a friendly German *Lektorin* that his "radical" views were not regarded favorably by the German Department, where *Gemütlichkeit* was the order of the day and hearty singing of German carols at the Christmas party was a surer road to success than reading Büchner ("Ach, Herr Gossman, was lesen Sie denn da?" the head of the department exclaimed in dismay when he found Gossman reading *Woyzzeck* in the university library), he decided that German, as taught at Glasgow anyway, was more provincial and narrow than anything he had ever experienced in Scotland, and that he should concentrate his efforts on French. Here the teaching staff were open, intellectual, and cosmopolitan—like the language and the literature themselves, it seemed. Among the scholars that the professor, Alan Boase—reputedly an active champion of the Republican cause during the Spanish Civil War—had gathered around him, were Sam Hackett, Francis Scarfe, Stephen Ullman, Alban Krailsheimer, and Norman Cohn, who then taught medieval literature but was already quietly working on his classic study of millenarianism, *The Pursuit of the Millennium*. Still, in the Cold War conditions of the time, the mere suspicion of Marxist influence in criticism could cause trouble, even in a broad-minded Department of French Studies, such as Glasgow then certainly was. Cohn had to reassure an alarmed Boase that there was no substance to a colleague's assertion that the terribly earnest and conventional study of "L'Idée de l'Age d'Or dans *Le Roman de la Rose*," which his favorite student had produced for Jean Frappier during a postgraduate year at the Sorbonne, was "Marxist." In the late forties and early fifties radicalism was not theoretical and it was anything but chic.

From his early training and acculturation Gossman believes he has retained a considerable inner tension between the continental habit of taking every intellectual question to its furthest extreme, which he found first in Lukács and a little later in Sartre, and which often goes hand in hand with an oppressive, potentially tyrannical *esprit de système*, and the native British tradition of moderation and skepticism, which emphasizes observation and attention to specifics, discourages radical speculation, and—wisely, perhaps—avoids pushing problems to their ultimate, dramatic, and often tragic consequences. In today's terms, that tension translates into a recognition of the value and interest of theory and at the same time a cautious holding back from it. From Wellek's delightful reminiscences of Princeton in the late 1920s, in the essay in this volume, it emerges that the only professor at Princeton at that time who had a theoretical interest—Morris Croll—was also the least tolerant of views that were different from his. Coming from Wellek, who has always affirmed the essential importance of literary theory, that testimony is particularly telling.

After a year at the Sorbonne, Gossman went on to two years of compulsory military service, during which he was given intensive training in Russian. Whoever was in charge of the program, the object of which was evidently to prepare for the next war, had had the eccentric, but by no means foolish idea that the Russian pronunciation of interrogators of future Soviet prisoners-of-war would be improved by having them recite Pushkin and Lermontov; and so it was that every Friday for an entire winter, in a cold, damp barracks in the soggy wilderness of Bodmin Moor, thirty boisterous young men in coarse khaki uniforms were initiated by an aging, elegant, and effeminate member of the former Czarist Pazhski Korpus to the art of reading and reciting Russian poetry. Three happy years at Oxford (where Gossman was the first and probably last student of French literature at the then newly founded St. Antony's College, a college intended for graduate students only, the vast majority of whom were foreign) led—miraculously in view of the complete absence of any mandatory course of instruction and the casual and infrequent, albeit kindly and encouraging, supervision he received from Jean Seznec—to the completion of a doctoral thesis on medieval scholarship in the Enlightenment.

Gossman has always felt, however, that the most important stage in his education occurred not at Paris or Oxford but in Baltimore, where, at the very moment Wellek was challenging positivist methods of literary study in his speech at Chapel Hill, he joined the Romance Languages Department of the Johns Hopkins University. He had not come to Hopkins expecting to be educated; armed with an Oxford D.Phil., he believed, foolishly, that he already was. Quite simply, during the year he spent in Paris preparing a *Diplôme d'études supérieures* under Frappier, he had formed a solid friendship with several American students, found himself more in tune with them intellectually and temperamentally than with the Europeans he knew, and in 1958, in a fit of restlessness and curiosity, had written to one of them, Jules Brody of Columbia, inquiring about a position in the United States. Three of them, including Brody, were waiting for him at the dock when he arrived in New York City in September 1958 on the S.S. *United States*, and a few days later he was driven down to Baltimore by Frank and Laura Randall. (Frank is the son of the philosopher who approved of Wellek's book on Kant.)

In 1958 there was no Comparative Literature at Hopkins. But Girard, Wardropper, Singleton, and Spitzer (who, though retired by then, was still a vocal presence in the hallways and at meetings of the Philological Association, and the History of Ideas Club) were anything but pedantic specialists of a national language and literature. Among younger colleagues, Thomas Hart had been trained as a comparatist. In any case, the old-fashioned philological basis of the Romance Languages Department made it inhospitable to the narrowest forms of literary nationalism. Students in Romance Languages at Hopkins at that time had to take seminars in French, Spanish, and Italian, and they had to pass exams in all three languages and literatures, as well, of course, as in

Latin and Romance Linguistics. Above all, the humanities at Hopkins in those days were like a single large department. Wellek's ideal of free intellectual inquiry unobstructed by "no trespassing" signs was there a reality. Though it had a veneer of southern gentility, the University was intensely aware of its intellectual traditions and its leadership role in graduate education, and determined to maintain its position at the forefront of scholarship. It was easy for an eager young assistant in Romance Languages to get to know colleagues and graduate students in English, German, Classics, Near Eastern Studies, Philosophy, History, and History of Art; in fact chairmen made a point of having their younger faculty members meet eminent senior scholars from other departments. Gossman was fortunate to have as mentors in the early years of his career Earl Wasserman and D. C. Allen in English, Fred Lane in History, Adolf Katzenellenbogen in Art History, Ludwig Edelstein, George Boas, and Maurice Mandelbaum in Philosophy (all three became close friends), and among the younger luminaries Hillis Miller (then still an ardent disciple of Poulet) and, of course, his own colleague in Romance Languages René Girard, infinitely fascinating, mocking, exhilarating, challenging, and disrespectful—and, despite the Christian direction of his work, seductively Mephistophelean. Among the younger members of the Hopkins faculty, he was a brilliant Dr. Coppelius, endlessly inventive, winding up all who came in contact with him and keeping them on their toes. To his unflagging stimulation was due in large measure an intense exchange of ideas among assistant professors and advanced graduate students: Tom Hart, Dick Macksey, John Freccero, John Wallace, Jay Levine, and many others. Gossman does not remember the issue of comparative literature ever coming up, except perhaps in conversations with Tom Hart, but the study of literature in *all* the departments in Gilman Hall was as comparative as you can get, in any sense of the word comparative. Gossman's own first Ph.D. student, Eugenio Donato, who had been admitted, as you could be at Hopkins in those days at least, on the strength of his obvious talent, even though he did not have a B.A., was inspired by a seminar on Molière to write his thesis on "literary rococo," with chapters on Molière, Marivaux, and Fielding. The chairman of the oral examination committee for this Ph.D. in Romance Languages was Earl Wasserman in English.

Fairly soon, of course, it became clear that in a large measure it was theory (or "methodology," as people still said at first, convinced as they were that the goal was to introduce self-consciousness to the practice of interpretation and not thinking that there might be anything else a literary scholar could do but interpret), that united all the departments in a common enterprise and provided the basis for a common discourse. Spitzer's "method" had been a challenge to Lovejoy's history of ideas approach to texts and was in turn challenged by later practices. The "phenomenological" approach of Georges Poulet, who had served for a brief period as chairman of Romance Languages, had intrigued Wasserman greatly, partly on account of the high regard, almost awe, in which he held his young colleague Hillis Miller. Thanks to scholars like Spitzer and Poulet, the positivist scholarship that Wellek attacked at Chapel Hill was already thoroughly discredited at Hopkins in the late fifties. At the Romance Languages lunch table at the Hopkins Club, making fun of "positivism" (represented for us by the fact-filled volumes of H. Carrington Lancaster's *History of French Dramatic Literature in the Seventeenth and Eighteenth Centuries*, one of the "monumental" achievements of the preceding generation of Hopkins scholars) was a great source of hilarity for several years and created a sense of solidarity and brotherhood that was as close as any one at that time could come to the exhilaration of the *jeune France* or the *junges Deutschland* of the last century.

Soon, under the influence of Girard and the benign chairmanship of Nathan Edelman, Romance Languages became a hotbed of theory. By the mid-to-late sixties, when Edelman left to go back to Columbia and Girard assumed the chairmanship, no one talked about "method" and "methodology" any more. Interest had come to focus more and more on theory for its own sake, independently of its value for criticism and interpretation. In fact, interpretation was already beginning to be seen as problematical, and literary works, referred to increasingly as "texts," were no longer thought of as having the wholeness and internal coherency that it had been simply assumed until then was the indispensable characteristic of every work of art or literature. When Georges Poulet returned to Hopkins to give a lecture, it was obvious that his time too had passed, and he was treated with the kindness reserved for aged veterans. (Several of the contributors to this volume, among them Thomas Greene and Victor Lange, relate a similar movement away from the centrality of the literary work and its interpretation). A succession of visiting professors in Romance Languages—Goldmann, Barthes, Derrida, Michel Deguy, Levinas, Serres, Marin, Lyotard—brought Marxist, structuralist, Heideggerian, and finally deconstructionist theories to the entire campus.

The highpoint of this movement was the pathbreaking International Structuralist Conference organized by Girard at Hopkins in 1966. This conference, at which papers were read by all the leading theorists of the day, and whose proceedings, edited by Richard Macksey and Eugenio Donato, have become a classic of literary theory and the history of ideas, had an enormous impact on literary study throughout the United States. Interestingly, it marked both the culmination of "structuralist" influence (the term was used broadly to embrace not only Lévi-Strauss's and Roman Jakobson's version of structuralism but the so-called "genetic structuralism" of Lucien Goldmann) and the announcement of its imminent displacement by "post-structuralism," for it was at this conference on structuralism that Derrida read a celebrated paper taking issue with Lévi-Strauss. By the time Girard left Hopkins and Yale took over leadership of the movement in literary theory, the somewhat eclectic intellectual ferment that had accommodated Goldmann and Jakobson, Lévi-

Strauss and Derrida, Barthes, Lacan, and de Man, had been rendered more systematic and monolithic. Because of that, it could also be influential in a different way. "Deconstruction" was spread from New Haven to the remotest campuses of the nation. The great days of theory at Hopkins, in contrast, while never free of intellectual terrorism, were marked by a good deal of variety and experimentation and by a vertiginous absence of disciplinary constraints. These were the times when Tony Wilden's Ph.D. thesis in Romance Languages, written under Girard's direction, and later published by the Johns Hopkins University Press, provided the first major translation and presentation of Lacan in English. Even after Girard left, the climate in Romance Languages and at the university as a whole, remained remarkably free and unconventional. At one time, two professors in the French section of the Department (out of a total complement of five) were teaching seminars, in the same semester, on Hegel's *Phenomenology.* Some barely audible rumblings about this from the Philosophy Department came to nothing. It was not the style at Hopkins to lay claim to academic turf. Certainly not in the expansive sixties and early seventies, when it seemed both in the U.S. and in Western Europe that there was no boundary that could not be transgressed, no limit that would not be passed.

Having spent his entire career in Departments of Romance Languages, first at Johns Hopkins and then at Princeton, Gossman has been under no pressure to define the goals and methods of Comparative Literature—or, for that matter, of Romance Languages. At Hopkins every one was free to pursue any intellectual curiosity, in virtually any field. Gossman was, if anything, conservative in his choice of seminar topics. At Princeton, under a tolerant administration and a succession of generous chairmen, he has felt no constraint on the kind of scholarly work he has chosen to do, while on his side he has always gladly taken on the teaching expected of him as a Professor of French. In addition, the university accommodates interdisciplinary, team-taught courses, and it was in one of those—a senior undergraduate seminar on "Society and Culture in Nineteenth Century Basle," taught with Carl Schorske—that he enjoyed the most stimulating teaching experience of his life. His "foreign" interests in German or English literature and culture have sometimes intersected with his "domestic" ones—as, for instance, when the *Christentum und Kultur* of Franz Overbeck, Nietzsche's close friend and colleague at Basle in the 1870s, afforded an illuminating insight into French classical tragedy—but this has usually occurred in an unplanned way. Gossman has not felt that all his scholarly work should be determined by or contribute to a single unifying theory. Moreover, as the nineteenth century philological foundation of the study of the Romance Languages was basically foreign to him—it never took hold in the United Kingdom as it did in the United States—he has usually thought of his own "discipline" as a fairly harmless administrative convenience which did not require intellectual justification and probably was incapable of it, but which, perhaps for that very reason, afforded a great deal of freedom to its practitioners, as well as a considerable degree of intellectual stimulation through the gathering together under one roof of specialists in three or four different languages and literatures.

Gossman's experience has thus encouraged, along with admiration for top-flight theoretical speculation, considerable skepticism about his own abilities in that area, and a cautious reticence with respect to the definition or theoretical grounding of his own work. He is aware of certain abiding concerns: for instance, he has often been drawn to writing which is situated at a boundary, like that between history and literature, and which tests that boundary without seeking to overturn it. Most recently, his interest has focused not so much on particular works that stand astride a boundary as on an entire frontier culture—that of the city of Basle in the nineteenth century. Wedged between France and Germany at the northern extremity of the Swiss Confederation, Basle has been a center of international culture and commerce for centuries. Long a virtually autonomous city-republic, it has jealously preserved its local traditions and pursued its own path while at the same time establishing ever wider connections with the larger world. It has been both intensely conservative and inward-looking and breathtakingly enterprising and resourceful. While its oligarchic elite of ribbon magnates moved smartly into the new chemical industry in the second half of the nineteenth century, founding giant companies—Hoffman Laroche, Ciba-Geigy, Sandoz—that are known the world over, and sought an accommodation with the social forces and political demands created by a modern economy, they provided a refuge at their university for an extraordinary group of scholars and philosophers (notably Bachofen in ancient history and mythology, Burckhardt in modern history and history of art, Nietzsche in classical literature and philosophy, and Franz Overbeck in theology) who had mounted a radical attack on the received wisdom of nineteenth century progressivism and the optimistic doctrines of modernism. What drew Gossman to study this unusual small city was not only its adaptability and resourcefulness, but its ability—not unconnected, perhaps, with its humanist, Erasmian traditions—to live with contradictions, to acknowledge and negotiate between contrasting truths and values. But he does not find it easy to justify this scholarly work theoretically and is fearful that a rigorously held to theory might oblige him to delimit its scope. A degree of intuitiveness, of theoretical and disciplinary indecisiveness, seems to him, in his own case, to be a condition of his doing it at all.

For that reason, he has not been unhappy with the fuzziness of "Romance Languages" as a professional discipline in today's academy or with the varied responsibilities departments of Romance Languages are called on to assume: instruction in French, Spanish, and Italian language and "culture" for the entire undergraduate constituency; inculcating, as any language department does, a sense of language as a complex system of signs and teaching students how to use them to communicate effectively; and introducing young people to the study of literature and to a number of enriching and challenging literary works in a foreign language. Such "comparative" courses as he has taught himself have tended to be federative rather than unitary, based on accretion rather than on a single well-articulated hypothesis. At Princeton, for instance, he instituted a seminar for undergraduate seniors majoring in Germanic, Romance, or Slavic languages and literatures on topics of common interest, such as "Italy in the Modern European Imagination," "Nietzsche and his European Reception," or "The Idea of Europe." But the seminar is taught by a team of teachers from the three language departments, each of whom teaches a work in his or her own field that bears on the seminar topic. Within his own department, Gossman has won acceptance for a similar course in which two or three teachers from different sections of the department, each teaching texts he or she knows intimately, explore a common theme, such as "France and Spain in the Age of the Counter-Reformation." "Comparative Literature" strikes Gossman as both more committed to and more directly dependent on theory than the kind of collaborative interdepartmental investigation he himself finds most congenial. More important, from his point of view, its focus tends to be more exclusively literary and its understanding of what literature is narrower, despite the cosmopolitanism rightly underlined by many of the contributors to this volume. As he was correcting the proofs of the volume, Gossman was reminded that he had expressed similar reservations about Comparative Literature in an Introduction to the Proceedings of the Charles Sanders Peirce Symposium on Semiotics and the Arts, which was held at Hopkins in 1975 to mark the university's 100th anniversary. Recalling that Earl Wasserman, who had begun planning the Symposium shortly before his untimely death, had intended it to point literary studies in a new direction by presenting Comparative Literature as the modern successor to the still predominant diachronic study of the national literatures, he noted then that "to those of us who took over from Earl after his death, it seemed that his intention might be even more effectively fulfilled if, instead of simply consecrating a reorganization that was already under way in many places, we could indicate a possible future direction of scholarship in the humanities that held the promise of greater interdisciplinary than Comparative Literature itself" (*MLN*, 91 [1967]:1425).

The recent revival of interest in historical criticism and the expansion of the range of texts literary scholars now study may well run counter to the strict definition of the field and the rigorous—often formalist—methods of analysis by means of which Comparative Literature sought to transform the study of literature from a branch of history, without a well-defined object or methodology of its own, and in many cases a mere instrument of nationalist ideology, into a genuine intellectual discipline as precise in its objectives and methods as any other scientific discipline. It remains to be seen how Comparative Literature will meet the challenge to its authority from new and aggressive fields like feminist studies or cultural studies. One can only point out that, since its very existence is connected with debate about the nature of literature and literary study, Comparative Literature should contain within itself the power to examine and renew its own tenets.

Gossman's own allegiance is probably to a far older conception of "literature" than that current in present-day university departments of literature, comparative or otherwise—a conception he evoked fumblingly in several essays of his own before finding it magisterially expounded by Marc Fumaroli in his recent *Age de l'Eloquence*. That older conception of literature embraced a wide range of discourses, extending from philosophical and political argument, to sermons, eulogies, and works of erudition. It included Machiavelli's *Prince* as well as *La Mandragola*; Guez de Balzac's *Le Prince* or Richelieu's *Testament politique* as well as Corneille's *Cinna*; Descartes' letters to princess Elisabeth and his *Discours de la méthode*; Pascal's *Pensées* as well as the fables of La Fontaine, the maxims of La Rochefoucauld, or the letters of Mme de Sévigné; Montesquieu's *Esprit des lois* as well as *Les Lettres persanes*; Constant's *De l'Esprit de conquête et de l'usurpation* as well as *Adolphe*. Such a humanist and cosmopolitan conception of literature—literature as public discourse aiming at enlightenment, persuasion, and the enhancement of the moral, intellectual, and artistic judgment of the individual and the community, the "culture of the mind and of the heart" in the celebrated words of Charles Rollin, the eighteenth century Rector of the University of Paris—survived, somewhat faint and worn, to be sure, in Gossman's own Scottish education and he remains in large measure faithful to it, even though for many years he could not identify it properly. It is a conception completely antithetical to the restrictive and purist post-Romantic idea of literature that has become generally accepted in our culture—and in departments of Comparative Literature certainly no less than anywhere else. Since the Romantics, to borrow Fumaroli's vivid metaphor, literature has become "the Kamchatka of an immense, fragmented technical and scientific culture, which has isolated it and turned it into a special reserve, while continuing to pay it formal respect." The preoccupation with the relations "between history and literature" that has recurred throughout Gossman's career now appears to him as the form taken by an often poorly understood effort to draw attention to what for him remains and ought to remain a problem to all who care about literature: the deep divide between the broad and varied but virtually abandoned territory of the older "rhetorical" literature, the literature of public discourse, and the austere, beleaguered outpost to which literature has been evacuated since the second half of the nineteenth century by its most devoted and uncompromising lovers. In his concern with this problem and with the idea of totality that doubtless underlies it, it may be that something survives of the utopianism of those wartime and immediate postwar years which Gossman feels left an indelible mark on him. If it does, it is a utopianism chastened by age, experience, and disappointment, and softened by acknowledgment of the diversity of literary and political cultures and the equal necessity and justice of competing values.

W. H. Auden provided the title of these reflections and will also provide their conclusion.

> We envy streams and houses that are sure:
> But we are articled to error; we
> Were never nude and calm like a great door,
>
> And never will be perfect like the fountains;
> We live in freedom by necessity,
> A mountain people dwelling among mountains.

16

Exile, Play, and Intellectual Autobiography

Mihai I. Spariosu

I was born at the Eastern edge of Central Europe, near Timişoara, the capital of Banat in southwestern Romania. Timişoara is situated at the border between three countries (Romania, Serbia, and Hungary) and is thus multilingual and multicultural, with all the advantages and disadvantages deriving from such a geographical position. Moreover, it had at one time been one of the most culturally sophisticated cities at the Eastern border of the Austrian-Hungarian empire, a cosmopolitan center with imperial architecture reminiscent of that of Vienna and Budapest, a fine neobaroque opera house, a modern cathedral quaintly combining a neobyzantine style with southern Romanian folk architecture, beautiful old parks, and the picturesque remnants of a late medieval and a baroque quarter. The languages spoken in the city were Romanian, Hungarian, German, Serbian, and Yiddish, and my childhood friends and playmates belonged indiscriminately to all of these linguistic worlds. I grew up in a cosmopolitan, multilingual, and pluricultural atmosphere conducive to tolerance and mutual respect among ethnic groups. (Unlike Transylvania, Banat is not beset with ethnic conflict between Romanians and Hungarians. This ethnic harmony was dramatically underscored during the 1989 anticommunist uprising, when Romanians and Hungarians formed a human chain around the Reverend Tökes Laszlo to prevent his arrest by Ceauşescu's security forces).

My life began not only at a geographical crossroads but also at a sociohistorical one. Born toward the end of World War II, I had the dubious privilege of witnessing the twilight of an old world and the ushering in of a new one, an experience that has undoubtedly contributed to my life-long skepticism toward violent recipes for social change. My early years were marked by the Communist revolution in ways that I am still trying to understand. My father, a well-read lawyer who spoke several languages and from whom I got my first lessons in French, had belonged to the privileged class of the old kingdom of Romania. Yet he had been sympathetic to socialism and leftist political ideals of social justice and had felt that all was not well in that kingdom. After a few years of the communist regime that he had helped consolidate by giving up his law practice and becoming a party activist, however, he had to concede that my mother (born into a modest family in the Transylvanian Alps and making her way from rags to riches, then back to rags after the war) was right: if the old dispensation was often unjust, the new one was doubly so. The former exploitees had proven, against the predictions of the Marxist fathers, to be more ruthless than their exploiters, because more hungry for power. Like so many leftist intellectuals of his generation, my father saw his dream of social justice come to nought, and he could not survive the disappointment. As my mother told me much later, her husband had asked her, on his deathbed, to keep me away at all costs from political involvement. But his last wish proved to be a very tall order, given the nightmarish nature of the nascent society that few of my father's generation (George Orwell being among those few) could really understand.

As a young schoolboy, I cried at the death of Stalin, whose ubiquitous portrait in all the classrooms and corridors of my primary school displayed the deceptively benign legend: "Comrade Joseph Stalin, Little Father of the Children of the World." My first publication, at the age of six, was a short poem entitled "To My Fatherland" which appeared in a national children's magazine (this publication—need I say?—is not listed in my *curriculum vitae*, even though it would give a new meaning to the American academic motto, "publish or perish"). My Stalinist period, however, ended at the age of twelve, with the death of my father violently marking my loss of innocence. I continued to write throughout high school but now, perhaps appropriately, my literary production consisted mostly of (equally embarrassing, but mercifully never published) imitations of French Romantic tragedies.

I received a solid, traditional, high-school education from competent, prewar professors who had not yet been purged or forcefully retired. One episode that sticks in my mind dates from the first week of my first year in high school. Our literature professor had assigned us the reading of *The Iliad*, and I became so absorbed in the world of the epic that I stayed up all night to read the book from cover to cover. Upon determining that I was the only student in the class to have completed the assignment, the old teacher, who had a city-wide reputation as a learned but strict and exacting shrew, called me to her desk and, to my acute embarrassment, kissed me on both cheeks in front of the whole (snickering) class. In addition to *The Iliad*, my favorite works in that course were *The Divine Comedy*, the poetry of Goethe and Schiller (which I had previously studied during my private German lessons with two German Notre Dame nuns), the plays of Shakespeare and, above all, the novels of Dickens— an author that motivated me to learn English and is therefore responsible for my subsequent career in English and Comparative Literature. All these foreign works were actually required reading in a course on Romanian literature: although she did not know it, my first literature teacher was teaching a Comparative Literature class. Perhaps she was, in some measure, responsible for my later forays across disciplinary boundaries and my distaste for narrow, positivistic fields of specialization. In high school, my favorite subjects were literature, philosophy, history, and classics, to the chagrin of my mother who, in keeping with my father's last wish, would have liked me to study mathematics, physics, and chemistry, on the assumption that these neutral, scientific subjects were not apt to lead me into political trouble. (As it turned out, that was an illusory assumption, because during the Ceauşescu era the pure and applied sciences were equally politicized and the body of Romanian scientists and technicians were ruthlessly purged of nonconformist elements.)

After graduating from high school, I decided to take the qualifying exams for the Faculty of Germanic Languages at the University of Bucharest. These examinations were made doubly difficult by the imposition of quotas to favor candidates with "healthy social origins," that is, sons and daughters of workers and farmers, over those coming from the middle class and the intelligentsia. Eventually it turned out that the Faculty of Germanic Languages catered not so much to the sons and daughters of the working class as to those of high party and government officials who wanted their children to learn foreign languages, especially English, just in case the political wheel turned again. (Their political foresight was, for once, admirable indeed, given the events of 1989 and the international fall of communism.)

Despite unavoidable bows to official ideology, the Department of English in which I worked toward a B.A. in the early sixties had somehow managed to maintain its prewar, high academic standards. Professors who grew up and were largely educated before World War II (some of them in England and the United States) offered their students a solid, traditional philological training, and I gratefully remember such dedicated educators as Ana Cartianu, Leon Levitzki, Dan Duţescu, Liliana Pamfil, and Ion Preda. Apart from courses in the History of English Language and Germanic Philology, linguistics, philosophy, aesthetics, and translation, I took required courses in English, German, Romanian, and World Literature. Again, there was no question of specializing in a national literature without acquiring some knowledge of Western literature as a whole. I remember vividly the courses in Romanian literature of George Călinescu, the great Romanian critic and novelist who was, in matters esthetic, a disciple of Croce, as well as those of Tudor Vianu, a professor of World Literature who had studied in Germany and represented a rigorous foil to George Călinescu's flamboyant critical impressionism. I also took courses from a younger generation of scholars, who like myself grew up under communism but had turned to the old teachers and the old humanistic values for guidance, such as Matei Călinescu, Virgil Nemoianu, and Ştefan Stoenescu. Călinescu and Nemoianu have since then built outstanding academic careers in Comparative Literature in the United States, precisely because they had never abandoned the Western cultural tradition that the new regime was trying, not entirely unsuccessfully, to annihilate. I am no less grateful to Dale Edmonds of the English Department at Tulane University, who was one of the first Fulbright professors to come to Romania and was instrumental in bringing me to the United States.

By the time I emigrated to the United States in 1971, my Romanian academic career was well under way. I had been teaching English literature at the University of Bucharest since 1967 and had completed all the doctoral requirements except for the defense of my thesis (on Laurence Sterne's *Tristram Shandy*). I had published a number of essays on English literature and Romanian translations of *Under the Volcano* (fragments), *Tristram Shandy* (coauthored) and Frye's *Anatomy of Criticism* (coauthored), as well as a collection of stories for children. I always looked at translation as being the best way of perfecting both one's literary skills and one's knowledge of one's own native language. Unfortunately, this linguistic apprenticeship remained largely unused because soon I went into exile and decided to write in the language of my adopted country. But, as it turned out, my early literary exercises did not go completely to waste. Much later I learned from a former graduate of the English department at the University of Bucharest (who had meanwhile become a distinguished journalist, translator and novelist) that the Romanian version of *Tristram Shandy* had become, in certain literary circles, something of a model of Romanian vocabulary and style to be opposed to the official *langue de bois* that had started taking over the Romanian literary magazines of the eighties.

In the United States I had to begin my academic career all over again, first at Tulane University, where I was offered a graduate fellowship and then a teaching assistantship in the English Department. After receiving an M.A. degree in English from Tulane, I decided to move into a Comparative Literature program in order to follow my interdisciplinary interests and take advantage of my linguistic background. Although I was accepted by several reputable northeastern schools, I decided to go to Stanford, particularly because I was intrigued by the counter-culture that was still in full swing in the California of the early seventies. What I found in Palo Alto was mostly a suburban, country-club atmosphere, so I moved to San Francisco as soon as I finished my course requirements for the doctoral degree. Rebellious and restless as I was in those days, I never integrated myself in the Californian counter-culture either, which I found rather naive, self-righteous, and shallow. The Buddhist-inspired, holistic mentality that animated the best part of it and had attracted me to it in the first place remains with me to this day, however, and I find myself returning to it again and again in my work.

At Stanford I found an atmosphere of intellectual and institutional freedom that appealed to me. Theory was now the rage, and I was very much attracted to French deconstruction, the work of Michel Foucault, and the anthropological theories of René Girard. They helped me understand certain aspects of the mentality of power that I had seen at work in my native Romania and that was operative in much more diffuse and benign forms in Western Europe and the United States as well. In the long run, however, I turned away from these theoretical trends for the same reasons that I had turned away from Marxism in my early adolescence. These theories were all too often employed by some of their supporters simply to gain cultural authority, replacing one kind of orthodoxy with another. To me what seemed most important, finally, was not so much this or that intellectual trend as the *ethos* or mode of behavior of its proponents. For this reason, my best teachers were not always the most brilliant or the most famous ones, and I found much truth in Matthew Arnold's words about Spinoza: "A philosopher's real power over mankind resides not in his metaphysical formulas, but in the spirit and tendencies which have led him to adopt these formulas."[1] In other words, it is a thinker's mentality, his mode of thought and behavior, not his theoretical pronouncements, that can in the end have an impact on humanity. This observation I had already found in Plato's autobiographical seventh letter.

Later on, I discovered that several of my senior comparatist colleagues around the country shared my ambiguous feelings toward critical and ideological "-isms." Then I began to understand how and why our similar life experiences had made us choose Comparative Literature as a field of study in the United States in the first place. Like me, many members of the older generation of comparatists were exiles—German, Spanish, Italian, and East European nationals who had looked for refuge from Fascist and, after World War II, Communist persecution. As Lionel Gossman and I suggest in our preface to this volume, in Comparative Literature they saw an opportunity to cross all the boundaries and "fenced off reservations" (in René Wellek's words) from which they had suffered so much in their native lands. But the exilic experience that had led these scholars to the (re)founding of our discipline also reveals the ambivalent nature of any foundational act. On the one hand, as young men and women, they saw America anew "as a land of unlimited possibilities with an exhilarating sense of freedom, allowing for the creation of a novel self and novel institutions. On the other hand, they experienced the deep-rooted, often unconscious fear of constant change and ceaseless upset that inevitably accompanies exile, and that fear was eventually mediated in personal and institutional terms as a need for continuity, for upholding a humanistic tradition that had nourished them and their predecessors."[2]

Being one generation younger than my senior comparatist colleagues, however, I thought I could learn from both their positive and their negative experiences. I turned away from the current critical orthodoxies in American academia, but without falling back on the old humanistic tradition. Instead I resolved to trace the history of several of our contemporary intellectual and cultural attitudes in order to understand them and myself a little better.

Before accepting a regular teaching position at the University of Georgia, I took several temporary jobs, moving from university to university largely as an itinerant scholar. My most fruitful *Wanderjahre* were the two years (1979–81) that I spent as Humboldt Postdoctoral Fellow at the University of Konstanz (where I worked most closely with Wolfgang Iser) and the University of Hamburg (where I worked with Karl Robert Mandelkow), and two other years (1978 and 1982) as a Mellon Fellow in Comparative Literature at Cornell University, during which period I completed my philosophical education. (At Cornell, the persons with whom I discovered most intellectual affinities were Giuseppe Mazzotta, Enrico Maria Santí, Dominick La Capra, Wolfgang Holdheim, and William Kennedy.) By that time it became obvious to me that I would be a perpetual exile and that this condition was far from being undesirable. It compelled me to confront my own void and understand what it means to be of two worlds and belong to neither. This is precisely the in-between world of play to which I have dedicated much of my research. My historical and philosophical investigations on exile and play have also led me to formulate my own answers to such central questions as: What is the nature of the interplay between poetry, ethics, and politics in the Western tradition? What is the nature of the interplay between art, culture, and power? Why has literary or fictional discourse been so often marginalized in the history of Western thought? How can literature contribute to the creation of new ethical and cultural values? I felt that the best way of approaching these questions was by tracing the history of several key concepts in Western thought, such as mimesis, play, exile, and utopia. After examining their origins in ancient Greek culture I came to realize that these concepts were all interrelated not only as forms of play but also as instruments of a mentality of power. And so I began, in *God of Many Names: Play, Poetry and Power in Hellenic Thought from Homer to Aristotle* and *Dionysus Reborn: Play and the Aesthetic Dimension in Modern Philosophical and Scientific Discourse,* to outline a history of mimesis and play in Western thought.

The two books start from the premise that Western communities, ancient and modern, share a mentality of power that, for descriptive purposes, can be divided into archaic and median. The archaic mentality is an aristocratic, warlike mode of thought and behavior, characteristic of the Homeric world, that may appear in individuals and social groups of later communities as well. A median mentality, on the other hand, finds initial expression in traditional gnomic poetry, for example in Hesiod and some of the Seven Sages (but also in Homer), as well as in such Delphic injunctions as "nothing in excess," "measure is best" and "know thy limits." This mode of thought and behavior later becomes associated mainly with what we moderns call "the middle class," but can equally be adopted by other individuals or social groups, including the aristocracy. The shift in emphasis from an archaic to a median mentality in ancient Greece seems to bring about the split of the holistic, mythopoeic language (still traceable in epic and lyrical poetry, in some Presocratic fragments, and in the choral parts of tragedy) into several autonomous discursive stretches. These stretches later develop into fields and disciplines, including what we moderns call philosophy, science, literature, theology, jurisprudence, history, rhetoric, and so forth. From the outset, these fields or disciplines engage in a contest for cultural authority.

But my studies also show that the shift from an archaic to a median mentality in the Western world is by no means complete or irreversible. Even when archaic values and beliefs become submerged, they can easily resurface, especially during massive migrations, invasions, wars, and revolutions. A modern political example of such a return of archaic values can be seen in the temporary victory of the so-called totalitarian regimes during most of the twentieth century. By setting themselves the task of destroying bourgeois political systems, these regimes actually eliminated median, rational values and went back to immediate forms of power or a might-makes-right mentality.

It is in this general cultural context that I construct my history of the concepts of mimesis and play in Western thought. The basic premises underlying this history are that, at least since Plato and Aristotle, mimesis and play have gone hand in hand, and that both these concepts can be traced back to, and have served as instruments for, a mentality of power. Through play, power conceives of itself in an archaic mentality as spontaneous, free, and arbitrary movement (for instance, in Homeric epic and Presocratic thought), and in a median mentality as reason, ideal form, and eternal order (for instance, in Platonic and Aristotelian philsophy). Mimesis in turn appears in an archaic mentality (for example, in ritual and Greek tragedy) as an ecstatic, Dionysian cosmic movement, and then in a median mentality (for example, in Plato and Aristotle) as a mere simulacrum of this movement. In median thought, play becomes "good" imitation and is made to serve Being as eternal order. This process works itself out in Western thought as a slow transition from "poetry" and "myth" to "philosophy" and "science" as the main authority of knowledge and truth.

In modern thought, it is Kant and German idealism in general that begin the long, uneven, and by no means irreversible process of restoring play to its pre-Platonic high cultural status, attempting at the same time to divorce it from mimesis (at least in its post-Platonic sense of imitation); this process culminates in the late nineteenth and the twentieth century in the work of Nietzsche, Heidegger and their post-structuralist heirs. From a suppressed epistemological prop of philosophy (controlled and regulated by mimesis), play turns once more into an indispensable cognitive tool or a fundamental way of understanding Being. In this context, mimesis also reverses its function: it is no longer an onto-epistemological instrument for subordinating the latter two to the former. Plato's nightmare of "bad" mimesis finally comes true: in such contemporary theorists as Bataille, Deleuze, Derrida, and Paul de Man, play no longer is "good" mimesis, installing Being and Truth, but, rather, mimesis is "bad" play, replacing Being and Truth with the eternal play of simulacra. Thus, on the one hand, play and art are subordinated to philosophy and science, and on the other hand, philosophy and science themselves become art and play. What was suppressed in Plato (art, play, the aesthetic) becomes privileged in Nietzsche and his twentieth-century followers.

In this light, literature itself becomes a power instrument, engaged in a dialectic of truth and fiction. Each historical power-configuration has its own official texts or truths, to the exclusion of all the others, but these may in turn be challenged and replaced by any of the others. What is treated as literature (fiction) in one age, may become science (truth) in a different age, while scientific stretches of discourse may in turn come to be regarded as literature. Thus, in Western culture, literature has often acted as a differential principle for other stretches of discourse. By openly displaying its fictionality, it has allowed other linguistic constructs, such as science, history, philosophy, ethics or religion, to be invested with the authority of knowledge and truth. In this context, the self-conscious or aestheticist moments in literary history were far from being flights from "reality"—on the contrary, they were often last-ditch attempts to reinforce a certain reality or truth. Literature has thus actively participated in the creation and establishment of certain states of affairs or power configurations in Western culture.

My cultural historical research has identified a mentality of power as being the main source of Western cultural values, but I have also tried to find ways in which one could turn away from this mentality and create new values. Of course, many people either are content with our mode of thought (if not always with our mode of behavior) or find it inevitable, so this part of my work addresses only those who, like myself, have found from their own life experience that the devastating emotional effects of a mentality of power outweigh its satisfactions. For me, the key to a radical change lies in the notions of exile and utopia, which I examine in my current work.

In our century, both exile and utopia have received increasing attention in the humanities mainly as a result of three factors: the massive human dislocations before and after the two world wars; the division of the political world into antagonistic ideological camps as a result of these wars; and finally, the growing public dissatisfaction with the prevailing global power configurations that have invariably shown disquieting totalitarian tendencies. Exile and utopia, however, have never been seen in correlation and have seldom been considered in a general sociocultural and philosophical context. I start from the premise that in Western culture exile and utopia have always acted as instruments of a mentality of power and that they can both be seen as forms of play. But I also explore the possibility of opening these notions to an alternative mode of thought and behavior (outside a mentality of power), to which they may have access precisely because of their ludic nature.

Although it is usually conceived as a political instrument of expulsion and neutralization, exile may have the opposite effect of providing a free space or playground between political systems and between cultures. Viewed in this light, exile becomes not only a form of play but also a form of utopia, if we use this term in the sense of "no-place" or "nowhere" (a meaning of utopia underlined in Samuel Butler's title, *Erewhon).* The neutral playground or no man's land opened by exile can in turn be used to effect radical changes upon both the expelling and the receiving political systems or cultures. Political examples are countless, ranging from the ostracized Athenian legislators, politicians, and generals in ancient Greece to Moses in Egypt and the land of Midian, to Aeneas at Carthage; from the popes at Avignon to the various emperors and kings in exile all over medieval and modern Europe; from Lenin in Switzerland and Trotsky in Mexico to the present-day P.L.O. leaders in the Middle East. Cultural examples are no less numerous, ranging from the Greek, Jewish, and Christian exiles in the ancient and the medieval world to the present-day "boat people."

In turn, utopia has been conceived as a form of exile, in the sense that it is invariably placed in a remote or imaginary land, in a distant past or future, that is, in a *neutral* space or playground. Though it is deliberately removed from the real world, it nevertheless maintains subtle and complex links with this world, being ultimately designed to effect radical changes upon it. Familiar examples include Plato's ideal Republic, Campanella's City of the Sun, More's Utopia, Bacon's New Atlantis, Prospero's magic island in the *Tempest*, Swift's Land of the Houyhnhnms, Voltaire's El Dorado, Butler's Erewhon, as well as the negative utopias (dystopias) of Zamyatin, Koestler, Huxley, and Orwell.

The view of exile as utopia and utopia as exile, and of both these phenomena as interrelated forms of play, allows us to value them as potentially positive cultural developments, once we separate them from a mentality of power. In his brilliant essay, "The Sun and the Self. Notes on Some Responses to Exile," Claudio Guillén draws a distinction between a "literature of exile" and a "literature of counterexile." For Guillén the prototype of a literature of exile is Ovid's *Tristia:* the Latin poet remains forever an alien among "barbarians," with his eyes perpetually fixed on Rome, his homeland, idealized as both an immobile center and a lost paradise. The literature of counterexile, on the other hand, finds its prototype in the Cynic-Stoic view of exile as cosmic freedom. Plutarch, among others, indicates that this view originates in the philosophical contemplation of the sun, the stars, and the other heavenly bodies, which allows individual gazers to detach themselves from their immediate historical and political circumstances and become at one with the cosmos, converted into a universal, all-embracing home. In a literature of counterexile, according to Guillén, "the poet learns and writes from his experience, moves away from it as situation or motif, while reacting to the social or political or, generally speaking, semiotic conditions of exile through the very thrust of the linguistic and ideological exploration that enables him to transcend the original condition."[3]

It is this second, positive and creative, attitude toward exile that I should like to stress here. In our age exile has all too often been regarded as a negative or even as a tragic development, and passionate testimonials of life in exile are not infrequent—see for example, Robert Boyers's collective volume, *The Legacy of the German Refugee Intellectuals* or, from a reverse perspective, Malcolm Cowley's *Exile's Return*. Without downplaying the emotional and cultural impact of exile on the individuals involved, one should nevertheless point out that the freedom, mobility, and multiple cross-cultural perspectives resulting from any radical uprooting may eventually contribute to the breakdown of traditional national and ethnic barriers, and to the creation of the kind of planetary communities that are currently to be found only in science fiction.

At the same time, we need to emancipate the concept of utopia from its negative, totalitarian ideological implications, emphasized for instance by Nicholas Berdyayev in the observation that Huxley used as an epigraph for his *Brave New World*: "Perhaps a new age will begin, an age when the intellectuals and the educated class will dream of ways in which to avoid utopias and return to a non-utopian society, less 'perfect' but 'freer.' " With this warning in mind, we could perhaps revaluate not only our concept of freedom but also that of utopia, imagining it as a product of a nonviolent, playful mentality, beyond ideology and politics. Then exile could also be understood as *atopia*, that is, as an experience of the void or emptiness. Far from being negative and threatening, this experience may be seen as an exploration of the unknown, both within and without, characteristic of all truly playful activity. Understanding and accepting one's exile may constitute a first step toward a no-man's land, or a turning away from our mentality of power, which may then bring about a much-needed ethical transvaluation of our crisis-ridden world.

Finally, we can reassess the value of literary discourse for a non-agonistic mode of thought. Ever since Plato and Aristotle excluded poetry from the realm of immediate power, literature as play can equally be seen as a form of exile and no man's land. If we emancipate it from a dialectic of truth and fiction, that is, from a mentality of power, literature can assume a culturally transcendental dimension, going beyond its immediate historical context of agonistic interaction with other modes of discourse. It can thus become a playground suitable for the creation and imaginative enactment of human values that often are incommensurable with those embraced by the community out of which the literary work arises and to which it is normally addressed. In other words, literary discourse could offer fresh cultural alternatives precisely because it is a ludic phenomenon, that is, an *as if* mode of activity and being, in which the world of actuality and that of the imaginary become interwoven and create an intermediary world separate from, yet contingent upon, the other two. This last issue stands at the center of my recent study, entitled *The Wreath of Wild Olive: Essays on Play, Literature, and Culture*, in which I demonstrate how aesthetic works, by staging a real or imagined state of affairs and presenting it from various perspectives, can contribute to a better understanding of the existential choices open to the polis and can play a significant role in proposing modes of historical change.

This brief intellectual autobiography shows, I hope, how my historical situation as an exile has shaped my thought and how my thought has shaped my historical situation as an exile. The exilic condition has taught me that I ought to define myself primarily neither as a Romanian nor as an American but as a citizen of the world, that is, as a human being. Although I now hold a senior position at the University of Georgia and, in many ways, lead a quiet and comfortable life, I have not given up my intellectual and existential quest. I continue to travel often to different parts of the globe, creating my own no-man's land between the world I inhabit in my North American community and any other world with which I come into contact during my travels. As a citizen of this no-man's land, I consider it my responsibility to disseminate the values of a peaceful, noncompetitive mentality throughout the communities to which I temporarily belong. It is as cosmopolitan citizens that students of literature, academics, and educators like ourselves could play an important role in our global communities. Education or *paideia* has always been a crucial factor in creating new worlds, a truth that Plato fully understood when he had Socrates elaborate his playful model of an ideal republic. On the other hand, the conceptual model I propose is neither ideal nor utopian, for it does not advocate, like Socrates, a particular kind of community or sociopolitical entity. Instead, it advocates a certain mentality or a certain way of responding to the world and to other beings, that is, a form of human responsibility that transcends national, ethnic, social, or political differences. This does not mean, however, that such a mentality cannot in turn create an infinite variety of national, ethnic, social, or political realities. For what my exilic experience has revealed to me is that the greatest freedom humans have is to create and recreate themselves anew.

NOTES

1. Matthew Arnold, "Spinoza and the Bible," *Essays in Criticism* (London and Cambridge: Macmillan, 1865), p. 209.

2. See Foreword, p. ix.

3. Claudio Guillén, "The Sun and the Self: Notes on Some Responses to Exile," in *Aesthetics and the Literature of Ideas* edited by François Jost and Melvin J. Friedman (Newark: University of Delaware Press, 1990), p. 265.

List of Contributors

Anna Balakian is Professor of French and Comparative Literature at New York University. Her books include: *Literary Origins of Surrealism; Surrealism: The Road to the Absolute; The Symbolist Movement: A Critical Appraisal; André Breton: Magus of Surrealism; The Fiction of the Poet: From Mallarmé to the Post-Symbolist Mode;* and *The Snowflake in the Belfry: Dogma and Disquietude in the Academic Arena.*

Stanley Corngold is Professor of German and Comparative Literature at Princeton University. He is the author of *The Fate of the Self: German Writers and French Theory; Franz Kafka: The Necessity of Form;* (with Irene Giersing) *Borrowed Lives;* and a volume provisionally entitled *Forms of Feeling: Tensions in German Literature.*

Lilian R. Furst is Marcel Bataillon Professor of Comparative Literature at the University of North Carolina at Chapel Hill. Her books include: *Romanticism in Perspective; Romanticism; Naturalism; Counterparts: The Dynamics of Franco-German Literary Relations 1770-1895; The Contours of European Romanticism; European Romanticism: Self-Definition; Fictions of Romantic Irony; Zola's "L'Assommoir": A Working Woman's Life; Through the Lens of the Reader; Explorations of European Narrative; Realism;* and the forthcoming *Home is Somewhere Else: Autobiography in Two Voices.* She co-edited *The Anti-Hero* and *Disorderly Eaters: Texts in Self-Empowerment.*

Gerald Gillespie is Professor of German Studies and Comparative Literature at Stanford University. He is the author of *Daniel Caspar von Lohenstein's Historical Tragedies; German Baroque Poetry; Ouzhou Xiaoshuo De Yanhua [Evolution of the European Novel]; Garden and Labyrinth of Time: Studies in Renaissance and Baroque Literature; German Theater before 1750;* and *Romantic Drama.* He is editor and translator of *Die Nachtwachen des Bonaventure: The Night Watches of Bonaventura* and *Der gestiefelte Kater;* and editor of *Herkommen und Erneuerung: Essays für Oskar Seidlin* and *Littérature comparée/littérature mondiale: Comparative Literature/World Literature.*

Lional Gossman is Professor of Romance Languages at Princeton University. He is the author of: *Men and Masks: A Study of Molière; Medievalism and the Ideologies of the Enlightenment; French Society and Culture: Background to Eighteenth Century Literature; Augustin Thierry and Liberal Historiography; The Empire Unpossess'd: An Essay on Gibbon's Decline and Fall; Orpheus Philologus: Bachofen versus Mommsen on the Study of Antiquity;* and *Between History and Literature.*

Thomas Greene is Professor of English and Comparative Literature at Yale University. His books include: *The Descent from Heaven: A Study in Epic Continuity; Rabelais: A Study in Comic Courage; The Light of Troy: Imitation and Discovery in Renaissance Poetry; The Vulnerable Text: Essays on Renaissance Literature; Poésis et Magie;* and (as co-editor) *The Disciplines of Criticism: Essays in Literary Theory, Interpretation, and History.*

Albert Guerard is Professor of English at Stanford University. He is the author of *The Past Must Alter; Robert Bridges; The Hunted; Maquisard; Joseph Conrad; Thomas Hardy; Night Journey; André Gide; The Bystander; Conrad the Novelist; The Exiles; The Triumph of the Novel: Dickens, Dostoevsky, Faulkner; The Touch of Time: Myth, Memory, and the Self; Christine/Annette;* and *Gabrielle.*

Thomas R. Hart is Professor Emeritus of Comparative Literature at the University of Oregon, and editor of *Comparative Literature.* He is the author of: *La alegoria en el Libro de Buen Amor; La España moderna vista y sentida por los españoles* [with Carlos Rojas]; *Cervantes and Ariosto: Renewing Fiction;* and *Cervantes' Exemplary Fictions.* He has also prepared several editions of Gil Vicente's Spanish and bilingual plays.

W. Wolfgang Holdheim is Frederic J. Whiton Professor Emeritus of Liberal Studies at Cornell University. He is the author of: *Benjamin Constant; Theory and Practice of the Novel: A Study on André Gide; Der Justizirrtum als Literarische Problematik; Vergleichende Analyse eines erzählerischen Themas; Die Suche nach dem Epos: Der Geschichtsroman bei Hugo, Tolstoi und Flaubert; The Hermeneutic Mode: Essays on Time in Literature and Literary Theory; Reflecties over het Detective-Verhaal; Schleiermacher en de hermeneutische traditie.* He is also translator of Max Scheler's *Ressentiment.*

Victor Lange is John N. Woodhull Professor Emeritus of Modern Languages at Princeton University. He is the author of *Kulturkitik und Literaturbetrachtung in Amerika; Modern German Literature; Thomas Mann: Tradition and Experiment; The Classical Age of German Literature; Bilder-Ideen-Bergriffe. Goethe-Studien;* and *Goethe* (Philipp Reclam ju., Stuttgart, 1992). He has edited, translated, and provided introductions to many volumes of Goethe's works.

Harry Levin is Professor of Comparative Literature at Harvard University. His books include: *James Joyce: A Critical Introduction; The Overreacher: A Study of Christopher Marlowe; Contexts of Criticism; The Power of Blackness: Hawthorne, Poe, Melville; The Question of Hamlet; The Gates of Horn: A Study of Five French Realists; Refractions: Essays in Comparative Literature; The Myth of the Golden Age in the Renaissance; Grounds for Comparison; Shakespeare and the Revolution of the Times; Memories of the Moderns;* and *Playboys and Killjoys: An Essay on the Theory of Practice of Comedy.*

Herbert S. Lindenberger is Avalon Foundation Professor of Humanities in Comparative Literature and English at Stanford University. His books include: *On Wordsworth's 'Prelude'; Georg Büchner; Georg Trakl; Historical Drama: The Relation of Literature and Reality; Saul's Fall: A Critical Fiction; Opera: The Extravagant Art;* and *The History in Literature: On Value, Genre, Institutions.*

Marjorie Perloff is Sadie Dernham Patek Professor of Humanities at Stanford University. Her books include *The Poetics of Indeterminacy: Rimbaud to Cage; The Futurist Moment: Avant-Garde, Avant-Guerre and the Language of Rupture;* and *Radical Artifice: Writing Poetry in the Age of Media.* She is editor of the forthcoming *Permission Granted: John Cage and the Making of Americans.*

Thomas G. Rosenmeyer is Professor of Comparative Literature at the University of California, Berkeley. He is the author of *The Masks of Tragedy; The Green Cabinet: Theocritus and the European Pastoral Lyric; The Art of Aeschylus; Senecan Tragedy and Stoic Cosmology; Deina Ta Polla: A Classicist's Checklist of Twenty Literary-Critical Positions;* and, with J. Halporn and M. Ostwald, *The Meters of Greek and Latin Poetry.* He is translator of Bruno Snell's *The Discovery of the Mind.*

Mihai I. Spariosu is Professor of Comparative Literature at the University of Georgia. His books include: *Literature, Mimesis, and Play: Essays in Literary Theory; Dionysus Reborn: Play and the Aesthetic Dimension in Modern Philosophical and Scientific Discourse; God of Many Names: Play, Poetry, and Power in Hellenic Thought from Homer to Aristotle.* He has edited several volumes of criticism including *Mimesis in Contemporary Theory: The Literary and Philosophical Debate.*

René Wellek is Sterling Professor Emeritus of Comparative Literature at Yale University. He is the author of *Immanuel Kant in England; The Rise of English Literary History; Theory of Literature; A History of Modern Criticism; Essays on Czech Literature; Concepts of Criticism; Confrontations: Studies in the Intellectual and Literary Relations between Germany, England, and the United States during the Nineteenth Century; The Disciplines of Criticism: Essays in Literary Theory, Interpretation, and History* (edited by P. Demetz, T. Greene,

L. Nelson, Jr.); *Discriminations: Further Concepts of Criticism;* and *The Attack on Literature and Other Essays.* He edited *Dostoievsky: A Collection of Critical Essays; Thomas Masaryk: The Meaning of Czech History;* and *Evidence in Literary Scholarship: Essays in Memory of James Marshall Osborn.*

Index of Names, Places, Institutions, and Events

Abrams, M. H., 30
Adams, Robert, 30
Adler, Mortimer J., 97n
Adler, Renata, 22
Adorno, Theodor, 33
Aeschylus, 59, 61, 128
Aldridge, A. Owen, 116
Allen, Don Cameron, 102, 198
Allen, Woody, 146
Alonso, Amado, 17, 101
Alonso, Dámaso, 100, 101
Alter, Robert, 15
American Academy in Rome, 19
American Association of Teachers of French, 80
American Comparative Literature Association, 17, 49, 79, 80, 83
American Philological Association, 49
American School of Classical Studies, 57, 58
American University, 129
Amherst College, 101
Amis, Kingsley, 33
Andersson, Theodore, 15
Andover, 150
Andrade, Mario de, 100
Ankara, 182
Antioch College, 144
Antwerp, 177, 181, 182, 184, 191n
Apollinaire, Guillaume, 131
Apollonius of Rhodes, 57
Aquinas, Thomas, 131
Arac, Jonathan, 188

Argentina, 184
Ariosto, Lodovico, 103
Aristotle, 130, 131, 211, 214
Arnim, Achim von, 78
Arnold, Matthew, 126, 209
Ashbery, John, 132
Association of University Teachers of German (Great Britain and Ireland), 119
Athens, 213. See also American School of Classical Studies
Atkins, Stuart, 15, 160
Auden, W. H., 33, 204
Auerbach, Erich, 9, 40, 41, 56, 65, 66, 100, 101, 102, 125, 136, 146, 162
Austen, Jane, 82, 130
Australia, 118
Austria, 126
Avignon, 213

Babbitt, Irving, 16, 17, 20, 21
Bachmann, Ingeborg, 135
Bachofen, Johann Jacob, 201
Bacon, Francis, 213
Baker, George Pierce, 14
Baker, John Ellis, 4
Bakhtin, Mikhail, 34, 70
Balakian, Anna, 164
Bald, R. C., 30
Baldensperger, Fernand, vii, 15, 16, 18, 125
Baltimore, 197
Balzac, Honoré de, 99

Band, Arnold, 22
Banerjee, D. K., 22
Bard College, 178, 184, 186
Barlach, Ernst, 160
Barnard College, 138
Barney, Nathalie, 83
Barr, Stringfellow, 97n
Barthes, Roland, 34, 85, 132, 134, 139, 163, 199, 200
Basle, 200, 201
Bassmett, Susan, 118
Bataille, Georges, 84, 211
Baudelaire, Charles, 61, 75, 76, 77, 109, 127, 131
Beall, Chandler, 103–104, 105, 121
Beckett, Samuel, 61
Beethoven, Ludwig van, 160
Behler, Ernst, 58
Belfast, Queen's University of, 110–114
Belgium, 184
Belgrade, 116, 165
Benfey, Christopher, 22
Benichou, Paul, 17
Benjamin, Walter, 33
Bentham, Jeremy, 127
Beowulf, 26, 131
Berdyayev, Nicholas, 214
Berenson, Bernard, 19
Berkeley, University of California at, 55, 57, 58–59, 62, 151, 167
Berlin, 50, 64
Berlin, Free University of, 25, 34
Berman, Ronald, 95
Bernheimer, Charles, 22
Berryman, John, 33
Bersani, Leo, 22
Betteridge, Harold, 194
Biggerstaff, Knight, 31
Binghamton, State University of New York at, 161, 162, 163, 166, 167
Bishop, Morris, 30
Blackmur, Richard, 33
Blake, William, 127, 130, 147–148
Blanchot, Maurice, 39, 61, 127, 190n
Bloch, Herbert, 20
Block, Haskell, 2, 164

Bloom, Harold, 31, 42, 118
Bloomfield, Leonard, 31
Bloomington. *See* Indiana, University of
Boas, George, 102, 198
Boase, Alan, 196
Boer War, 89
Bohemia, 2
Böhme, Jakob, 6
Bonnefoys, Yves, 33
Boorsch, Jean, 100
Bordeaux, 165
Borges, Jorge Luis, 100
Borgese, Giuseppe Antonio, 97n
Bossuct, Jacques-Bénigne, 90
Boston, 119, 121, 184
Boston University, 6
Boundary 2, 167
Bourdieu, Pierre, 134
Bouterwek, Friedrich, 100
Bové, Paul, 167
Bowman, Herbert, 15
Bowra, C. M., 19, 21
Boyers, Robert, 214
Boym, Svetlana, 16
Brady, Patrick, 21
Brandeis University, 65
Brandenburg [Ger. historian], 26
Brecht, Berthold, 84
Brent, Jonathan, 139
Breton, André, 78
Bristol, University of, 117, 165
British Society for Comparative Literature, 118
Brody, Jules, 197
Brombert, Victor, 86
Bronte sisters, 82
Brooklyn, New York, 180
Brooks, Cleanth, 30, 39, 40, 99, 130
Brooks, Peter, 22, 43
Brooks, Van Wyck, 16
Brower, Reuben, 15
Browne, Sir Thomas, 46
Browning, Robert, 132
Bruneau, Charles, 100
Bruneau, Jean, 19

Brussels, 181, 184
Bryn Mawr College, 102
Bucharest, University of, 207–208
Büchner, Georg, 152, 153, 195
Buck, Paul H., 18
Budapest, 165, 205
Bunker, Archie, 127
Burckhardt, Jacob, 201
Burckhardt, Sigurd, 160
Burke, Edmund, 91
Burke, Kenneth, 130
Burke, Peter, 43
Butler, E. M., 27
Butler, Judith, 135
Butler, Samuel, 213

Cage, John, 135, 139
California, University of, 182
California Institute of Technology, 7
Călinescu, George, 207
Călinescu, Matei, 136, 207
Camargo Foundation, 101
Cambridge University, 27, 51, 52,
   109–110, 109, 110–111, 112, 118, 179,
   180. *See also* Churchill College,
   Girton College, Jesus College, New
   Hall
Campanella, 213
Campbell, O. J., 15
Camus, Albert, 77, 92
Canada, 52–53, 54
Canadian Broadcasting Corporation,
   53; Havelock, Eric, 54
Čapek, Milič, 7
Caribbean, 166
Carpentier, Alejo, 103
Carré, Jean-Marie, vii, 17, 19
Carthage, 213
Cartianu, Ana, 207
Case Western Reserve University, 122
Cassirer, Ernst, 49, 128, 163
Catholic University of America, 19,
   129, 130–131, 138
Ceausescu, Nicolae, 205, 207
Cendrars, Blaise, 131
Centeno, Augusto, 127, 128, 139

Cervantes, Miguel de, 103, 105, 106
Cesaire, Aimé, 82, 83
Chafe, Wallace, 130
Chapel Hill. *See* North Carolina,
   University of
Chartier, Roger, 136
Chateaubriand, Alphonse de, 129
Chaucer, Geoffrey, 106, 128
Chekov, Anton, 28, 128
Chicago, 8, 120, 153
Child, Francis James, 13
Chou, Lily, 22
Churchill College, Cambridge, 116, 118
Cicero, 53, 130
Clarke, Howard, 22
Claveria, Carlos, 101
Clements, Robert, 80, 81
Cleveland, 159
Clifford, James, 128
Clüver, Claus, 133
Coelho, Joaquim-Francisco, 20
Cohn, Norman, 196
Cohn, Robert, 10
Coleridge, Samuel Taylor, 3, 127, 148
Colie, Rosalie, 128
Collège de France, 60, 85
College of William and Mary, 122, 123
Cologne, University of, 20
Colorado, University of, 99
Columbia University, 4, 14, 76, 80, 118,
   126, 130, 178–181, 189, 191n, 197
Comparative Literature, 10, 17, 103–106,
   120, 169
Comparative Literature Studies, 116
Conant, James B., 18
Condorcet, Marie-Jean, Marquis de, 91
Conrad, Joseph, 92
Constance, University of, 136, 210
Constant, Benjamin, 203
Constantinople, ix, 75. *See also*
   Istanbul
Cooper, Lane, 30
Corneille, Pierre, 56, 203
Cornell University, 27, 29, 30–32, 65,
   169, 177, 178, 181, 183, 186, 187,
   192n, 210

Corngold, Stanley, x
Crane, Stephen, 92
Croce, Benedetto, 3, 207
Croll, Morris, x, 3, 197
Cross, Samuel Hazzard, 22
Cuba, 161
Culler, Jonathan, 38
Curtis, Simon, 118
Curtius, Ernst Robert, 8, 30, 66, 146,
  152, 161, 162
Czechoslovakia, 2, 7, 8, 18, 195

Daiches, David, 30
Damon, Philip, 59, 169
Dana, Henry Wadsworth Longfellow,
  22
Dante, 13, 126, 148, 206
Darmstadt, 161
Dartmouth College, 116, 120
D'Aubigné, Agrippa, 90
Davenport, Guy, 132
Davidson, Donald, 61
Davie, Donald, 118
Davis, Herbert, 29
Deconstruction, 163
Degas, Edgar, 193
De Gaulle, Charles, 187
Deguy, Michel, 199
De Kiewiet, C. W., 31
Del Valle, Rosamel, 79
Deleuze, Gilles, 134, 211
De Man, Paul, 19, 34, 42, 43–44, 127,
  140n, 163, 169, 177–190, 190n, 191n,
  192n, 200, 211
De Man, Hendrik, 177, 185
Demetz, Peter, 42
Demus, Otto, 52
De Rachewiltz, Siegfried, 22
Derrida, Jacques, 18, 34, 44, 59–60,
  132, 162, 163, 167, 169, 170, 190n,
  199, 200, 211
Dersofi, Nancy, 22
Descartes, René, 127, 203
De Stael, Germaine, 82
Detienne, Marcel, 60
DeVane, William C., 8

Deyermond, Alan, 101
Diacritics, 188
Dickens, Charles, 126
Dieckmann, Herbert, 101
Donato, Eugenio, 198, 199
Donegal, 160
Donne, John, 130
Dostoevsky, Fyodor, 92, 126, 129
Doughty, Charles, 28
Dragomoschenko, Arkadii, 138
Dreyfus Case, 89
Driesch, Hans, 26
Dryden, John, 126, 131
D'Souza, Dinesh, 10
Ducasse, Isidore, Lucien (pseud.
  Lautréamont), 37, 41
Duke University, 123
Duke University Press, 167
Duncan, Isadora, 38
Dunkirk, 52
Durham, University of, 117
Durling, Robert M., 22
Duțescu, Dan, 207

East Anglia, University of, 117, 118
Ecole Normale Supérieure, 18, 59
Edelman, Nathan, 102, 103, 199
Edelstein, Ludwig, 198
Edmonds, Dale, 208
Egypt, 213
Eichendorff, Joseph von, 4
Eisenhower, Dwight D., 178, 181
Eisenstein, Sergei, 135
Eliot, George, 126
Eliot, Thomas Stearns, 16, 33, 41, 68,
  127, 148, 160
Else, Gerald, 55
Emerson, Ralph Waldo, 127, 132
Emory University, 103
England, 2, 9, 51, 52, 101, 107, 115, 117,
  120, 121, 127, 182, 185. *See also*
  Great Britain
Engle, Paul, 55
Epicurus, 53
Erasmus, Desiderius, 202
Essex, University of, 117, 118

Estève, Edmond, 19
Etiemble, René, 163
Euripides, 128
Europe, 2, 162, 163, 166, 167, 168, 171, 172, 173, 177, 181, 182, 183, 186, 187, 188
Exeter, University of, 117

Fackenheim, Emil, 52
Fairley, Barker, 27–28
Falk, Eugene, 83
Fang, Achilles, 22
Fanger, Donald, 15
Farmer, Bette-Anne, 119
Faulkner, William, 92, 105, 127, 151
Fédération Internationale des Langues et des Littératures Modernes (FILIM), 116
Felsted, England, 159
Fichte, Johann Gottlieb, 91
Fielding, Henry, 92, 106, 198
Fish, Stanley, 132
Fitts, Dudley, 15, 159
Fitzgerald, F. Scott, 92
Flaubert, Gustave, 19, 84, 92, 99, 126
Fleming, Raymond, 22
Flesch, William, 192n
Fletcher, J. B., 14
Foerster, Norman, 5, 6, 16, 55
Fokkema, Douwe, 21
Fontane, Theodor, 126, 195
Ford Foundation, 78
Formalism, 130, 153, 162, 174
Foucault, Michel, 31, 34, 45–46, 134, 135, 163, 167, 170, 208
France, 2, 39, 65, 66, 97n, 159
France, Anatole, 77
Frank, Joseph, 21, 134
Frank, Roberta, 22
Fränkel, Hermann, 57
Frankfurt School, 33
Frappier, Jean, 196, 197
Freccero, John, 102, 198
Frenz, Horst, 162
Freud, Sigmund, 47, 59, 61, 100, 162
Freyer, Hans, 26

Fribourg, Switzerland, 57, 165
Friederich, Werner P., 17, 77, 83, 104, 161
Friedländer, Paul, 57, 61
Friedländer, Walter, 125
Frye, Northrop, 21, 42, 85, 103, 147–149, 162, 208
Fuentes, Carlos, 21
Fulbright Fellowships, 39, 101, 208
Fumaroli, Marc, 203
Furst, Lilian, ix, 16, 21

Gadamer, Hans-Georg, 26, 44–45
Gallaudet College, 130
Garber, Frederick, 163
García, Márquez, Gabriel, 105
Gaskell, Elizabeth, 131
Gates, Lewis E., 16
Gauss, Christian, 33
Geneva, University of, 118
Geneva School, 163
George, Stefan, 4, 109
George Washington University, 129
Georgetown University, 129
Georgia, University of, 210, 215
Germany, 2, 172, 182
Giamatti, A. Bartlett, 42, 81
Gicovate, Bernardo, 22
Giddens, Anthony, 135
Gide, André, 92, 190n
Gillespie, Gerald, 122
Gioia, Dana, 22
Giovannini, Giovanni, 129, 131
Girard, René, 102, 198, 199, 200, 209
Girton College, Cambridge, 109, 112
Glasgow, Scotland, 160, 193
Glasgow, University of, 194–196
Godwin, William, 91
Godzich, Wlad, 21
Goethe, Johann Wolfgang von, 27, 29, 53, 57, 65, 73, 106, 126, 127, 129, 130, 131, 194, 195, 206
Goetz, Walter, 26
Goheen, Robert F., 32
Goldmann, Lucien, 199, 200
Gombrich, Ernst, 125

Gombrowicz, Witold, 139
Goncourt, Edme and Jules de, 99
Góngora, Luis de, 9
Gossman, Lionel, 102, 209
Grabowicz, George, 22
Graham, Martha, 38
Great Britain, 108, 113, 116, 117, 118–119,
  159, 160, 194. *See also* England,
  Scotland, United Kingdom
Greece, 210, 213
Green, F. C., 29
Green, Richard H., 103
Greenblatt, Stephen, 45
Greene, Graham, 92
Greene, Thomas, 83, 199
Greet, W. Cabell, 128
Grillparzer, Franz, 161
Griswold, Whitney, 8
Guattari, Felix, 134
Guérard, Albert L., 89–91, 97n
Guez de Balzac, Jean-Louis, 203
Guggenheim Fellowships, 83, 123, 167
Guillén, Claudio, 19, 81, 125, 162, 164, 213
Guyard, Marius Francois, vii

Habermas, Jürgen, 34, 135, 136
Hackett, Samuel, 194, 196
Hafley, James, 131
Hahn, Reynaldo, 193
Hale, Dorrit, 10
Hall, Stuart, 134
Hamburg, 50
Hamburg, University of, 210
Hampshire, Stuart, 34
Handke, Peter, 33, 61
Hardy, Thomas, 92, 105
Harper, George MacLean, 1
Harrington, Katherine, 22
Hart, Thomas R., 8, 10, 121, 169, 198
Hartman, Geoffrey, 42, 43, 48, 81, 125,
  127, 162
Harvard Society of Fellows, 9, 18, 178, 184
Harvard Summer School, 116, 119
Harvard University, 3, 10, 13–23, 54,
  91, 101, 116, 121, 122, 129, 145, 160,
  161, 178, 183, 184, 186, 192n

Hatcher, Anna Granville, 102
Hatzfeld, Helmut, 129–130, 135
Hawkes, John, 92, 94
Hawthorne, Nathaniel, 127
Hazard, Paul, 76, 77, 78
Hazlitt, William, 160
H. D., 46, 83
Hebdige, Dick, 135
Heckscher, William, 55, 61
Hegel, Georg Friedrich, 34, 70, 127,
  200
Heidegger, Martin, 34, 60, 61, 127, 153,
  163, 167, 170, 186, 199, 211
Heidelberg, 182
Heijinian, Lyn, 138
Heine, Heinrich, 126, 127, 131, 136
Heller, Deborah, 22
Hemingway, Ernest, 190n
Herder, Johann Gottfried von, 91
Hesiod, 210
Hirch, E. D., 31
Hitler, Adolf, 6, 50, 54, 77, 185
Hoboken, 1
Hocquard, Emmanuel, 139
Hofmannsthal, Hugo von, 126
Hölderlin, Friedrich, 131, 136, 153, 195
Holdheim, Wolfgang, 210
Holland, Norman, 132
Hollander, John, 15
Holmberg, Arthur, 22
Holquist, Michael, 43
Homer, 41, 106, 206, 210, 211
Horace, 130
Hughes, Glyn T., 118
Hughes, Merrit Y., 7
Hugo, Victor, 193
Hull, University of, 117
Humboldt Fellowships, 210
Hume, David, 127
Humphries, Rolfe, 15
Hungary, 107, 160, 205
Hunter College, 75
Huntington Library, 7
Hüsserl, Edmund, 34, 161
Hutchins, Robert M., 89, 97n
Huxley, Aldous, 213, 214

Ibsen, Henrik, 138
Illinois, University of, 116. *See also* Urbana
Imbert, Enrique Anderson, 101
Indiana, University of, 10
Ingarden, Roman, 128
Innis, Harold A., 97n
Innsbruck, 165
International Comparative Literature Association, vii, 57, 78, 79, 80, 83, 84, 85, 116, 125, 164, 165, 194
Iowa, University of, 5, 6, 7, 18, 55, 56, 99
Iowa City, 4, 6, 7, 8, 55
Ireland, 2, 101, 159, 160, 172
Irvine, University of California at, 169
Iser, Wolfgang, 34, 210
Istanbul, 75
Ithaca, NY, 186
Ivanov, Viacheslav, 136, 137

Jaanus, Maire, 22
Jabotinsky, Ze'ev (Vladimir), 51
Jackson, Robert L., 8
Jacobs, Barry, 22
Jaeger, Werner, 17
Jakobson, Roman, 15, 17, 19, 100, 101, 125, 200
James, Henry, 92, 103, 126
Jameson, Fredric, 21, 33
Jasinski, René, 160
Jauss, Hans Robert, 136
Javitch, Daniel, 22
Jena, University of, 27
Jesus College, Cambridge, 52
Jews, Jewish, 3, 50, 64, 68, 107, 110, 111, 126, 181–182, 185, 191n, 193, 196
Johns Hopkins University, 30, 60, 101–102, 129, 169, 178, 187, 197–200
Johnson, Barbara, 20
Johnson, Josephine, 92
Johnson, Samuel, 130, 150
Joyce, James, 18, 41, 84, 92, 115, 131, 132, 138, 151
Jung, C. G., 162, 163

Kafka, Frank, 127, 177, 178, 180, 190n, 195
Kahler, Erich, 97n

Kaiser, Walter, 15, 19
Kansas, University of, 14
Kant, Immanuel, 34, 127, 197, 211
Katz, Wilbur G., 97n
Katzenellenbogen, Adolf, 198
Kayser, Wolfgang, 160, 162
Kelleher, J., 178
Keller, Gottfried, 126
Kennedy, William, 210
Kenner, Hugh, 49
Kermode, Frank, 118, 134
Kernan, Alvin, 43
Kinkeldey, O., 30
Kirkpatrick, Susan, 22
Kis, Danilo, 139
Kittler, Friedrich, 136
Kittredge, George Lyman, 17
Kleist, Heinrich von, 153
Koelb, Clayton, 22
Koestler, Arthur, 213
Korea, 38
Korean War, 145
Korff, August Hermann, 26, 195
Körner, Karl Theodor, 126
Krailsheimer, Alban, 196
Kristallnacht, 51, 191n
Kuhn, David (David Mus), 22
Kumin, Maxine, 22
Kybal, Milič, 7
Kyle, Regina, 121

Lacan, Jacques, 31, 34, 59, 61, 200
LaCapra, Dominick, 210
LaDrière, J. Craig, 19, 129, 130, 131
La Fontaine, Jean de, 203
Lake, Kirsopp, 21
Lancaster, H. Carrington, 199
Lane, Frederic, 198
Lange, Victor, 104, 169, 199
Langer, Susanne, 128
Langer, William, 160
Lapesa, Rafael, 100
La Rochefoucauld, François, Duc de, 203
Laszlo, Tökes, 205
Latin America, 166

Lautréamont. *See* Ducasse, Isidore Lucien
Lawrence, D. H., 41, 103, 190n
Le Soir, 181, 184
Leach, Henry Goddard, 15
Leavis, F. R., 152
Leeds, University of, 117
Lehmann, Phyllis, 56
Leipzig, 25
Leipzig, University of, 25, 26
Lejeune, Philippe, 188
Lenin, Vladimir Il'ich, 213
Lenneberg, Eric, 49
Leopardi, Giacomo, 126
Lermontov, Mikhail Iur'evich, 197
Lévi-Strauss, Claude, 59, 103, 163, 200
Levin, Harry, 92, 93, 104, 110, 116, 120, 129, 131, 159, 160, 162, 169, 184, 185
Levinas, Emmanuel, 199
Levine, Jay, 198
Levitzki, Leon, 207
Lewis, Janet, 92
Leyerle, John, 22
Lida, Raimundo, 101
Linacre College, Oxford, 101
Lindenberger, Herbert, 93, 134, 195
Liverpool, University of, 117
Locke, John, 127
Lohenstein, Daniel Casper von, 161
Lohner, Edgar, 10
London, 119, 129
London University of, School of Slavonic Studies, 5, 117; School of Oriental and African Studies, 52; Royal Holloway College, 109
Longfellow, Henry Wadsworth, 13
Longinus, 130
Lorca, Federico Garcia, 128
Lord, Albert, 15, 18–19, 20
Los Angeles, University of California at, 16, 57, 90, 137
Los Angeles, 57
Loti, Pierre, 77
Lovejoy, Arthur O., 20, 102, 199
Lowell, James Russell, 13
Lowell, Robert, 131

Lowes, John Livingston, 3
Luhmann, Niklas, 136
Lukács, Georgy, 34, 152, 194, 195, 196
Luke, David, 109
Lyons, University of, 19
Lyotard, Jean-François, 34, 167, 199

MacArthur Foundation, 83
Machiavelli, Nicolo, 203
Mack, Maynard, 41
Macksey, Richard, 198, 199
Magoun, Francis P., 18, 19
Mailer, Norman, 18
Malevich, Kazimir Severinovich, 132, 135
Malkiel, Maria Rosa Lida de, 101
Mallarmé, Stéphane, 10, 19, 77, 127, 131, 160, 186
Malone, David, 161
Malory, Sir Thomas, 117
Malraux, André, 182
Manchester University, 108, 114–116, 118, 121, 123
Mandelbaum, Maurice, 198
Mandelkow, Karl Robert, 210
Manet, Edouard, 193
Mann, Thomas, 18, 92, 131, 183, 189
Mannheim, Karl, 63
Marin, Louis, 199
Marinetti, Filippo Tommaso, 132
Maritain, Jacques, 33
Marivaux, 198
Marseilles, 7
Marsh, Arthur Richmond, 14
Martin, Harold C., 19
Martz, Louis, 41
Marx, Karl, and Marxism, 61, 100, 162, 163, 167, 170, 173, 206, 209
Maryland, University of, 182
Massey, Irving, 22
Mathesius, Vilem, 5
Matisse, Henri, 38
Matlaw, Ralph, 22
Matthiessen, F. O., 20
Maxwell, Baldwin, 6
Mayhew, Lewis, 95

Mayoux, Jean-Jacques, 21
Mazzotta, Giuseppe, 210
McCabe, Colin, 118
McCannell, Juliet Flower, 185
McCarthy, Senator Joseph, 56, 160
McCullers, Carson, 131
McDiarmid, John, 56
McGalliard, John C., 6
McIlwain, Charles H., 97n
McMaster University, 53
Mellon Fellowships, 167, 210
Melville, Henry, 92, 127
Menner, Robert James, 8
Mensel, Heinrich, 3
Merivale, Patricia, 15
Metro-Goldwyn-Mayer, 129
Mexico, 213
Michelet, Jules, 90
Miller, J. Hillis, 92, 198
Milosz, Czeslaw, 21
Milton, John, 29, 41, 106, 126, 128, 147
Miner, Earl, 173, 174
Mintz, Ilse, 126
Mintz, Maximilian, 126
Mistral, Frédéric, 101
Modern Language Association, 4, 8,
    10, 81, 83, 90, 104, 120
Molière, Jean-Baptiste Poquelin, 128,
    198
Montaigne, Michel de, 103
Montale, Eugenio, 131
Montesquieu, Charles de Secondat,
    Baron de la Brède et de, 77, 90, 203
Montpellier, University of, 101
Montreal, 53–54, 165
Moore, George, 92
More, Paul Elmer, 16
More, Sir Thomas, 213
Morize, André, 17
Morris, Charles, 130
Moses, 213
Muir, Edwin, 15
Muir, Willa, 15
Mumford Jones, Howard, 160
Munich, 161, 165, 167
Munich, University of, 25, 26

Munn, James B., 22
Münster, University of, 20
Murray, Henry A., 20
Musset, Alfred de, 129, 135

Nabokov, Vladimir, 15, 30
Naddaff, Sandra, 22
Nagy, Gregory, 15
National Endowment for the
    Humanities, 123, 168
National Humanities Center, 123
Naumann, Walter, 160, 161
Navy School of Oriental Languages, 99
Nazis, 50, 161, 191n
Neilson, William Allan, 3
Nelson, Lowry, Jr., 9, 42
Nemoianu, Virgil, 16, 136, 207
Netherlands, 65
New Britain, CT, 75
Newburn, Harry K., 103
New Criticism, 39, 55, 60, 130, 141,
    145, 147, 148, 159, 160, 162
New Hall, Cambridge, 118
New Haven, 5, 8, 37
New Historicism, 155, 159
New Literary History, 167
New School, 126
New York, 126, 139, 142, 144, 165, 177,
    180, 195, 197
New York, State University of,
    Stonybrook, 116
New York Graduate Center, 116
New York Times, 116
New York University, 80, 81, 163
Nichols, Stephen, 116
Nietzsche, Friedrich, 26, 34, 56, 60,
    126, 127, 162, 167, 201, 202, 211, 212
Nims, John Frederick, 21
North Carolina, University of, vii, 6,
    17, 77, 78, 79, 83, 84, 85, 123, 161,
    165, 194, 197, 199
Northampton, MA, 3
Northwestern University Press, 139
Notre Dame University, 99

O'Brien, Justin, 15
O'Connor, Flannery, 131

O'Hara, Frank, 131
Oberlin College, 127, 138, 139
Ohio State University, 101, 160
Oklahoma A & M, 99
Olsen, Stein Haugom, 60
Ong, Walter, 94
Oppenheimer, J. Robert, 185
Oregon, 120–121, 123
Oregon, University of, 8, 10, 17, 103–104, 120
Orwell, George, 182, 206, 213
Osborn, James Marshall, 5
Osgood, Charles Grosvenor, 1, 2
Ottawa, 165
Overbeck, Franz, 201
Ovid, 106, 213
Owen, Stephen, 16
Oxford University, 101, 108, 118, 197. *See also* St. Antony's College, Somerville College

Packard, David, 91
Palencia-Roth, Michael, 22
Palestine, 51
Palmer, Michael, 138
Pamfil, Liliana, 207
Panofsky, Erwin, 55, 125
Pares, Sir Bernard, 5
Paris, 38, 59, 118, 153, 160, 161, 165, 167, 168, 185. *See also* Ecole Normale Supérieure
Paris, University of, 17, 19, 37, 196, 197, 203
Parker, A. A., 101
Parker, Frank, 38
Parrot, Thomas Marc, 1, 2, 5
Parry, Adam Milman, 9
Parry, Milman, 19, 20
Parschchikov, Alexei, 138
Pascal, Blaise, 203
Pasinetti, Pier, 9
Pasternak, Boris, 131
Patton, General George S., 7
Pavel, Thomas G., 21
Paz, Octavio, 21
Peacock, Ronald, 108

Pearl Harbor, 6
Pearson, Norman Holmes, 99
Peirce, Charles Sanders, 130
Pennsylvania, University of, 7
Pentagon, 183
Perec, Georges, 135
Perry, Bliss, 14
Pessoa, Fernando, 100
Petrarch, Francesco, 59
Peyre, Henri, 8, 40, 64, 100
Pfuhl, 6
Phillips Academy, 159
Picasso, Pablo, 160
Piero della Francesca, 38
Pike, Burton, 22, 164
Pinder, Wilhelm, 26
Pirandello, Luigi, 128
Plato, 38, 130, 211, 213, 214, 215
Plutarch, 213
PMLA, 155
Poe, Edgar Alan, 61
Poggioli, Renato, 18, 21, 93, 125, 184, 185
Poland, 18, 107
Pope, John C., 3, 8
Pope, Alexander, 1, 2, 126, 130
Postmodernism, 163, 167
Poststructuralism, 163
Potter, M. A., 14
Pottle, Frederick A., 8
Poulet, Georges, 102, 152, 198, 199
Pound, Ezra, 129, 132
Prague, 4, 5, 8, 153, 177
Prague, Charles University of, 1, 2, 3, 5, 8
Pratt, Mary Louise, 95
Prawer, Siegbert, 118–119, 124n
Preda, Ion, 207
Priest, G. M., 4
Princeton University, 1–3, 4, 20, 32–34, 169, 200, 202
Principia College, 37
Prospero, 213
Proust, Marcel, 18, 84, 92, 126, 127, 129, 131, 132, 135, 162
Pusey, Nathan M., 18
Pushkin, Aleksandr, 197

Quine, Willard V., 15
Quinones, Ricardo, 15
Quint, David, 185

Raabe, Wilhelm, 28
Radcliffe College, 19
Raimondi, Ezio, 163
Raimund, Friedrich, 126
Rand, E. K., 20
Randall, Frank, 197
Randall, John Herman, 4
Randall, Laura, 197
Redfield, Robert, 97n
Regnier, Mathurin, 90
Remak, Henry, 164
Renan, Ernest, 90
Renoir, Alain, 22, 57, 58
Reverdy, Pierre, 132
Revue de Littérature comparée, 17
Reykjavik, 182
Riasanovsky, Nicholas, 55
Rice University, 90
Richards, I. A., 29, 38, 194
Richard, Jean-Pierre, 132
Richardson, Samuel, 84
Richelieu, Cardinal, 203
Ricoeur, Paul, 33, 61
Riffaterre, Michael, 125
Rilke, Rainer-Maria, 4, 52, 109
Rimbaud, Arthur, 77, 132, 134
Robertson, D. W., Jr., 102
Robinson, F. N., 14
Rochester, University of, 99
Rockefeller Foundation, 83
Rolland, Romain, 52
Rollin, Charles, 203
Romania, 205–208, 209
Rome, 213. *See also* American Academy
Ronsard, Pierre, 41
Rooney, William, 130
Root, Robert Kilburn, 1, 2, 5
Rorty, Richard, 34
Rose, Marilyn G., 166
Rosenblat, Angel, 101
Rousseau, Jean-Jacques, 61, 91, 127,
    185, 186, 187, 190n

Roussel, Raymond, 132
Royet-Journoud, Claude, 139
Ruskin, John, 132
Russell, P. E., 101
Ryan, Judith, 20

Sabin, Margery, 22
Sade, Marquis de, 84
Saintsbury, George E., 29
Said, Edward, 21
Salinas, Pedro, 101
San Diego, University of California at,
    20
San Francisco, 120, 208
San Marino, CA, 7
Sand, George, 82, 129, 135
Sandburg, Carl, 39
Santayana, George, 15
Santí, Enrico Maria, 210
Sappho, 59
Sarraute, Nathalie, 85
Sartre, Jean-Paul, 77, 159, 182, 196
Saussure, Ferdinand de, 30, 31
Scarfe, Francis, 196
Sceve, Maurice, 41
Schiller, Friedrich, 52, 126, 194, 195,
    206
Schlegel, Friedrich, 126
Schleiermacher, Friedrich, 34
Schofield, W. H., 15, 17, 18
Schopenhauer, Arthur, 127
Schorske, Carl, 200
Schramm, Wilbur, 6
Schücking, Levin, 26
Schüller, Richard, 126
Schütz, Alfred, 126
Schweitzer, Albert, 30
Scotland, 101, 193–194
Scott, Sir Walter, 131, 153
Sears, Robert, 94
Seattle, 56, 144
Sebba, Gregor, 103
Sebeok, Thomas, 130
Second World War, ix, 63, 141, 160,
    161, 162, 185, 193, 194, 203, 205,
    207, 209

Sedgwick, Eve Kossofsky, 135
Segal, Erich, 15, 81
Seidlin, Oskar, 160
Sein, Ana Fernandez, 22
Sen, Nabaneeta, 22
Senelick, Laurence, 22
Serbia, 205
Serres, Michel, 199
Sévigné, Marie de Rabutin-Chantal,
    Marquise de, 203
Seznec, Jean, 197
Shaffer, Elinor, 118
Shaftesbury, Anthony Ashley Cooper,
    1st Earl of, 4
Shakespeare, William, 1, 10, 26, 45,
    126, 127, 139, 148, 155, 179, 206, 213
Shaver, Chester, 128
Shaw, George Bernard, 26, 139
Sheldon, E. S., 14
Shelley, Percy Bysshe, 140n, 153
Sherman, Stuart P., 16
Sieburth, Richard, 22
Siegen, University of, 136
Simmons, E. J., 15
Simon, John, 22
Singleton, Charles, 101, 102, 198
Sismondi, Simonde de, 100
Skinner, B. F., 160
Slusser, George, 22
Smith College, 3–4, 56
Smithsonian Institution, 130
Snell, Bruno, 55–56, 61
Socrates, 215
Solmsen, F., 30
Somerville College, Oxford, 109
Sophocles, 52, 127
Southampton, University of, 117
Southern California, University of, 132,
    161
Southern Methodist University, 122
Spain, 20, 159, 160
Spanos, William, 167
Spargo, J. W., 15
Spariosu, Mihai, 137
Spenser, Edmund, 1, 103, 148
Spingarn, Joel Elias, 14

Spinoza, Benedictus de, 209
Spitzer, Leo, 8, 30, 66, 100, 101–102,
    117, 125, 127, 136, 146, 198, 199
St. Antony's College, Oxford, 197
Stalin, Josef, 172, 206
Stallknecht, Newton, 162
Stanford Humanities Center, 123
Stanford University, 57, 90, 91, 93–95,
    122, 133–138, 145, 168, 208
Starobinski, Jean, 16, 33, 132
Stein, Arnold, 147
Steinberg, Leo, 125
Steiner, George, 21, 118
Stendhal, 92, 99, 126
Sterne, Laurence, 208
Stimson, Henry, 7
Stoenescu, Ştefan, 207
Stone, George Winchester, 81
Storm, Theodor, 4
Strasbourg, 116
Strich, Fritz, 26
Striedter, Jurij, 16
Structuralism, 162, 163
Sussex, University of, 9, 117
Svevo, Italo, 115
Swarthmore College, 51
Swift, Jonathan, 29, 213
Switzerland, 185, 187, 213
Syracuse University, 77
Szanto, George, 22

Taine, Hippolyte, 90
Tate, Allen, 33, 39
Tennyson, Alfred, Lord, 126
Texas, University of, 117, 121–122, 123
Thackeray, William Makepeace, 126
Thatcher, Margaret, 116
Theocritus, 57
Thibaudet, Albert, vii
Thierry, Augustin, 77
Thomas, Henri, 190n
Thompson, Flora, 103
Thompson, Stith, 20
Thorlby, Anthony, 8, 9–10, 118
Thucydides, 53
Ticknor, George, 13, 100

Tieck, Ludwig, 126, 167
Tillich, Paul, 160
Times Literary Supplement, 126
Timişoara, Romania, 205
Todorov, Tzvetan, 132
Tokyo, 165
Tolstoy, Lev, 126
Tompkins, Jane Parry, 42
Toronto, 4
Toronto, University of, 4, 15, 25–29, 32, 53, 54
Torrance, Robert, 22
Tracy, Robert, 22
Train, John, 22
Trakl, Georg, 134
Transylvania, 205
Trilling, Lionel, 118, 178, 182
Trotsky, Lev, 182, 213
Truman, Harry, 144
Tübingen, University of, 160
Tulane University, 208
Tuxwell, Rexford G., 97n

Ukraine, 180
Ullmann, Stephen, 196
Unamuno, Miguel de, 150
Underdown, David, 46
Union College (Schenectady, NY), 19
United States, 3, 65, 116–117, 123, 125, 127, 132, 159, 163, 169, 170, 171, 172, 174, 177, 178, 185, 187, 200
United Kingdom, 201. *See also* Great Britain
Urban VIII, Pope, 172
Urbana, 116. *See also* Illinois, University of
Utrecht, 165

Valdés, Mario, 81
Valency, Maurice, 81
Valéry, Paul, 39, 100, 130
Van Tieghem, Paul, vii, 125
Venice, 78, 165
Verlaine, Paul, 127, 193
Vernant, Jean-Pierre, 60
Versluys, Kristiaan, 22

Vianu, Tudor, 207
Vicente, Gil, 10, 102
Vico, Giovanni Battista, 162
Vidal-Naquet, Pierre, 60
Vienna, 107, 126, 132, 205
Vietnam War, 167, 188
Viëtor, Karl, 17
Villa I Tatti, Florence, 19
Vinaver, Eugène, 108, 109, 114, 116, 117, 118
Virgil, 103, 148
Vivien, Renée, 83
Voeglin, Erich, 126
Voltaire, 213

Wach, Joachim, 26
Wais, Kurt, 160
Wales, University of, 118
Walker, Janet, 22
Walker, Steven, 22
Wallace, John, 198
Wallerstein, Ruth, 7
Wardropper, Bruce, 101, 102, 198
Warnke, Frank, 58, 161
Warren, Austin, 6, 10, 18, 30, 55, 162
Warren, Robert Penn, 30
Warwick, University of, 117, 118
Washington, DC, 78, 129, 144
Washington, University of, 56, 57–58, 145, 147
Washington University, St. Louis, 65
Wasiolek, Edward, 21
Wasserman, Earl, 102, 198, 199
Weber, Max, 63
Weinstein, Arnold, 22
Weisberg, Liliane, 22
Weisstein, Ulrich, 164
Wellek, René, vii, viii, x, xi, 17, 18, 21, 30, 38, 40–41, 61, 84, 99, 100, 101, 104, 113, 116, 117, 118, 125, 127, 129, 133, 159, 160, 161, 162, 163, 197, 198, 199, 209
Wellek, Olga, 5, 7, 8
Wellek, Alexander, 8
Welty, Eudora, 131
Wendell, Barrett, 14

Wescott, Glenway, 92
West, Nathanael, 92
West, Thomas, 118
Wharton, Edith, 92, 126
Whinnom, Keith, 101
Whiting, B. J., 15
Whitman, Walt, 127, 132
Whittier College, Los Angeles, 7
Wilde, Johannes, 52
Wilde, Oscar, 26
Wilden, Anthony, 200
Williams College, 90
Williams, Raymond, 134
Wilson, Edmund, 21
Wilson, Edward, 101
Wilson, Woodrow, 2, 32
Wimsatt, William K., Jr., 38, 39, 40, 42, 130
Wind, Edgar, 56
Winternitz, Emmanuel, 126
Wisconsin, University of, 20, 116
Witke, Charles, 22
Wittgenstein, Ludwig, 31, 136, 152, 163
Woodberry, George Edward, 14

Woodhouse, A. B., 29
Woolf, Virginia, 38, 112, 131
Wordsworth, William, 56, 126, 127, 131, 140n, 150, 151, 152, 153
Wormhoudt, Arthur, 6
Wright, Louis B., 7

Yale University, 3, 5, 7, 8, 9, 10–11, 17, 37, 38, 40–42, 45, 63, 64–65, 66, 83, 99–100, 101, 130, 145, 160, 169, 178, 188, 200
Yalom, Irvin, 94
Yearbook of Comparative Criticism, 118
Yeats, William Butler, 19, 41, 43, 127, 131, 140n, 178

Zamiatin, Evgenii, 213
Zanzotto, Andrea, 139
Zholkovsky, Aleksandr, 136
Ziolkowski, Jan, 20
Zionism, 51
Zola, Emile, 92
Zurich, University of, 102, 187
Zurich, 178